This is an Honour Song:
Twenty Years Since the Blockades

This is an honour song

TWENTY YEARS SINCE THE BLOCKADES

An anthology of writing on the "Oka Crisis"
Edited by Leanne Simpson and Kiera L. Ladner

ARBEITER RING PUBLISHING • WINNIPEG

Copyright ©2010 Leanne Simpson and Kiera L. Ladner

Arbeiter Ring Publishing
201E-121 Osborne Street
Winnipeg, Manitoba
Canada R3L 1Y4
www.arbeiterring.com

Printed in Canada by Trancontinental
Design by Relish Design Studio

 MANITOBA ARTS COUNCIL
CONSEIL DES ARTS DU MANITOBA

 Canada Council
for the Arts
Conseil des Arts
du Canada

 Canadian
Heritage
Patrimoine
canadien

 Manitoba

With assistance of the Manitoba Arts Council/Conseil des Arts du Manitoba.

We acknowledge the support of the Canada Council for our publishing program.

ARP acknowledges the financial support to our publishing activities of the Manitoba Arts Council/Conseil des Arts du Manitoba, Manitoba Culture, Heritage and Tourism, and the Government of Canada through the Canada Book Fund.

Arbeiter Ring Publishing acknowledges the support of the Province of Manitoba through the Book Publishing Tax Credit and the Book Publisher Marketing Assistance Program.

Printed on 100% recycled paper.

LIBRARY AND ARCHIVES CANADA CATALOGUING IN PUBLICATION

    This is an honour song : twenty years since the blockades / edited by Leanne Simpson & Kiera L. Ladner.

Includes bibliographical references and index.
ISBN 978-1-894037-41-9

    1. Québec (Province)--History--Native Crisis, 1990. 2. Mohawk Indians--Québec (Province)--Kanesatake Indian Reserve--Government relations. 3. Native peoples--Canada--Government relations.
I. Simpson, Leanne, 1971- II. Ladner, Kiera L., 1971-

FC2925.9.O6T45 2010   971.4004'975542   C2010-901057-4

INDEX OF ARTWORK

Acknowledgements

Chi'miigwech to all of the Ancestors who survived, resisted and lived through the past 400 years of colonialism so that we might be here today.

To all of the Kanien'kehaka from Kanehsatà:ke, Kahnawà:ke and Akwesasne, naiwen'kowa.

Chi'miigwech to all of the contributors—the writers, the visual artists, the activists, community leaders, scholars, curators, graphic designers, poets, playwrights and musicians—who contributed to this project.

Chi'miigwech to Tracey Nepinak and Tina Keeper for Doug's play.

Chi'miigwech to John Samson, Rick Wood and the editorial collective at Arbeiter Ring Publishing for their unwavering support of this vision and the book.

Chi'miigwech to Damien Lee and Andrea Gallagher for editorial assistance.

Chi'miigwech to the MacKenzie Art Gallery, the McMichael Gallery, the Walter Phillips Gallery, and the Ottawa Art Gallery for assistance with obtaining images of the artwork.

Chi'miigwech to Nishna and Minowewebeneshiinh Simpson for hanging out with Steve while we worked on the book, and to Steve for your presence, engagement, profound love, and continual support..

Ekosi!

This is an Honour Song

KIERA L. LADNER AND LEANNE SIMPSON

The summer of 1990 brought some strong medicine to Turtle Island. For many Canadians, "Oka" was the first time they encountered Indigenous anger, resistance and standoff, and the resistance was quickly dubbed both the "Oka Crisis" and the "Oka Crises" by the mainstream media. But to the Kanien'kehaka (Mohawk) people of Kanehsatà:ke, who were living up to their responsibilities to take care of their lands, this was neither a "crisis" at Oka, nor was it about the non-Native town of "Oka." This was about 400 years of colonial injustice. Similarly, for the Kanien'kehaka from Kahnawà:ke and Akwesasne who created "crises" by putting up their own barricades on the Mercier Bridge or by mobilizing and/or mobilizing support (resources) at Kanehsatà:ke, this really had nothing to do with Oka, a bridge or a golf course. This was about 400 years of resistance. Like every Indigenous nation occupied by Canada, the Haudenosaunee have been confronting state/settler societies and their governments since those societies began threatening the sovereignty, self-determination and jurisdiction of the Haudenosaunee. It was not a beginning. Nor was this the end. This was a culmination of many, many years of Onhkwehonwe resistance resulting in a decision to put up barricades in defense of, and to bring attention to, Haudenosaunee land ethics, treaty responsibilities and governance.

Although the mainstream media focused on the white town of "Oka" and the "warriors," the Kanien'kehaka resistance was envisioned and carried out by Kanien'kehaka people from Kanehsatà:ke, Kahnawà:ke and Akwesasne. Although the mainstream media focused on masked warriors, the resistance began in March as a peaceful blockade on a snow covered dirt road with the simple intent of blocking the Oka golf course's planned expansion into the Pines or the commons: a small piece of land that the people of Kanehsatà:ke had been fighting to have recognized as theirs for at least 270 years. Further, while the media tried to focus solely on the warriors, in actuality, the resistance was carried out by countless men, women and children behind the lines and behind the scenes mobilizing support and resources. True, it was a critical act of resistance, but it was also a vision of reclamation, revitalization and restoration of Haudenosaunee lands, treaties, political traditions and responsibilities. Such vision and resistance served to inspire countless individuals and communities across the country as they put up their own blockades in solidarity with the Kanien'kehaka and/or to empower other struggles of resistance.

The summer of 2010 marks the twentieth anniversary of the Kanien'kehaka resistance at Kanehsatà:ke and Kahnawà:ke. And 2010 also marks the anniversary of a 290 year long resistance at Kanehsatà:ke which has seen countless generations of Kanien'kehaka fight to have their rights to their lands (including the commons/the Pines) acknowledged and respected. We thought it was time to observe these anniversaries.

But why "Oka"? Why a book marking this anniversary and honouring this particular resistance when Indigenous Peoples have been resisting colonialism as individuals, communities and nations since the dawn of colonization? People throughout the Americas have been engaged in an almost constant struggle for the reclamation, revitalization, and restoration of lands, treaties, political traditions and responsibilities. It is a struggle that began soon after the discovery of Europeans in Indigenous territories; about the time that the Europeans and their offspring societies proved themselves to be an invasive species that just wouldn't go away and one that just couldn't be respectful of another's territory, traditions, spiritual beliefs, economy or political system. Such struggles are anything but new. They have taken a multiplicity of forms from legal actions to public marches or demonstrations on the lawns of government buildings, and from Métis armed insurrections to protesting uranium exploration. Such struggles have even presented themselves as suicides. As Richard Wagamese wrote during that summer of 1990:

> Fourteen years ago, in May 1976, a young man died. Dressed in full traditional manner of his Peigan people, he travelled beyond the borders of this reality forever. He carried with him the love, respect and honour of his people. He carried with him an intimate knowledge of the realities of native life in Canada. And that is why he died.
>
> Nelson Small Legs Jr. shot himself through the heart. He left behind notes to his family and friends as well as a note to the news media.... [T]hose brief words to the press ring as heavily today as they did then.
>
> *'I give up my life in protest to the present conditions concerning Indian people in southern Alberta. For 100 years Indians have suffered. Must they suffer another 100 years? My suicide should open the eyes of non-Indians into how much we've suffered.'*[1]

So why a book on this particular resistance and not one about Small Legs or Listuguj or Ipperwash or Haida Gwaii? These were critical, influential mobilizations. While all of these nations threw stones in the water that generated a ripple effects, Kanasatà:ke was different. Not because of the ripple, but because we saw those powerful images every night on the news for months—images that became a defining moment for many of us. Images that generated unprecedented Indigenous response in the form of solidarity blockades across Turtle Island. The answer is quite simple—the mobilization of Kanien'kehaka that summer was such a powerful image and such a defining moment for so many of us (Indigenous and Canadian alike). But while it was such a powerful image and while it empowered so many individuals, communities and nations engaged in their own struggles, like the story of Small Legs it is important to understand that resistance often has an underbelly—stories of a community divided and stories which serve to divide a community. It is important to acknowledge that underbelly, but in putting together this book we seek to honour both the mobilization and the communities involved in their entirety.

Honouring and revealing Indigenous resistance is of critical importance to our communities, because these struggles are not well documented in mainstream Canadian history, they are manipulated by mainstream Canadian media and are hidden from Canadians and often Indigenous Peoples alike. Every single Indigenous nation in Canada has a long history of resistance. This resistance has been recorded in particular and unique Oral Traditions, spanning centuries and often documenting individual acts of resistance, in addition to wider-scale mobilization. Indigenous nations have a long and honourable history of standing up for justice, for peace and for the protection of their territories and citizens. They have been organizing, contesting, dissenting, and mobilizing since the invasion began, and the proof lies in the fact that we stand here today, connected to our lands as *Indigenous* Peoples.

The impetus for this book project was an academic conference in Montreal attended by both Ellen Gabriel and me (Kiera Ladner). During her talk, Ellen spoke of the opportunities that she has had to travel across the country (and beyond) and how her travels have allowed her to hear stories about the importance and the impact that their resistance has had far beyond the borders of Kanien'kehaka territory. As I sat and listened to her speak of the importance of such stories, it struck me how many people in the communities never had such opportunities or had never heard the voices from across the country speak of the resistance or its impact, and I knew I wanted to do something. But what that something was I did not know. Most importantly, I didn't know if this was something that I, as an outsider, should be doing.

After speaking with Ellen in Montreal and Ottawa over coffees, breakfasts and even birch bark basket making, I began to understand my responsibility and made a commitment to do something to publicly address the impact of the so-called "Oka Crisis." This sense of commitment and responsibility only intensified when I visited Kanehsatà:ke several months later. That day afforded me the opportunity to speak with people, other then Ellen, about the resistance in 1990, its impact on the community, and this project. It also provided the opportunity to tour the community long besieged by the loss of land and its checkerboard pattern, to see the commons—to see those Pines still standing and to hear the sound of the wind through the trees as if it were a constant Honour Song for the people who had stood strong nearly twenty years ago. It was an emotional moment spent driving with Ellen down the dirt road where the original blockade had been, thinking of the people who had stood there all those years before. A moment spent thinking of images and the woman I saw on my television every night for months. A moment recalling how the events at Kanehsatà:ke and Kahnawà:ke and how the people of Kanehsatà:ke, Kahnawà:ke and Akwesasne changed my life. And thus it was a day that I will never forget, for the people that I spoke with and the tour of the community reminded me of so very much about my own journey, why I was doing this project and the responsibilities that I carry.

So I put down my tobacco and I called Leanne—just as I always do when I am struggling with something big. After many, many conversations with Leanne, Ellen, and numerous Haudenosaunee and non-Haudenosaunee scholars and activists, the idea for the book was born. We would mark the anniversaries with a book honouring the impact of the resistance with stories from across our Island. I hope that we have accomplished this and that our Honour Songs are heard with the intent and respect with which all of our contributors wrote them.

When Kiera first presented the idea to me, I (Leanne) was initially reluctant. Not because the resistance at Kanehsatà:ke and Kahnawà:ke wasn't deserving; it most certainly is. This event changed my life. But because culturally, Nishinaabeg people are taught to tread very, very carefully and to avoid interfering with the affairs of others. I knew the pain and division the "crises" had created, fostered and reinforced in these communities. I knew as a citizen of the Nishnaabeg nation that I was an outsider to both the resistance and to the pain and division. So I put my tobacco down, and asked for guidance from my Ancestors, and the direction came. The Kanien'kehaka and Haudenosaunee people I spoke with were supportive. The Elders I spoke with were supportive. John Samson of Arbeiter Ring expressed his unwavering support of the project, calling Oka "the greatest political education of his life," and doors just opened.

While the project began with a trip to Montreal for Kiera, it ended with a trip to Montreal for me. During the last few days approaching our publisher's deadline, I travelled to Montreal with my children to accompany my partner who was attending a workshop at Concordia University. These things never happened by chance. As I was making my way back from the hotel pool with my children, Minowewebeneshiinh and Nishna, I ran into Ellen Gabriel in the elevator of our hotel. This was the first time I had met her. I introduced myself, and we exchanged a few words. I was wet, having just been in the pool, more dishevelled than normal, and I was caught by surprise. But as I looked into her blue eyes, I remembered. I remembered being a young 19-year-old Anishinaabekwe. I remembered seeing her on TV, and I remembered what that image had taught me and why I carried it through the next twenty years. I remembered that this was the woman responsible for waking me up. For sending me on a path that led me to learn my culture, my language, my political traditions. This was the woman that challenged me to find my voice and to use it.

The second image I took from that trip came form the stop of that sacred mountain in the middle of Montreal. As I looked out over beautiful Kanien'kehaka territory, my eyes focused on the Mercier Bridge, and I felt the enormity of the parallel mobilization at Kahnawà:ke. The Mercier Bridge leading in and out of Montreal, the traffic chaos, the white anger, the shear number of people their intervention affected.

Throughout the project, I have carefully listened to the guidance and concerns of Ellen Gabriel through Kiera. I have also consulted with my friend and colleague Taiaiake Alfred, and am thankful to both of these individuals for providing us with honest, forthcoming advice and perspectives. Kiera and I have tried to the best of our abilities to honour the contributions of individuals and communities involved in the most respectful way possible, in a way that does not further entrench any divisions in the community. Any mistakes or missteps are our own.

This book represents an Honour Song in the tradition of the Nishinaabeg and Nehiyaw nations, sung by a diversity of writers, scholars, activists and artists to honour all of the people that participated in the resistance from Kanehsatà:ke, Kahnawà:ke and Akwesasne. Honour Songs in Indigenous traditions are sung to publicly honour and acknowledge all the beautiful things, all the good, these individuals and communities have brought to the people, and to honour the positive impact this "crisis" had on Indigenous Peoples and Canada.

We also undertook this project to acknowledge the pain and the sacrifices made by the people of Kanehsatà:ke, Kahnawà:ke and Akwesasne. Pain and sacrifices these communities continue to live with. Twenty years is not long enough to heal a wound this large—particularly when these communities continue to be punished for the action by police, military, locals, surrounding municipalities, Quebéc and Canada. Twenty years is not long enough to heal divisions between families and friends. Twenty years is not long enough to heal divisions within communities, let alone those between nations.

We also undertook this project to bring attention to the fact that twenty years later the issues that resulted in the so-called "Oka Crisis" have not been resolved. People of Kanehsatà:ke are constantly forced to fight for the commons and what remains of their lands. Kanien'kehake in each of these communities continue in their efforts to rebuild and revitalize their nation, their government, their relationship to their lands and their treaty relationship with settler societies and governments. Something must be done!

Something must be done now—before another twenty years pass. As Patricia Monture wrote almost twenty years ago on the heels of the Kanehsatà:ke resistance, "I am frightened by the violence that we saw this summer at Kanehsatà:ke. In twenty years time, I do not want to turn on the television set and see one of my two boys standing there holding a gun. That is not what I want for their future."[2] We are haunted by these words and the echoes of these same words that have been spoken by countless generations of Indigenous mothers, grandmothers and aunties since the dawn of colonization. Those two boys are now towering young men (both well over six feet tall) with a younger brother. Though these boys have changed, the realities of resistance and the situation in Kanehsatà:ke have not. There are still episodes of Indigenous resistance, and young people are actively mobilizing in numerous communities as we write. Our hope is that something is done. This is not what we want for future generations.

We began this project in earnest during the summer of 2009. Our deadlines were extremely tight in order to get it out by the spring of 2010. As such we relied heavily on our own networks, drawing upon people from outside of the communities involved who had both an honour song to sing and the time to write it. Every single person we spoke with about writing for the book, whether they ended up contributing or not, indicated that the "Oka Crisis" was a defining moment in their lives. It was important to us to include a diversity of voices— from community activists and traditional people to young activists and emerging academics to poets and visual artists and scholars from Indigenous communities across Turtle Island and from Canadians. While we are missing several key voices (like Québécois) due to the inescapable time constraints, mid-stream dropouts, and the limits of our networks, we nevertheless hope that we have accomplished this. There was a fantastic response from the Indigenous artistic community, and we were only able to include a very small portion of that response—the artists whose practice lends itself to print media. Oka not only inspired artists to write songs, performances, theatrical works and contributions to the visual arts, it impacted the practices of a generation of artists who continue to create works today.

It is our hope that this book honours the resistance and resurgence of the Kanien'kehaka, and its influence on the resistance and resurgence movements of other Indigenous nations and its influence on Canada. Indigenous Peoples and their nations have been resisting and struggling against the colonialism since the very beginning. The Ancestors not only fought, blockaded, protested and mobilized against these forces on every Indigenous territory in Turtle Island, they also engaged in countless acts of hidden resistance and kitchen table resistance aimed at ensuring their children and grandchildren could live as *Indigenous* Peoples. The Grandmothers, Mothers and Aunties were particularly adept at keeping us alive, and passing down whatever traditions they could so we would have warmth in our hearts and warmth in our bellies. We believe it is important to reveal the legacy of resistance in order to not only shatter mainstream Canada's image of Indigenous Peoples as "passive victims" of colonization, but also to demonstrate to future generations that they exist because of the responsibility, sacrifice, courage and commitment of their Ancestors. Ultimately, and with the utmost humility, we undertook this project to help us pass on the legacy of resistance, of resurgence and of peace to our children, who will inherent this legacy and to the generations yet to be born.

Note on Terminology

Although the "Oka Crises" is known to most Canadians as the "Oka Crisis," the term is offensive to many involved in the struggle because it refers to the non-Native town, and because the term was manufactured by the mainstream media. We agree. However, in editing a collection from a group of such diverse writers, we have left the language up to individual writers. Like it our not, Indigenous or Canadian, people identify with the term "Oka Crisis" in a far greater way than they do to phrases such as "the resistance at Kanehsatà:ke" or the "standoff at Kanehsatà:ke and Kahnawà:ke." Still, we feel it is important to disrupt colonial labels, and have encouraged writers to decolonize their use of language where appropriate.

---

1 Richard Wagamese (1996), *The Terrible Summer*, Toronto: Warrick Publishing, p. 65.

2 Patricia Monture (1997), "Notes on Sovereignty" in Andrea P. Morrison (ed.), *Justice for Natives: Searching for Common Ground*, Montreal & Kingston: McGill-Queens University Press, p. 198.

Bad Indians

RYAN RED CORN

I was told by those old ones
that every song has a special time and a place where it's sang
this is our song
and this our time
they used to say the only good indian is a dead indian
i must be a no good at being indian
cuz I feel alive and kicking
we are the bastard reject children of manifest destiny
the offspring of fornicating aimsters
raised by our grandparents who told us
not to confuse being warriors with gangsters
the edward curtis groupies get jazzed by anyone fitting the bill
and America gets jazzed by every Bury My Heart at Walmart film
here i stand before you
this crowd of nations
this life of sanctions
an awkward patience
like five hundred BIA buildings vs. a father's' unfiltered hate
right next to the IHS building with a two and a half week wait.
a cinderblock battlefield where few are left standing
and the people it's failing, its marginalized estate.
i am armed to the teeth with words from the ivory tower
and those good **indians** told me it's borrowed power if...

if i talk loud enough
if i talk clear enough
that i would be heard
that for some talking is singing
that for some singing is praying
but i guess that depends on who is doing the talking
and i guess that depends on who is doing the listening
...so understand me in english,
you have been robbed of your tongues
the taproot of thought
in the middle of resisting
the language got caught
and she only shows her face during ceremony
like she's ashamed of her scars
like what she has to say is never really heard. at all.
and the violence she knows is enough to never sing again
but i killed the cameraman and stripped him of his lense.
i photographed the body and asked him to forgive.
forgive me as i cut out your tongue
forgive me as i put you in this powdered wig
forgive me when i put your body in a museum
forgive me of all my sins
for not being a good indian
the balls of your forefathers will be traded for whiskey
to fuel the molotov cocktails to be tossed at your cities
and the breasts of your mothers severed and bloody
will be sold to the freak show for the revelers money
your children will witness their whole world collapse
as kidnapped siblings must erase names off maps
so forgive me of all my sins
for not being a good indian
i was taught better than that
i have more respect than that
there is no history book with my story
there is no newspaper to give me my glory
because no one has heard this language in years
cept kokopelli, dream catchers and a trail of beers

my voice is a small pox blanket
that spreads like fire on the prairie
infecting both fist and hatchet
in the spirit of fucking crazy

Niimkiig

LEANNE SIMPSON

When the Canadian state mobilized its armed forces against the Kanien'kehaka at Kanehsatà:ke in the summer of 1990, their action confirmed everything every non-assimilated Indigenous person already knew—that given the opportunity, Canada would not hesitate to use its military power to crush Indigenous nations and our aspirations to be peaceful, responsible, self-determining neighbours. This reality seemed to somehow shock Canadians as they clung to a finely manicured image of themselves as "peacekeepers," marching around the UN-sanctioned world like boy scouts doing altruistic good turns for the world's so-called "less fortunate."

The circumstances that led to, at the time, the largest Canadian military mobilization since the Korean War have remained remarkably consistent over the past twenty years. With Canada still gleefully promoting the occupation and destruction of Indigenous territories. With Canada still cheerfully watching as our languages die while sinking billions into the promotion of the French language. With Canada still ardently criminalizing those who attempt to defend Indigenous lands in the face of white Windigo greed, all the while arrogantly defending Canadian sovereignty and borders on land that it does not own, it merely occupies.

The lengths the Canadian state would go to in order to defend its inability to share, its commitment to injustice and its poisoned diplomatic relationship with the Indigenous nations it continually chooses to occupy did not shock us. It was just the latest bit of evidence in more than 400 years of our resistance—from Mistahimaskwa to Obwandiyag (Pontiac) to Deskaheh and a list far too long to recount here. Indigenous Peoples knew that the "Oka Crisis" stemmed from over four centuries of neglect, violence, illegal occupation and subjugation. We knew that this was an accumulation of calculated Kanien'kehaka resurgence rooted in Haudenosaunee political traditions. We knew that although we were seeing a handful of Kanien'kehaka on the front lines, there were thousands of others working strategically, politically, logistically—their work in band offices, at negotiating tables and around kitchen tables unnoticed, their sacrifices unsung. We knew that many residents in those Kanien'kehaka communities did not want to be thrust into the media limelight, but were dragged along whether they wanted to be or not. And we knew that the people of Kahnawà:ke, Kanehsatà:ke and Akwesasne would live with the sacrifices, the divisions, the sorrow, and the pain of those sacrifices for years to come. We knew, one way or another, Canada would make them pay. Canada always makes us pay.

Yet every act of resistance and resurgence, even ones that are small and seemingly insignificant (and the resurgence at Kanehsatà:ke and Kahnawà:ke was neither small nor insignificant), holds at its core transformative energy that has the power to influence well beyond the immediate impact of the original act. And the events that led to the Kanien'kehaka resurgence at Kanehsatà:ke and Kahnawà:ke have now influenced a second generation of Indigenous Peoples to reclaim, relearn and rebuild our nations according to our own political traditions.

For Nishnaabeg people, mobilization and dissent have always been a cornerstone of our political traditions. Collective mobilization and mass movement throughout our territory was required to maintain our treaty and diplomatic relationships with animal nations and with our neighbouring Indigenous nations. Mobilization and collective movement were required seasonally for spiritual and economic purposes and established relationships that formed the foundation of our governance. Dissent, vision, commitment and action were the pillars of our political processes. And after centuries of practice, we got good at it.

The impetus for mobilization and change was not often lead by our middle-aged men, although they too carried the responsibility for action. Oftentimes, instructions from the spiritual realm came to those most closely connected to those forces—children, women and our Elders. In particular, our intellectual traditions have within them a library of examples of young women and children transforming our political culture and diplomatic relationships through visions and dreams, and a collective culture based on committed listening, validation and action. Chibimoodaywin, our great migration, and our largest collective political and mass mobilization, ensured we survived colonialism and carried our people through 500 years of committed collective action toward a common goal.

Nishnaabeg Elders often use an everyday image to talk about building resurgence and acts of resistance. They talk of throwing a stone into a body of water. The stone and the act of throwing, represents both intent and action. The impact upon the water is the result of that action. When the stone hits the water, there is an immediate and dramatic impact. There is sound and displacement.

But long after the stone sinks to the bottom, the concentric waves of displaced water radiate outward, carrying the impact of the action through time and space. The impact of the initial disruption is carried across different realms by these concentric rings, interacting with the other elements of Creation in synergy. Many Elders believe that the success of these acts of resistance depends upon not only our intent and our action, but also on directly asking the spiritual realm for assistance. Once those spiritual forces have been approached, it then becomes impossible for humans to predict the spiraling impact of that act of resistance as its influence broadens. From a Nishnaabeg perspective, resistance and resurgence is about strategy, decisive action, commitment and responsibility supported by the mobilization of spiritual forces.

When the Onkwehonwe collectively threw their stone into the lake in the summer of 1990, there was no way of telling the tremendous gift and opportunity they gave to Indigenous Peoples. There was no way to tell that their action was going to influence generations of Onkwehonwe from all different Indigenous nations to commit to building a culturally based resurgence. There was no way to know that it would influence Canadian politics, the Charlottetown Accord, the Final Report of the Royal Commission on Aboriginal Peoples and police response at Ipperwash, Burnt Chruch, Ardoch, Caledonia, Dump Site 41, Grassy Narrows and Kitchenuhmaykoosib Inninuwug. There was no way to predict that the resurgence at Kanehsatà:ke would challenge the Indigenous solidarity movement to finally contest the foundations of the Canadian state. But the concentric circles keep radiating. The circle grows bigger.

The Kanien'kehaka resurgence at Kanehsatà:ke galvanized a generation of people, of individuals who were educated by the event, who woke up and changed their lives. I have now met countless people, both Indigenous and non-Indigenous, who changed their careers, invigorated their politics, got out of relationships, got into relationships, learned their language, committed to their culture or to decolonizing themselves. The summer the Kanien'kehaka took on the Canadian army and won continues to inspire. It continues to bring us hope.

The resurgence at Kanehsatà:ke taught me that we all have the responsibility to stand up and to live up to our lives based on our gifts and our collective responsibilities for self-determination. It is our responsibility to fight for justice, just as our Ancestors did. To uphold the visions our Grandmothers and Grandfathers had for a peaceful and just co-existence with a Canadian state that acknowledges our sovereignties, nations and our independence. And in doing so, the Kanien'kehaka resurgence at Kanehsatà:ke shook up my generation. It defeated our chronic ambivalence and the distraction of identity politics. It forced us to choose which side of the fence we were on, and who we were going to be. What our legacy was going to be. For Nishnaabeg, it challenged us to relearn our song "Aambe Maajaada!," reminding us to commit to a resistance and resurgence that is ultimately about benevolence.

The summer of 1990 was a powerful one. Lots of Niimkiig flew over Gdoo-Naaganinaa, Our Dish, that year. Those powerful, beautiful thunderbirds carried with them their responsibility to protect the Nishnaabeg, the Onkwehonwe, and our lands. Those Niimkiig have long been angry with our colonizers for how our people and our lands have been treated. And so every summer, they come to us in solidarity, bringing us healing, cleansing our land. Their lightening striking distinctively and with clarity. Their voices carrying messages to those that can listen. Their power bringing rain to cleanse our mother. And when we are lucky enough to have them fly over our lands, we know that they are taking care of us because they love us and because they see what has happened. They see the injustice and their intent is clear. They embody action. The Onkwehonwe, like their Niimkiig relatives, take their responsibilities to protect their lands seriously. So to those families of Onkwehonwe, the ones from the last 400 years and the ones yet to be born, I say Miigwech! Miigwech! Miigwech! Miigwech for carrying the burden of Peace.

Mnaajtoon Ngamowin[1]

---

1 I am honouring a song to you. Miigwech to Nokomis Shirley Williams for Nishinaabemwin spelling assistance.

How Far Would You Go?

A Women's Perspective on the Twenty Years Since the "Oka Crisis"

HARMONY RICE

In the small and crowded Moosonee airport, Lillian Trapper sits patiently waiting for a flight. Moosonee is a small town situated near the mouth of the Moose River close to James Bay in northern Ontario. Trapper is on her way to her camp, or trapline, where she will meet some of her family and spend some time out on the land. Trapper, a Cree woman from Kattawagami, works as the Lands and Resources Manager for the Moose Cree Nation in Moose Factory. Her long hair rests on her green fleece pullover, while she sits and quietly reflects with me on the near twenty years since the "Oka Crisis" in 1990.

In conversations I had with people about the twenty-year Oka anniversary approaching, people were surprised to hear it has been so long. With a bewildered look on their faces, they wondered where did the time go and what (if anything) has changed. Witnessing those bewildered looks of wonder, I decided to delve into it a little further with several Indigenous women whose territory is within the province of Ontario, to ask them that very question: what has changed?

I approached women who have made commitments to working for the land, the water, culture and future generations, women whom I have such great respect and admiration for. They included Land and Resources Manager Lillian Trapper, land rights activist Chrissy Swain, Métis artist Christi Belcourt, Water Walker Josephine Mandamin and Longhouse Clan Mother Jan Hill. Each woman shared their experience with me, their thoughts on self-determination, and they each recalled where they were when they heard the news.

Trapper recalls living in Hull, Quebéc, at the time, pregnant with two young children and back in school. She says her children experienced the negative effects of the ignorance that was seeping out across the nation. Young non-Native children were hitting and spitting on her children because of the events at Oka. The media was all over Oka, and in Hull, while some people were trying to understand what was happening, others, out of fear or ignorance, may have taught their children otherwise. "What kind of parents would allow their children to be like that?" Lillian wonders, adding, "It is such a big thing for kids to treat one another like that. There might have been racist messaging in the homes; the perception was that First Nations were doing something wrong. And in Hull, we were only an hour away."

While the media reported one version of the story, we know now the stories of the community members and the people that travelled to stand in solidarity with the people of Kanehsatà:ke. We've watched the documentaries entailing many of the details that went unreported in the mainstream media, and we've read in books and articles about the way the Elders were treated, the way the youth were hurt, the way the women stood up and the way the men were targeted.

"Oka brought a lot of First Nation land issues to the forefront; people started to understand that it was two different societies, one looking from a recreational point of view, the other taking a sacred stance on it. They didn't want a golf course to be made there," says Trapper about what sparked the "Oka Crisis." She adds, "I think it nudged the nation to say you have to stand up for your rights."

Trapper has been working for her nation and the protection of their traditional territory since 2000. She has been developing a Land Use Plan for the Moose Cree that incorporates responsible management of traditional territory. Trapper says she has personally experienced the effects of resource development on traditional Cree lifestyle.

"I think we've come to a place in time where we've said this is our homeland, we have a history here. You have to come and talk to us if you want to deal with us. Slowly they've come to honour that. Our homeland is defined by the family areas out on the land, before they came to be based on reserve. We based our responsibility to the land from the political and social structures that we had and the way things were done. We weren't just wandering hunter gatherers, we had our own life cycle for how we lived from season to season," says Trapper.

When asked about being self-determining, Trapper says, "I truly believe we're born into this world with an inherent responsibility to take care of the land. Some of us realize it, some of us don't. With the settlers here, they're born, they choose a car, they buy a house, they plan their retirement. Our inherent responsibility is much bigger than that. I like to think of us as outside of the box. That's the perspective that I carry now, and it gets passed on to my child."

In my home community of Wasauksing, we lit a sacred fire to show our solidarity with the people at Oka. Like Lillian Trapper in the summer of 1990, my mother was pregnant, too. What kind of world are we bringing this baby into I wondered, and through my twelve-year-old sadness for Oka, I stayed committed to the fire with what little understanding I had of the events that were occurring.

I was just one of many youth who were questioning the many serious issues that led to the "Oka Crisis." Chrissy Swain shared her experience with me. Swain is a land rights activist, mother and young woman from Asubpeeschoseewagong, Grassy Narrows in Treaty Three territory in northwestern Ontario. A strong, passionate and dedicated leader, Chrissy shared with me the early struggles in her life. "During the time of Oka, I was eleven and I had just tried to commit suicide. I ended up in the hospital. When my dad picked me up, he took me to Winnipeg to my aunt. She took me to the protests, rallies and ceremonies for what was going on in Oka. That's where this part of my life began."

Chrissy remembers attending a pipe ceremony for the first time, watching women sing songs on the handdrum and people speak about Oka, sovereignty and land defense in ways she had never heard before. She says, "I had never felt so alive as I did then and I knew that was going to be my path for the rest of my life. Seeing those women and men standing up, I remember being in awe. I thought this is me, this is who I am. I had found myself. I was only 11 years old!"

Since the summer of the "Oka Crisis," Chrissy has grown into a leader for the community of Grassy Narrows. She has stood up against logging companies, walked to Parliament Hill in Ottawa and speaks all over the country about the devastating effects of resource development and extraction on her community and traditional territory. Grassy Narrows traditional land use area spans 2,500 square miles outside of the reserves' 14 square miles. Recently, Grassy Narrows trappers decided to challenge the Province in court on the granting of permits to the many corporations that enter Grassy Narrows territory.

"There is a big movement growing. Young people really are speaking out, standing up, and I hear people always bringing up Oka, remembering that it was Oka that educated them. I feel the movement really grew after Oka," says Swain.

When asked about what we've learned since Oka, Swain says, "We have to keep standing up. We have to start waking up our brothers and sisters. Getting them to burn that medicine and wake up that spirit inside of them. What we're doing already is a tool, that's where we have to go first with our own people. Even if it's one person in the community. It starts off with one and it just grows. The young are standing up by using our songs, using our medicines and taking back our ceremonies. They really are living the true Anishnaabe life." She adds, "Canadians should be educated in their schools about whose territory they are living on, who we are and the real history of this country."

The way these women have shared their experience, the way they have opened up about some of the most painful experiences we've faced as Indigenous people living in this country, brings back much of that pain, that sadness, that in some way we continue to carry. What I'm curious to know is how do we take that pain and use it as a tool in a proactive, positive way. I posed this question to Métis artist Christi Belcourt, who recollected her experience for me. Christi remembers wanting to go to Oka like many others. While buses were headed in that direction, those who couldn't make it watched the unfolding events on the news.

"I was watching it intensely on television and I was horrified to see the racism of Quebecers and Canadians come out, particularly seeing rocks being thrown at cars with grandmothers and children inside. It was ugly and shameful. I think it shocked many people, myself included, to realize Canadians were capable of this. Can you imagine if we were the ones throwing rocks at cars with grandparents and children of Quebecers inside—how we would have been demonized?" says Belcourt. She adds, "I think it taught me that racism exists within Canada and it is only covered by a very thin and fragile veneer—and that if we as Aboriginal people become unified or assert our rights in a physical way it cracks their veneer and they allow their deep feelings of hatred for us to show."

Belcourt is a Métis painter and writer, living and working in northern Ontario. Belcourt's work is focused on the depiction of floral patterns inspired by Métis and First Nations historical beadwork art; she studies plants and medicines and continues to apply that traditional knowledge to her work. Belcourt says that while seeing little change in Canadians perception of Aboriginals, she maintains a great sense of hope for the future.

"The racism that existed then still exists today. Our Prime Minister Harper just finished telling the United Nations that Canada doesn't have a colonial history! If another Oka happened tomorrow, I'm sorry to say, but I actually think Canadians' reactions would be worse and less tolerable today than they were in 1990," says Belcourt. adding, "I'm not advocating violence or protest for protest sake. I just think that if mother earth is being threatened, for example, as is the case with Site 41, then we need to physically stand up against violence being done to her in a non-violent way. And if that means blockades and standoffs, then so be it."

When we think of the many land struggles since Oka, we can see that while government has not been successful in negotiating and settling land claims with First Nations people, our guiding principles continue to be the protection of our land and its precious resources.

And this is where Elder and Grandmother Josephine Mandamin enters the story. Mandamin has walked around each of the five Great Lakes and up the St. Lawrence to the Atlantic Ocean, carrying a pail of water and the message that water is life, our most valuable resource. She says the events at Oka were a part of a reawakening and that it continues today.

Mandamin says, "I remember very clearly the summer of Oka. Those of us in Thunder Bay had demonstrated at the border crossing. It triggers my mind how Oka was broadcast on the news all across the country. And everywhere we went people were ready. Everybody was just waiting for something to happen—the government knew the Indians were restless."

Where did that restlessness and readiness go and why doesn't it sit at the tip of the toes of our politicians? Change appears to have occurred at the community level, but as the women in my interviews have noted, change hasn't been made with leadership in dealing with government, but rather with case law and the application of our traditional forms of government, and with youth reclaiming culture.

"As long as we, Aboriginal people, 'create partnerships' with governments and take their money, sadly I think it means we are kept under control, we are not autonomous nor self-governing," says Belcourt. "The minute we say 'no, we will not accept money in exchange for land, we actually want the land'...and if we stand up for that right, we have power...and that's when they don't know what to do with us and they panic. They are accustomed to us being 'reasonable' and 'complacent.'"

Trapper agrees that change hasn't been determined by the INAC band councils we have but rather on our traditional laws and customs, and our inherent responsibilities to protect the land.

Trapper says, "The most notable progress that's been made since Oka would be case law. We've come to a point of consultation and accommodation and yet the government still scrambles to figure how to deal with that. These are events in time that will one day speak to the treaty, little do they know it's coming to implementation."

When we see the success in the people of Kahnesatà:ke standing up for their land, we are educated in how Aboriginal Peoples are a self-determining people. More recent examples of this include the community of Kitchenumukoosib Innuwunnug and their experience with a mining corporation trying to enter and explore their traditional territory, another example is Site 41, which both Christi Belcourt and Josephine Mandamin have referred to.

"Our awareness was being raised. They were doing things we would never do with their cemeteries. There was no respect from the non Natives toward the Natives," says Mandamin. She adds, "Now I sense Aboriginal people are uniting in their own way—with the loss of our precious resources. We now have input into what goes on. For example, look at Site 41. That was a very monumental success for the people in those communities. It was non-Native and Native communities coming together for one specific reason: to protect the water."

Mandamin has been the focus of documentaries, news articles and widespread media, but more importantly, she shares her traditional knowledge, knowing that future generations will benefit from culture, language and a continued responsibility that we carry today as Indigenous people.

"All I can say from my perspective is that I sense there is a unity forming. When we walked with the water, you could sense a unifying force—like water, we are many rivers—all coming together as one. I think that Native people are really awakening, we just need to do more. We need to raise more awareness to our people, to our children, to our grandchildren, to our communities. About our whole sense of identity—of who we are, that we've never been colonized. If we're going to keep our culture, we need to keep our language."

Jan Hill is a clan mother from Tyendinaga Mohawk Territory who travelled to Oka with a delegation sent from Tyendinaga to sit in on the negotiations in 1990. Jan says that Canadians eyes were opened during the crisis. She says Canadians realized then that Aboriginal people wouldn't stand back and allow the government to continue to ignore their existence and responsibility as land protectors.

"The army stood against our people who had lived here on this land forever," says Hill. "For the Haudenosaunee, we've always maintained our traditional forms of government since before contact. We still have our governments. If we all understood our languages, there would be no confusion about our traditional laws and governance structures. If we know them in English, we understand them in English. We have difficulty understanding those teachings in English. We have so much educating to do with our people. There are many interpretations about role and responsibility and how we're supposed to work together, all because of our lack of language."

The history of the Indigenous experience and the traditional laws that exist among all of our nations maintain principles that have never changed, and we need this message— that Indigenous people have preserved and protected the land—now more than ever. They will continue to make a stand for the rights of mother earth. When I asked them my one final question, this is what they shared with me:

"How far would you go, Josephine?"

"Around the Great Lakes, to the ocean and back. As far as it's required. As we carry the water, that's what we talk about. Water is the greatest way to bring life to the people. I would go to any length—to even lay my life on the line for that."

"How far would you go, Lillian?"

"As far as I could go."

"How far would you go, Jan?"

"I believe our land is our land. I would stand on the land till death because that's our responsibility, to take care of the earth and to make sure there is a place for our children."

"How far would you go, Chrissy?"

"It's our natural responsibility as Anishnaabe, as a mother, grandmother, sister, auntie. It's a natural instinct, that motherly way that is inside of all of us, and that no matter what, we do it out of love. Love for land, love for the people, love for our children, love for our Ancestors, love for the creator."

"How far would you go, Christi?"

"History will record for our children what we do, and what we don't do. If we let things slide, they will know, they will see that we did nothing. In the case of Oka, the people stood up for what they believed, and although they suffered and paid a price for it, they won. And we are all better for having witnessed it. It called us all to action."

Meegwetch, Nya:weh to those women and men who, in their daily lives, continue to be the life force that makes our communities healthy, our ceremonies alive, our children knowledgeable, our language strong, and our land and water safe and protected. I feel so fortunate to walk this earth as an Anishnaabekwe. This is my women's Honour Song with gratitude and humility, all for you.

Oka to Ipperwash:

The Necessity of Flashpoint Events

PETER H. RUSSELL

Flashpoint Events: Their Nature

Oka and Ipperwash are what Aboriginal scholar John Borrows calls flashpoint events.[1] Three conditions produce flashpoint events. First, an Aboriginal people believe that the government, federal or provincial or both, have violated a treaty obligation or an obligation arising out of other Canadian laws. Second, efforts extending over many years, often decades or even centuries, to resolve the issue through political or legal means have been fruitless. Third, the federal or provincial government or a municipal government authorizes developments to proceed or continue on the land or waters that are at the heart of the dispute. The flashpoint event occurs when members of the Aboriginal community see that government, without settling the long-standing dispute, is permitting activities to take place that ignore Aboriginal interests in the area and, in effect, deny Aboriginal or treaty rights. Under these conditions, members of the Aboriginal community may decide to take direct action to stop the activity and produce a flashpoint event. Usually the direct action takes the form of occupying land and blockading public access to the land.

There is a regular pattern to the media and public reaction to flashpoint events. The general public reacts primarily to the images—

which are frightening and provocative. For the aroused public, the immediate concern is the restoration of what they call "law and order." The images convey no information about what lies behind the disturbing scene, about the circumstances that finally led the Aboriginal people to occupy the land or set up the barricade. The news story is all about the immediate conflict. The pressure on government is to restore the status quo as quickly as possible and get back to business as usual. But the standoff continues because the Aboriginal people have found that doing business as usual with "the crown" means continuing to have their rights and interests ignored.

Oka and Ipperwash were major flashpoint events. The prolonged standoff at Oka between Mohawks and the Canadian army through the summer of 1990 attracted enormous media coverage nationally and internationally. Television coverage of Oka may well have cost Canada an Olympic bid. In September 1996, Bob Rae, Ontario's newly elected premier, went to Osaka, Japan, with Lieutenant Governor Lincoln Alexander to lobby the Olympic Committee to support Toronto's bid for the 1996 summer Olympics. When Rae walked into the Osaka hotel where the Olympians were meeting, he looked up at television monitors mounted in the lobby running CNN footage, over and over again, featuring an army tank rolling over a barricade defended by bandana-wearing people of colour. As members of the Olympic committee entering the hotel asked where this disturbing scene was taking place and were told it was in Canada, Rae says he knew that Toronto's bid was dead in the water.[2] Political interest in the much briefer confrontation at Ontario's Ipperwash provincial park in 1995 was more localized, but it did have major implications for Ontario premier Mike Harris, whose instruction to the police "to get the fucking Indians out of the park" was widely thought to have led directly to the death of Aboriginal protester Dudley George.

The frequency of flashpoint events has been increasing in recent years. The *Report of the Ipperwash Inquiry* lists 24 "major aboriginal occupations and protests" in Canada between 1974 (the Anishinabe Park in northern Ontario) and 2007 (Caledonia near Brantford, Ontario).[3] During this period they have occurred in every part of Canada. Most have occurred since 1990. Notwithstanding the hot feelings manifest on both sides of the barricades aroused by a flashpoint event, a research study carried out for the Ipperwash Inquiry by Don Clairmont and Jim Potts notes the low level of violence that actually occurs in Aboriginal blockades and occupations.[4] The death of Quebéc Security Corporal Marcel Lemay at Oka and of Dudley George at Ipperwash are tragic exceptions. In part the low level of violence stems from a change in police policy from an emphasis on simply removing the Aboriginal protestors and the barricades to keeping the peace and encouraging a negotiated resolution of the issues in dispute.

Although interpersonal violence in these flashpoint events is relatively rare, they often lead to considerable property damage and, more seriously, serious social disruption and stress among the Aboriginal people involved and in the non-Aboriginal local community. Often these events are very divisive for the Aboriginal community which is directly involved and the feelings of anger and resentment they arouse leave a long-standing legacy of bitterness and disrespect between Aboriginal and non-Aboriginal communities. Flashpoint events are not a pretty way of dealing with the concerns of Aboriginal Peoples. Indeed, if we do not recognize the causes and the consequences of flashpoint events we might well conclude that they are an inappropriate way of improving relations with Aboriginal Peoples, rather than, as I claim, a necessary way of achieving just relations with Aboriginal Peoples.

Flashpoint Events: Their Causes

Underlying every major flashpoint event is an unresolved dispute—usually about land and resources—that has been simmering for a very long time. The issue that triggers the occupation or blockade is typically something more focused and immediate, such as disrespect for a traditional burial ground or exclusion from a harvesting right. But it is the unresolved dispute about how lands and waters and resources are to be shared between an Aboriginal people and settler authorities that lies at the base of the grievance.

Of course, if those who think there is no need to resolve these disputes other than by applying the superior power of the settler state's security forces, then when members of an Aboriginal community show that they will no longer accept the settler state's treatment, their eruption should be put down by force. For a great many years, after the military superiority of the settler state was secured, this was generally how Aboriginal protests were handled. A noisy segment of the Canadian public and some of their media supporters would have the state handle them that way today. But, increasingly, in an age when the winds of decolonization have been blowing for some time, Canadian governments and a part of the electorate that supports them aspire to more consensual relations with Aboriginal Peoples. Canadian and provincial governments have become somewhat more respectful of undertakings their predecessor governments made to Aboriginal Peoples back when they were valued military allies and economic trading partners and their goodwill was needed for peaceful settlement.

The dispute at the base of the Oka flashpoint event in 1990 can be traced back to 1717 when the Governor of New France granted priests of the Seminary of St. Sulpice a seigneury on the north shore of Lake of Two Mountains a few kilometres west of the Island of Montreal for the purpose of establishing a permanent mission to Indians at "a site far from the evils of civilization," where the Indians could fish and hunt and farm.[5] The Indians who began to settle on the land near the seigneury were mostly Iroquoian, although some were Algonquins. For many centuries before the arrival of French settlers, the lands where the seigneury was established was part of the traditional territory of the Mohawks and other nations of the Iroquoian confederation. In 1717, the French Crown's grant of land to the Sulpicians and another in 1735 were for the use and benefit of the Indians on the express condition that title would revert to the Crown if the Indians vacated the mission. A wampum belt fashioned by the Mohawks records the terms on which the Kanehsatà:ke settlement at Lake of the Two Mountains was formed.[6]

After the fall of New France, the British Crown in the *Act of Capitulation of Montreal* promised the Indians who had been loyal to the French that they could remain on their lands except for those parts which had been formally surrendered to the Crown. The Mohawks and Algonquins living at Kanehsatà:ke hoped that the lands they had settled on would be protected by this undertaking. They also considered that this commitment was strengthened by King George III's broader promise in the Royal Proclamation of 1763 that British settlement on Indian lands would take place only on the basis of treaties with Indian nations. But although the Mohawks at Akwesasne along the St. Lawrence and at Kahnawà:ke immediately south of Montreal were able to secure reserves of land, the British refused to recognize any land rights of the Kanehsatà:ke Mohawks. The British Superintendent of Indian Affairs rejected the Mohawk wampum belt as worthless. In 1840, the British colonial regime, in appreciation of the Suplicians' assistance in quelling the Rebellion of 1837–38, passed legislation unilaterally recognizing the seminary's title to the seigniorial lands.

The Mohawks of Kanehsatà:ke never accepted this unilateral denial of their land rights. Many converted to Protestantism. They quarreled bitterly with the Suplicians and petitioned British authorities for recognition of their land rights. After Confederation, there seemed to be a breakthrough when William Spragge, Canada's new Commissioner of Indian Affairs, proposed that the government negotiate with the Suplicians to have the seigneury transferred to the Crown and held in trust for the Indians of the Lake of Two Mountains. But nothing came of this. The Kanehsatà:ke Indians continued to press their claim by petitioning and, when petitions were ignored, through flashpoint events that were put down by force. They then resorted to the courts. In 1912, three Mohawk Chiefs managed to get their claim before the Judicial Committee of the Privy Council. Not surprisingly, the British law lords upheld British legislation confirming the Sulpcians' title to the lands. This British tribunal knew nothing of the recognition of common law native title that underlay the 1763 Royal Proclamation. In 1889, at the high tide of European imperialism, the JCPC had ruled that the only rights of Aboriginal people were those granted to them by the sovereign imperial authorities.[7]

As urban sprawl, transportation and industrial development continued to encroach on the Aboriginal Peoples' land, the federal government offered them reserve lands elsewhere. In 1869, the Algonquins of Kanehsatà:ke moved to lands set aside for them at Maniwaki in northwestern Quebéc. In 1881, 35 of the 120 Mohawk families at Kanehsatà:ke moved to land reserved for along the Gibson River between Georgian Bay and Muskoka in Ontario. But most of the Mohawks wished to remain on what remained of their lands. By the latter part of the twentieth century, their community of just under a thousand lived on a checkerboard of lots in the town of Oka and surrounding farm lands which had been purchased from the Sulpicians in 1945. This area constituted 1% of the original lands assigned by the Sulpicians for the Indians use and benefit.

When the government of Canada, following the Supreme Court of Canada's decision in *Calder*, initiated a comprehensive land-claims process for First Nations which have never made land treaties with the Crown, the Mohawks of Kanehsatà:ke joined with the Mohawks of Kahnawake and Akwasasne to submit a comprehensive claim. This claim was summarily rejected by the government because the federal government asserted that the Mohawks could not prove their occupation of these lands "from time immemorial." In 1977, the Mohawks of Kanehsatà:ke submitted a specific claim with respect to their rights to the seigneurial lands. After nearly a decade of deliberations and appeals, the federal government, which was legislator, judge and jury in the process, decided that the claim did not meet its criteria of "specific claims."

The spark that ignited the 1990 occupation and barricades at Oka was the decision of the town of Oka's council to support a project that would add nine holes to a private golf course by encroaching on land known as the Pines. The Pines are sandy hills on the northern boundary of the town of Oka on which the Mohawks had planted pine trees many years earlier to keep sand from sliding town on the town and the lake below. The Pines "are the heart of the territory the people of Kanehsatà:ke called their own for more than 270 years."[8] Their burial ground is at the edge of the Pines. For several months, federal Indian Affairs officials had been working with the band council and the municipal council to broker a deal that would save the Pines. Then, in early March 1990, the Oka Council voted to proceed with the golf course extension. This triggered a Mohawk demonstration at the golf club on March 9. The following day, a few Mohawks dragged a fishing shack into a clearing in the Pines and began to build a camp. They were soon joined by members of the Mohawk Warrior Societies from Kahnawà:ke and Akwasasne. In April, when the fishing shack was vandalized, Mohawks blocked the south entrance to the dirt road running through the Pines off Highway 344 and the north entrance connecting to a back road into Oka. The flashpoint event had begun.

The Ipperwash tragedy has its genesis in the failure of Canada to honour treaty arrangements entered into with Anishnabek-speaking peoples in the early years of the nineteenth century. The treaty in question is known as the Huron Tract Treaty and was signed in 1827 by representatives of the British Crown and chiefs representing the Ojibwa and Chippewa peoples who had played a crucial role as Great Britain's allies in the War of 1812.[9] Under the terms of this treaty, four parcels of land were reserved for the exclusive use of the peoples of the First Nations. One of these parcels of land was the Stoney Point reserve where Dudley George's people had lived until 1942 when the Government of Canada appropriated it for military purposes. The Stoney Point lands run along a sandy stretch of the southeastern shore of Lake Huron. The Kettle Point reserve is just south of it. The other two reserves were in the Sarnia area. In return for these four reserves and a small annual payment, the First Nations agreed that European settlement would be permitted on the remaining 2.7 million acres of their traditional lands—virtually all of southwestern Ontario.

Although there were verbal and, later on, written undertakings in all of these "land cession" treaties that the Aboriginal people would be free to continue their economic pursuits in lands they agreed to share with newcomers, British and Canadian authorities regarded off-reserve lands as "surrendered" lands and, as the settler economy developed, left no room for an Aboriginal economy. "Indians," as the Ojibwa, Mississauga, Odawa, Pottowatomi, Delware and members of other First Nations were called, were confined to their postage-stamp reserves. And on these reserves they were made subject to legislation, culminating in the *Indian Act*, that aimed to prepare them for assimilation into settler society.

By the twentieth century, Dudley George's people, the Stoney Pointers, and the Kettle Point people were experiencing the full force of this colonialist regime. Now a community of several hundred, they relied for survival entirely on the produce of their small reserves. They were not even allowed to sell firewood in neighbouring towns. In the 1920s they came under pressure to sell their beachfront property to realtors eyeing its summer cottage potential. In a transaction facilitated in 1927 by a developer's cash payments to members before a band vote, part of the Kettle Point beachfront was surrendered to the Crown (aka the Government of Canada) for $15 an acre. The following year all of the Stoney Point beach front, with its magnificent sand dunes, was surrendered for $35 an acre. The surrendered lands, of course, were sold for development at several times the amount paid to the people on the truncated reserves. In 1936, the Ontario government paid developers $100 an acre for a part of the Stoney Point lakefront to establish Ipperwash Provincial Park.

Some band members, at the time, questioned the legality of these transactions. But at this time the Indian Act made it a crime for a lawyer to be an advocate for Indian land issues in the courts. Many years later, when Aboriginal people gained access to the courts, Judge Gordon Killeen of Ontario's Superior Court found that while the transactions were legally valid, they had about them the "odour of moral failure."[10] The Ontario Court of Appeal found that the "tainted dealings" might support a case for breach of fiduciary duty against Canada. These decisions were upheld by the Supreme Court of Canada.[11] The Stoney Point people are still awaiting monetary compensation for breach of the Crown's fiduciary obligation.

Being swindled by the federal government was by no means the only difficulty Dudley George's people had to endure. The Ontario government rejected archeological evidence and refused, again and again, a band request to protect their old burial site in Ipperwash Park. This cruel and disrespectful treatment of their sacred site built up a bitter sense of resentment among the Stoney Pointers.

But the people of the Stoney Point reserve were to suffer an even greater indignity. In 1942 the Government of Canada appropriated the entire Stoney Point reserve for military purposes. The Stoney Point people were squeezed into the Kettle Point reserve, their houses moved or destroyed. This was done under the *War Measures Act*, against the clearly expressed wishes of the Kettle and Stoney Point people, at a time when their young men in disproportionately high numbers were serving in Canada's armed forces, and despite the availability of other land in the area. In reviewing this appropriation, Judge Sidney Linden, who conducted the Ipperwash Inquiry, comments that what he found so disturbing is "the stark contrast between the ease with which First Nations people gave their loyalty and trust to the government and the ease with which the Government of Canada betrayed that trust."[12]

After the war, the Department of National Defence promised to return the reserve to the Kettle and Stoney Point band as soon as it was no longer needed for military purposes. But, despite many, many efforts to get it back, many government promises to return it and a parliamentary committee calling for its return, nothing was done. The Canadian government pig-headedly just hung on to the land even though it no longer had any use for it.

By 1993, a group of Stoney Pointers that included Dudley George and many members of his family lost patience with the decades of fruitless negotiations and broken promises and began living on their reserve. On July 29, 1995, they drove an old school bus into an empty barracks building, in effect taking back the land reserved for their people by the Huron Tract Treaty of 1827. The caretaker crew of soldiers left peacefully after helping the "occupiers" operate the base equipment.

On September 5, 1995, after the Ipperwash Provincial Park had closed down for the season, a few Stoney Point people came into the Park to mark off and secure their burial ground. The next night, Dudley George and other Stoney Pointers were enjoying an evening barbeque in the land alongside the parking lot between the part of their reserve they had recovered and the provincial park. They were in no mood to be pushed around by the police. Suddenly confronted by a phalanx of 30 helmeted police banging truncheons on their shields, the men and boys in the group, some brandishing sticks, charged at the police. To Kenneth Deane, an OPP sharpshooter hiding in the bush, Dudley George's stick looked like a gun. He riddled him with bullets. Thus did this flashpoint event come to a sudden and tragic end.

Though the details of the events that led to both of these flashpoint events are different, they both manifest the same underlying factors. The historical base of both is a failure of European authorities—at Oka the French, at Ipperwash the British, and their Canadian successor governments—to live up to undertakings they made in order to have peaceful and mutually beneficial relations with First Nations. Both involved massive dispossession of the Indigenous Peoples and severe economic marginalization. The loss of land in both cases was legally justified by the imperial powers and their successor Canadian governments and courts, which ignored the legal basis on which relations Indigenous Peoples were originally based. This legal opportunism was accompanied by actions on the part of non-Indigenous governments that gave priority to projects of minor importance to the non-Indigenous majority—a golf course extension at Oka, an unnecessary military base at Ipperwash—over vital interest of Indigenous Peoples. Finally, in both cases, members of the Aboriginal community seeing that political negotiations and litigation over a great many years were getting them nowhere, decided to seek justice by taking action. Analyses of the many other flashpoint events that have occurred in recent years would reveal a similar pattern of causal conditions.

Flashpoint Events: Their Consequences

The immediate consequence of the flashpoint events at Oka and Ipperwash was a reversal of the actions by non-Aboriginal authorities that sparked them. The federal government paid $5.28 million for 40 acres of disputed land at Oka to put an end to the golf course expansion plan. Soon after Judge Sidney Linden' released his Ipperwash Inquiry report, the Ontario Government announced that it was returning the Ipperwash Provincial Park lands to the Chippewas of Kettle and Stoney Point First Nation with a plan for co-managing the park to be worked out with the First Nations and local communities. The Stoney Pointers continued their "occupation" and enjoyment, free of police interference, of their lands that for 63 years had been used by Canada as a military base.

But these reversals of the government actions that provoked the countering actions by Indigenous Peoples are only the most immediate consequences. What about the larger issues in dispute?

Certainly the confrontations at Kanehsatà:ke and Kahnawà:ke did not lead to a resolution of the underlying conflict between the Mohawks and Canada about sovereignty and land rights. Ottawa and Québec continued to reject the Mohawks' position that they form a sovereign nation which has never agreed to being subject to British or Canadian sovereignty. Federal Ministers of Indian Affairs have tried to treat the communities at Kanehsatà:ke and Kahnawà:ke as bands subject to *Indian Act* regulations. This has involved federal government interventions at both Mohawk communities aimed at imposing *Indian Act* forms of government and opposing government based on Mohawk constitutional principles. These interventions added to the divisive impact the events of the summer of 1990 had on both communities.

After Oka the Quebéc government was even more blatantly negative in resisting Mohawk self-government. John Ciaccia, the Quebéc Minister of Native Affairs and the only cabinet member who showed any understanding of the underlying issues, towards the end of the crisis was completely sidelined. The standoff at Oka was much longer and far more provocative to the non-Aboriginal community than the brief two days that culminated in Dudley George's death at Ipperwash. It began with the death of a Canadian soldier, continued through the long hot summer of 1990, involved violent altercations between Mohawk warriors and the Quebéc and the threat of more serious conflict between warriors armed with AK-47s and Canadian armed forces, the spread of Mohawk resistance to Kahnawà:ke and the closing of the Mercier Bridge entrance to Montreal. All of this certainly soured relations between the Mohawks and members of the non-Aboriginal community whose leaders did nothing to enlighten them about the underlying issues. The provincial government treated the Mohawk actions entirely as a law and order problem, arresting and charging many of the Mohawk warriors, and directing the *Sûreté du Québec* to patrol the Mohawk communities.

These negative consequences should not blind us to the positive gains for the Mohawk Nation. Above all, and despite much internal stress and conflict, the Mohawks' resistance at Kanehsatà:ke and Kahnawà:ke strengthened those societies' sense of being responsible for their own future. They had held off the Canadian army and a provincial police force. By showing their determination and ability to defend their vital interests they asserted their own sense of sovereignty. While the Mohawks' resistance did not secure recognition of their sovereignty by the Government of Canada, it convinced that government that the time had come for a fundamental examination of relations with Aboriginal Peoples. It was the "Oka Crisis" that spurred Brian Mulroney and his government to establish the Royal Commission on Aboriginal Peoples with a mandate to conduct a comprehensive study of the conditions of Aboriginal Peoples and their relationship with Canada. The Mohawk communities have continued to build on the sense of agency strengthened by their action in the "Oka Crisis." This is particularly evident with the larger community of Kahnawà:ke that has been able to secure control over its schools, social welfare and security through pragmatic agreements with Ottawa and Quebéc City—agreements in which none of the parties concede an ounce of sovereignty.[13]

The political context of Ipperwash was significantly different from Oka, and this difference affected the way in which the larger issues underlying that flashpoint event were treated. The denouement of the Ipperwash crisis came swiftly with the death of an Aboriginal man, Dudley George. This tragic death immediately provoked a wave of public sympathy for the Aboriginal community. Even though the provincial government of the day, the recently elected Harris Conservative government, denied any responsibility for Dudley George's death and treated the entire episode as a law and order issue, there was much political criticism of the Harris government's response to Ipperwash and demands for a full public inquiry, a demand that the Liberals promised to carry out if they were elected to government. The McGuinty Liberals honoured that promise when they defeated the Harris government in the 2003 provincial election.

The fact that there was so much political criticism of the Harris government's treatment of Ipperwash reflects change taking place in the wider Canadian political environment. I would characterize this change as an increased acknowledgement on the part of non-Aboriginal political leaders of Canada's failure to establish just and fair relations with Aboriginal Peoples. There is evidence of this change in the inclusion of a large section of the proposed *Charlottetown Accord* devoted to facilitating Aboriginal self-government and honouring treaties. Granted that package of constitutional proposals was rejected by 54% of the Canadian people voting in the 1992 referendum, still the fact remains that these provisions were supported by the federal government and all ten provincial governments and were not a significant factor in the *Charlottetown Accord's* referendum defeat[14] indicates that since Oka, Canada had moved further along the decolonizing path. This change in the political climate was surely a factor in the McGuinty Liberals unrelenting attack on the Harris government for its performance at Ipperwash.

There was also a *little* progress in the courts and at the federal level in remedying the violations of treaty rights that were a crucial part of the events leading up to Ipperwash. In the 1990s when the Kettle and Stoney Point people finally gained access to the courts, they were able to secure the court finding referred to above that the transactions through which they had been conned into surrendering their valuable beach properties were tainted with "the odour of moral failure." This ruling was upheld by the Supreme Court of Canada, as was the lower court's ruling that this breach did not undermine the legality of the tainted surrenders. Subsequently, the Indian Claims Commission found that the federal government's dealings with these lands constituted a breach of the Crown's fiduciary obligations and recommended that the federal government negotiate with the First Nation to work out an appropriate remedy for its moral failure. Judge Linden reports that at the time of writing (May 2007) no settlement had been reached.[15] In 1985 the Government of Canada signed an agreement with the Kettle and Stoney Point Band which was approved by 80% of the band members. The agreement calls for a return of the army camp "when not required by Defence" with compensation of $2,490,000. The Department of Defence did not require it then nor ten years late later when Dudley George and others from his community repossessed the lands. The federal government has still not formally returned the army camp lands to the First Nation. Part of the problem has been difficulty in determining whether the lands should be turned over to the Kettle and Stoney Point First Nation which the federal government recognizes or to the Stoney Point First Nation which it does not recognize. This is a lingering legacy of federal government interference in the internal affairs of Aboriginal Peoples.

Policing is another area in which the Ipperwash flashpoint has resulted in a policy gain. The horrific use of an armed tactical response police unit to break-up a family picnic and barbeque beside a provincial park demonstrated clearly to senior officers of the Ontario Provincial Police, if not to their political masters, that a new approach for policing Aboriginal occupations was needed. Soon after the Ipperwash tragedy, OPP Commissioner Gail Boniface began a process of reforming the policy for policing Aboriginal occupations and blockades based on a peacekeeper approach developed by the RCMP. This approach recognizes that breaches of laws at issue in these events are not simply violations of trespass and public convenience laws but violations of treaties and other laws governing Canada's constitutional relations with Aboriginal Peoples. The police intervention in these situations should aim at minimizing violence while a credible process of resolving the underlying issues through negotiations between Aboriginal and non-Aboriginal governments is mounted. Judge Linden reports progress in applying this policy in various flashpoint events across Canada and strongly recommends such a policy for Ontario.[16]

The OPP employed the peacekeeping approach in policing the Six Nations peoples' occupation of a building site at Caledonia near Brantford, Ontario, in 2006–07. This approach was in stark contrast to Sûreté du Québec response to the Aboriginal occupation at Oka. However, it was clear from the virulent public criticism it attracted that mainstream opinion continues to view these flashpoint events in narrow law-and-order terms. Political leaders in Ontario have made no effort to enlighten the public. The Conservative opposition in the Ontario legislature sniped at the Liberal government for not insisting on tougher policing at Caledonia. For its part the McGuinty Liberal government appointed a new OPP Commissioner, Julian Fantino, who has shown no understanding at all of the peace-keeping approach recommended by Judge Linden and practiced by his predecessor.

A significant consequence of both Oka and Ipperwash was the establishment of major commissions of inquiry into relations with Aboriginal Peoples. It was the Oka affair's stark demonstration of the clear absence of policy mutually acceptable to Aboriginal and non-Aboriginal Canada that moved Prime Minister Mulroney to commission retired Chief Justice Brian Dickson to consult with Aboriginal Peoples on the terms of reference of a commission on inquiry and to advise him on the composition of such a commission. The result was the Royal Commission on Aboriginal Peoples (RCAP), composed of four commissioners: George Erasmus, Viola Robinson, Mary Sillett and Paul Chartrand, who were leaders in each of the main streams of Canada's Aboriginal community (status Indians, non-status Indians, Inuit and Métis); and three non-Aboriginal commissioners (Rene Dussault a Québec jurist; Bertha Wilson, the first woman jurist to sit on the Supreme Court of Canada; and Alan Blakeney, a former Premier of the Province of Saskatchewan). Their mandate covered virtually all aspects of Aboriginal Peoples' relationship with Canada and their current social and economic conditions. The Commission conducted a process of public consultation that took it to over 100 Aboriginal communities and towns and cities in every part of Canada. RCAP was the first time in any settler country that there was an effort to have Aboriginal and non-Aboriginal people review their past relationships, study their present conditions and develop a plan for going forward together.

The Ipperwash Inquiry fulfilled a promise made by the Liberal party when it was in opposition and was established soon after the McGuinty Liberals gained power in 2003. The Ipperwash Inquiry was led by a single judge, Sidney Linden, who carried out an extensive program of public consultations with both Aboriginal communities and non-Aboriginal communities in Ontario and invited and received submissions from many Aboriginal and non-Aboriginal organizations. The Ipperwash Inquiry's mandate was two-pronged: it was to conduct a full inquiry into the circumstances that led to the death of Dudley George, and it was to make recommendations on policies that would lessen the likelihood of such tragic incidents occurring in the future. This was the first time a province had established such a broad mandate for examining relations with Aboriginal Peoples. In focusing on Ontario, the Inquiry was dealing with the Canadian province that has the largest Aboriginal population, and a province which is covered almost entirely by historic treaties.

Of course, with commissions of inquiry the question always arises of the extent to which their ideas and recommendations were implemented. In the case of RCAP, only a very small number of the hundreds of recommendations in the commission's final report were implemented. The commission reported to a different government from the one that had established it. Although the Chrétien Liberal government did not commit to carrying out chapter and verse of the commission's report, its official response to RCAP, *Gathering Strength*, supported the commissioners' central proposals, promising to work with Aboriginal Peoples on agreements concerning self-government and resources, to honour treaty obligations and to close the gap between the living conditions of Aboriginal Canadians and non-Aboriginal Canadians. Royal Commissions, particularly those like RCAP that are assigned broad policy mandates, should not be judged solely, or even mainly, in terms of the number of their recommendations that are implemented. Their primary value in the broadest sense is educational. RCAP provides a statement of how relations with Aboriginal Peoples must be reformed if they are to be just and mutually beneficial.

The policy recommendations in Judge Linden's Ipperwash Report focused on policing and treaty relations. As noted, there has been some progress in implementing its recommendations on policing, although the Ontario government has done little to ensure that the changes in policing Judge Linden recommended are official and enduring. Judge Linden's report makes it clear that the underlying cause of the Ipperwash tragedy was a failure to honour treaty relations. The educational thrust of his recommendations is to help the people of Ontario understand that "we are all treaty people" and to show how the promise of the treaties on which Ontario is founded can best be fulfilled. The key instrument recommended for doing this is a Treaty Commission to monitor treaty relations, facilitate the fair and expeditious resolution of treaty disputes and educate the people of Ontario about treaty relationships. The McGuinty government welcomed the report and committed itself to implementing its recommendations which, in contrast to RCAP's, did not try to dot every "I" and cross very "T" and were modest in number. It quickly implemented Linden's recommendation to establish a Ministry of Aboriginal Affairs. Moving beyond that to the establishment of a Treaty Commission will take time as it involves working with the federal government which is, in effect, a party to all of the treaties in Ontario and with the other party to those treaties, the Aboriginal Peoples in Ontario. In the two years since the Ipperwash report was released some progress has been made. Ontario's Aboriginal Peoples have shown a capacity to work together on the Ipperwash proposals through several province-wide and regional organizations, and the federal government's participation has made implementation a three-cornered process. It is too early to determine how fruitful this complex process will be. But there is no doubt of the educational value of the Ipperwash report in providing an understanding of the treaty relations on which Ontario was founded and on which a mutually beneficial relationship with its Aboriginal Peoples depends.

Flashpoint Events: Their Necessity

For those of us who seek justice in Aboriginal relations, flashpoint events are a necessity. These events do not result in a total remedy of the conditions underlying the particular situation that sparked the event. They do not deliver full justice, but they do put a stop to furthering an injustice. And what is the alternative for Aboriginal Peoples who have exhausted the possibilities of having an injustice dealt with through political negotiations or the courts? Should they just continue to lump it and say "aw shucks, let's hope that someday those white folks and their governments will stop doing that stuff to us." That's not advice that I could give.

Besides stopping the perpetration of a particular act of injustice, these flashpoint events yield other deeper benefits. As can be seen from the analysis of Oka and Ipperwash, these acts of Aboriginal resistance serve as wake-up calls to governments. They are sharp and clear signals that Aboriginal Peoples are not going to take it on the chin any more, that there are fundamental flaws in the conditions of Aboriginal communities and the treatment of their rights that governments must address. For Aboriginal Peoples they strengthen a sense of agency, a sense that their communities and their governments have the primary responsibility for protecting their rights and advancing their interests.

The Aboriginal initiatives that trigger flashpoint events, of course, are not the only way of protecting rights and advancing interests. They certainly have their downside. They can be very stressful and divisive for the Aboriginal community involved. They can create much inconvenience for the non-Aborginal community. Occasionally they lead to property damage, personal injury and, as at Oka and Ipperwash, death. They always put a strain on relations between Aboriginal and non-Aboriginal communities. But so long as political negotiations and litigation fail to stop injustices or provide timely and adequate resolution of disputes about the rights of Aboriginal Peoples and the treaty obligations of governments, flashpoint events, despite their adverse aspects, will be necessary. As Aboriginal Peoples gather their political strength, they may become more frequent, unless, as I hope, Canadian governments and the people who vote for them can move more expeditiously along the path of decolonization.

---

1 John Borrows (2007), "Crown and Aboriginal Occupations of Land: A History & Comparison" Research Paper prepared for the Ipperwash Inquiry, <www.ipperwashinquiry.ca>.

2 Story told to the author.

3 *Report of the Ipperwash Inquiry* (2007), Vol. 2, p. 21, <www.attorneygeneral.jus.gov. on.ca/inquiries/ipperwash/report/vol_2/index.html>.

4 *Ibid.*, p. 23.

5 Geoffrey York (1991) and Loreen Pindera, *People of the Pines: The Warriors and the Legacy of Oka*, Toronto: Little Brown, p. 86.

6 See York and Pindera, (1991) and the sources they list in chapter 6 on the history of Kahnawà:ke.

7 *Cooper v. Stewart* (1889) 14 App. Cas. 286.

8 York and Pendera, (1991) p. 43.

9 The historical account that follows is based on evidence given at the Ipperwash Inquiry and is summarized by Judge Sydney Linden in Volume 1 of the *Report of the Ipperwash Inquiry*, <www.attorneygeneral.jus.gov.on.ca/inquiries/ipperwash/report/ vol_I/index.html>

10 *Chippewa of Kettle and Stoney Point v. Canada*, (1995), 24 OR. (3d) 654, at 690

11 *Chippewa of Kettle and Stoney Point v. Canada*, (1998) 1 S.C.R. 756.

12 *Report of the Ipperwash Inquiry* (2007), Vol 1.

13 See Martin Papillon (2008) "Canadian Federalism and the Emerging Mosaic of Aboriginal Governance," in Herman Bakvis and Grace Skogstad, eds., *Canadian Federalism: Performance, Effectiveness and Legitimacy*, 2nd edition, Toronto: Oxford University Press.

14 But a significant number of First Nations rejected the Aboriginal rights section of the Accord because they did not accept the process as a legitimate way of dealing with the rights of their nation. Many Aboriginal women also opposed the Accord because their Canada-wide association was excluded from the process.

15 *Report of the Ipperwash Inquiry* (2007), Vol. 1, p. 63.

16 *Report of the Ipperwash Inquiry* (2007), Vol. 3, ch. 9, <www.attorneygeneral.jus.gov.on.ca/ inquiries/ipperwash/report/vol_3/index.html>.

Cowboys and Indians

WAB KINEW

The summer of 1990 was the summer that we stopped playing Cowboys and Indians and started being warriors. Growing up on a reserve called Ojibways of Onigaming, which is on the east side of Lake of the Woods in North-Western Ontario, my friends and I would play war games outside every day. For most of our lives we had played the conventional game with roles inspired by westerns or whatever action movie was hot at the time. However, when we started to see images of the warriors in The Pines standing up for our people and for our land, we were inspired to emulate them. Not only was this a watershed moment in our lives as we became politicized for the first time, it was also the start of a much larger shift: it was the moment in which struggle for Native rights became ingrained into the fabric of Anishinaabe society for my generation.

I was nine years old at the time. Most of my friends and cousins that I played with were between eight and twelve. It's difficult to underline how radical of a shift it was for us to identify with the warriors. For our entire lives we had been raised to think of ourselves as Canadian. We sang "O Canada" every morning in school. Though we lived in a community that was economically deprived and faced a number of social problems, we were not aware of any inequality. We figured everyone in Canada lived as we did and we fully embraced the vision of ourselves as citizens of this country. We were also taught a profound respect for the men and women that serve in the Armed

Forces of both Canada and United States. Every time we went to a pow-wow, we saw the grand entry led by veterans. The pow-wow would stop for a flag song as the veterans retired the colours, and then, typically, an Anishinaabe song to honour all servicemen and women. To put it simply, we all respected people in uniform and held them in high esteem.

It was shocking then to see the Canadian Army deployed against people that looked like us, with their military vehicles moving into a community that reminded us a lot of our home. I asked myself "Why would my country be trying to fight it's own people?" The only plausible answer was that perhaps we were not thought of as other Canadians—that the Canada I grew up believing in didn't believe in me. That's when something changed. For the first time I realized that my Anishinaabe identity superseded my role as a Canadian citizen. I saw my friends come to similar realizations as we all identified with the people of Kanehsatà:ke. The "Oka Crisis" was an event that forced people to choose sides, and we did not have to think twice about which side we were on. We were with the warriors.

We were the warriors. Everyday we would disappear into the forest of our reserve to play warriors. At night we'd run home to watch the days update from Kanehsatà:ke and cheer for our heroes. The next day we'd imitate what we'd seen on CBC's *The National*. On the first night of the blockade, we saw a Warrior driving a front-end loader and fortifying the barricade. The next day we tipped over a hockey net that I had in my backyard, and that became our barricade. We piled lumber, sticks and random junk onto that hockey net and hunkered down. On the night that the army raided the long house in Kahnawà:ke, we sat and stared in awe at footage of a big Mohawk man in a red shirt. The next day we all wore red shirts. I'm exaggerating about the red shirts, but you get the idea.

We had a new set of role models: role models that were fighting for something bigger than themselves, role models that were fearless and role models that were proud to be Native. In turn, we became proud of ourselves as Anishinaabe and sought out the role models that we had closer to home. I started talking to my parents about Native rights. My father told me about the demonstration in Kenora in 1965 that my uncle Fred had been instrumental in organizing. My mother told me about my father's history as community organizer and political leader. My friend Makwa's dad, Seymour, started to wear his red beret again. That is a symbol of the fight Native rights that was made popular by the American Indian Movement. He told his boys about his time as a member of the Ojibway Warrior Society in the 1970s. My cousin Waylon's father, Makate Kiniw, was also a member of that organization when he was young. These were stories we had never heard before, and I do not know if our parents would have ever told us about them if it had not been for the stand that the people of Kahnesatà:ke made.

One of the stories that we heard that summer was about the occupation of Anicinabe Park. As it turns out, one of the first armed occupations in Canada had taken place in our backyard, at a place that we drove by every time we went to the pow-wow in Rat Portage. In July of 1974, some 16 years before Oka, the Ojibway Warrior Society had occupied Anicinabe Park on the south side of Kenora. It was the culmination of years of racism in the area. Native people were often beaten and then dumped into the lake near what is now Harbourfront. Native people were banned from eating in most restaurants other than Ted's cafe and Ho Ho's. Native women were subjected to rape and abuse at the hands of non-Natives. That summer the tension boiled over, and the young people of Treaty 3 entered the park for a youth conference and decided to make a stand. My dad was the Grand Chief of Treaty 3 at the time and worked behind the scenes for a peaceful resolution. My friend's dad, Seymour, and my cousin's dad, Makate Kiniw, were there as warriors, taking up arms to fight for our people. These were guys that we saw every day growing up on the Rez. We knew them as mild mannered men who carried themselves with the quiet stoicism and humility that is typical of Lake of the Woods Anishinaabe. And yet, they had a history of taking up arms just like the warriors we were now emulating. How cool was that?

When you hear about the oral traditions of Anishinaabe people you often think of Nanaboozhoo stories or the Midewin legends, but our oral tradition also includes stories of resistance and struggle. We heard about how the Ojibway Warrior Society would sing on the pow-wow drum every day in Anicinabe Park. Apparently, that drove the town people of Kenora insane. Some of the stories were funny, others serious, others even a bit scary. But people were talking about things that had been dormant for a long time. Old feelings were starting to surface.

As young people, we started to feel new things as well. I started to wonder whether we didn't deserve better than the Rez life was offering us. Over the course of that summer the feeling that we had to do something became very intense. When I came to Winnipeg I saw the peace village that had been set up in front of the Manitoba Legislature. I looked at the tipi in front of the building, studied the tents that were pitched in Memorial park and read the signs that people had made in support of the Mohawks. I had been to the Legislature a couple of times before. Once, after the murder of J.J. Harper, I went with my mom to a demonstration there. I remember that because my nephew Jay and I both showed up with the same placard. It read "policeman are you my friend?" I had also been there for another demonstration around the time of the Meech Lake accord wearing an Elijah Harper T-shirt that my aunt Karen had made for me. Back on the Rez, we watched news stories about railroads and highways being blockaded in other parts of Canada. We heard about protests further east in Ontario that were being held to show solidarity with the Mohawks. We felt like we were missing out.

The "Oka Crisis" changed the way we played "war" by forcing us to think for the first time about what we were fighting for and who our allies were. This was the moment when the struggle for Native rights became ingrained into the fabric of Anishinaabe society for my generation. War games have been played by Ojibway children for millenia teaching them both practical skills like aim and balance, while also informing them of broader societal notions like courage and valour. Suddenly, the vehicle that delivered those lessons to us had an American Indian Movement bumper sticker on it. Instead, the games we played were now teaching us to become warriors who would stand up for our people, our land and our rights. I have heard some activists talk about having an "Oka" on every Rez and how that would be a "revolution." Oka changed the definition of Warrior for my generation. To me that is the real "revolution."

In the years following Oka, I have watched the strides that our people have taken on the journey toward equality. Some followed directly from the crisis, like the Royal Commission on Aboriginal People. Others followed indirectly but benefited from the change in attitudes that Oka brought about, like the apology to Residential School Survivors.

At the same time I have made my own strides. I have gone to school and received an education. I have become a responsible father. I have sundanced for a decade for change. I have a deep respect for those that serve our country in the military and for my relatives who serve in the American armed forces. I fully embrace the vision of Canada as a multicultural society and I strive to be positive force within that. Before I am any of those things though, I know that I am an Anishinaabe. And I can trace that attitude in large part to the summer of 1990, the summer that we stopped playing Cowboys and Indians and started being warriors.

Dust[1]

WAUBGESHIG RICE

It was a summer afternoon sometime in the mid-1980s and I was just a kid. My little brother couldn't have been older than three. Our Mom loaded us into the family's Dodge Reliant K and drove us up to meet Dad. She didn't explain to me exactly where we were going or what we were doing, but I could tell by the nervous urgency in her voice that it was important.

We tore up the dusty rez roads, and in a few minutes made it to one of the sandpits near the old CN line. The trains hadn't run through here in years, but apparently there was a CN crew there with trucks, attempting to load them up with sand. There were dozens of our own community members there as well, trying to block them, holding up signs and chanting things like "This is OUR land!"

This was a few years before a group of Mohawks took their own stand at a place called Oka. A stand that changed how this country viewed and treated Aboriginal people. There was no template for resistance for the people in my community on that summer day, and what they were doing was on a much smaller scale than what those Mohawks pulled off years later. Still, it was driven by a universal passion and dream of reconnecting with the land.

In my youthful naiveté I didn't see what the big deal was. It was just sand—and there was lots of it there. But as the afternoon went on I slowly understood what my community was standing up for. As Elders and children alike blocked the machinery, I saw for the first time the strongest bond that I've ever witnessed or felt in my life: between my people and the land.

The crew members in their hard hats and jeans stood around, cracking jokes and pointing. They didn't really care, because they didn't have to work. TV crews showed up, and so did the cops and all kinds of other officials to try to diffuse the situation. Emotions ran high but everything remained peaceful. Eventually the trucks left, empty.

To them, it was just sand. But to us, it was all we had left to hold on to. These grains of sand under our feet had sustained us for thousands of years. They held us up as our old ways of life were brutally uprooted and left to wither. It wasn't just sand they were trying to dig away at. It was identity. Tradition. And the strongest bond that there is—between Mother Earth and her children.

And at that point it was a bond that breathed new life into our community. At a time when the traditional Anishinaabe way of life was hanging by a thread; just memories in the hearts and minds of the Elders. The seeds were in the ground, but we had been toiling through a devastating drought for decades. This unified stance and this unbridled passion are what finally brought the rain.

After that I saw things like the drum. I heard the Ojibwe language louder than I ever had before. I can't legitimately say that our community's cultural renaissance is tied back to this one solid moment, but it was a catalyst. We became Anishinaabe people once again by taking a stand, and once again understanding the power of land.

---

1 A previous version of this essay entitled "The Power of the Land" was published in *Spirit Magazine* (Winter 2007) and is reprinted here with permission.

When Hope Can be a Lie

AL HUNTER

You're being pacified,
lied to.
Understand hope.
Your hope is a lie,
It's a big carrot on a stick,
an illusion,
designed
to keep you running
in circles
while all around you
your prison walls close in
You're being pacified
Lied to.

Understand hope.
Your hope is a lie,
A fire
A funeral pyre
To burn you dead or alive
Your own cremation
At the hands of the nation
Subjugation for your blind participation
In Hope.

You're being pacified
Lied to.

You're being pacified,
tied to
the gallows
while your own fingers tie down a knot
in the noose.
Bust loose
while you can
the prison is not what they create
it's what you create
in your mind.
Bust loose
stop running in circles, look
at the hook
that rips out of your skin
set yourself free
the wound is worth it
the scar is worth it
bust loose
you'll see
it's your own choice
to free your voice
to voice your freedom
to say no to the noose
bust loose
hope is not a word
it's but a tool for your pacification
stop running in circles
stop your never ending gyre
stop the fire
for your own funeral pyre
Stop.
Look.
Listen.
See what's real

To reveal and to heal
Hear the chorus of voices
That say we have choices
That say to be pacified
To be lied to
Will not be my life
I will not
be the sacrifice
At the altar of Hope.

Watch their world fall away
When you see that

You control
Your own
Destiny.

I control
My own
Destiny.

We control
Our own
Destiny.

We control
Our own
Destiny.

Hashinoqwah

JUDY DA SILVA

When I think of the "Oka Crisis," I think of all of the similar struggles my own family and my own community have faced and are facing. I live in Treaty 3, and I am an Anishinaabekwe. My experience has been different from the Kanien'kehaka, but I know, like all of the women that have come before me, and the ones yet to be born that our fight to protect our lands, our way of life, and the health of our families is the same. In this paper, I want to honour all the women who have sacrificed to make our lives better, especially the ones who are criminalized for protecting the land. Women are the carriers of our nations, and because of this they often bare the brunt of colonial anger, racism, and violence. The women of Kanehsatà:ke, Kahnawà:ke and Akwesasne are my sisters, and I sing my Honour Song to them, by sharing my own experiences and the experiences of the women in my family. My idealism and my strength comes from my grandmother Hashinoqwah. She passed into the Spirt World May 7, 1984—a day I will never forget and a day I learned to live from death.

Sacred Fire

In 2002, some people in my communty of Grassy Narrows started a blockade to protect our lands against clear-cut logging. Since then, many fire keepers have passed through our land in support of our blockade. The sacred fire is one tool our people use to pray. A sacred fire can be made anywhere at anytime. Before you start the fire, you put tobacco on the earth and ask the Grandmothers/Grandfathers to come and hear your prayers. This is how I start the sacred fire.

We kept that sacred fire buring through our blockade. These fire keepers had different routines on how to start the fire—use only wooden matches, start with birchbark, walk clockwise around the fire, use only seven rocks for the firepit, use only thirteen rocks for the firepit, use only poplar, use only spruce, use only pine, pour water on the rocks surrounding the firepit, put tobacco around the rocks surrounding the firepit, use tobacco flags with the four direction colours of broadcloth around the fire, do not throw garbage in the sacred fire, do not gossip around the sacred fire, speak only of good things by the fire, only men can make the sacred fire, women on their moon cycles not allowed near the sacred fire, women on their moon cycles do not put tobacco on the sacred fire, women on their moon cycles do not put firewood into the sacred fire and on and on and on. There are many different ways to start sacred fires, but the purposes is always the same.

To break the chains of colonialism from our minds and our actions, we remind people when they come and sit with us at this sacred fire, there are no rules except to respect the sacred fire. We sing by the sacred fire, we talk by the sacred fire, we eat by the sacred fire, we drink our teas by the sacred fire and we cry by the sacred fire. We allow women of all colours to sit with us by the sacred fire even when they are on their moon cycles.

Like Creator, the sacred fire is a very gentle, soothing, healing energy that can take away erratic static thoughts and help you get grounded and gain strength in your solitude. I think it has to do with the gentle crackling sounds, or the heat, or the dancing light. It is mesmerizing and hypnotic, but at the same time, not all engulfing of spirit.

The sacred fire is a tool that can be used to protect the land and the future. We make the sacred fire to protect the land/Mother Earth and also hold full moon ceremonies there.

Mothers and Grandmothers

Some of my stregnth comes from the women in my family. But it has not been easy for them. My mother is a woman that suffered very much in her life. She is Anishinaabekwe from Shoal Lake, Ontario. She is the eldest of her siblings. My mother lived through abuse in residential school and now lives with those thoughts that were driven into her mind. My mother is a woman that never experienced childhood and was seen as a woman at a very early age. She was a child doing woman's work. She was a child having child's thoughts raising seven children with no time for herself. This is the woman that raised me until I was eight years old. She left with a thoughtful look at her seven children before walkingout the door. My 16-year-old sister was crying quiet tears by the door at the mom that walked out on herself. My mom, a misunderstood woman, a disrespected woman, a frightened insecure young woman—I now understand her better than I did as an eight-year-old child. My mom was a mom-child— she had no parenting lessons, or positive Anishinaabekwe role models, only residential school. The nuns' stern looks, the priests silently pulling teenage Anishinaabekwe girls by the wrists to a place where their screams or cries won't be heard. The big long dormitory cold and dark and sad with little baby girls wimpering in the night. These were my mom's parents.

I now understand the legacy my people live with; residential school did the job. It made us landless people with the residential school as our mom and dad. The residential school bred neocolonialism into our genes—loss of culture, loss of language and loss of hope. As I filter through all these thoughts of residential school, my main worry right now is the little children that were buried at those residential school sites. They never made it home. The way they died was never disclosed to parents. This was the holocaust of my people. My 83-year-old dad was in residential school in the 1930's and he told us a story of a little boy he was particularily fond of. All of the Anishinabek kids loved him. One day, the older boys went by the beach and there was the little boy laying face down, all wet. My dad said they grabbed him, layed him face up and starting pumping the water out of his lungs, putting pressure on his little tiny chest. My dad said his heart was still beating and he was warm. Suddenly, a nun came running down and yelling "Leave him alone, he is dead, leave him alone!" She pushed the boys away and grabbed the little tiny boy. My dad said they buried him alive; my dad said they just dug a hole in the earth and put the little tiny boy in there and covered him with earth. What horrific tradegy my dad's twelve-year-old eyes had to see and feel. This is the legacy of our people.

Protectors

We, the Anishinabek people, are the protectors of the earth. We were the last ones to walk from the Creator and we can still communicate with him/her directly through fasting, meditation, and ceremony. My family is Lynx Clan and we are told we are the protectors of the people, the scouts. There are many Indigenous nations that have the warriors of their peoples, such as the Lonefighters, Lynx Clan, Wolf Clan and so on. This is not a thought process for these warrior societies to act on being a warrior, it is our responsibility. This is knowledge that we carry through our bodies, our minds, and our spirits. I think out there in the big cities, there are our people that have lived in cities all their lives and do not have any connection to themselves as the Indigenous people of the land. But somewhere, deep inside, they get this feeling when they go to a pow-wow or Indigenous gathering. It is like a homecoming, it is hearing their heart beat in unison to the drumbeat. I also think it is tears welling up in their eyes for a reason they do not understand. Almost a deep longing. As the drum beat fades, so does their memory of their connection to the heartbeat of the our Mother the Earth. It is our responsibility to carry on the knowledge of our Ancestors— our songs ceremonies, namegiving, water ceremonies, and medicine gathering. This knowledge will always remain with us and we will never lose it, because it will always come to us through our dreams and visions. You can change our thought processes, you can change our clothing, you can change our values, but you can never take the Anishinabek/Pikani/Onkwehonwe out of us.

Full Moon

There are 13 moons in one year according to my people. With every moon there is a cycle of the land that prepares our people for their cycle in their life as a community. I do not know all the names of the moons by heart, but I am fully aware of the wild rice moon. This is when the wild rice is ready. After the full moon of the wild rice moon, that is when the rice is ready to harvest. This is the time our Anishinabek families used to go and set up camps way out towards the rice fields and pick rice for two weeks. It was a time to reconnect to families and socialize as a community. Everyone would cook together, and even some men would go hunting and bring back meat, then the women would dry some meat. It was a good time. I think for me, the last time I was part of a wild rice camp, I was fifteen years old and I was the babysitter for my family of wild-rice pickers.

The full moon is a very significant part of my people. Currently, a few of us women go to the blockade site and make a sacred fire in the wigwam and have a full moon ceremony. We do not have lines and regimens of how the full moon ceremony happens. We just say, "Full moon tonight!" Then we meet there in the evening when the moon is high; sometimes we just bring our teas, snacks, and hand drums and we sing songs.

Sometimes we just sit around the fire and share stories. We started using the full moon ceremony as a time to reconnect to the cycle of the earth and reconnect to the land for our land protection initiatives. One of my friends that lives in the city uses a candle and then smudges herself and puts her tobacco offering in the smudge dish. She tells me she is lighting her little sacred fire.

My grandmother Hashinoqwah used to say "this is when the babies are born" as she looked up at the full moon with her small telescope. She allowed us to look at the moon with this little telescope, and it was amazing to see the shadow of holes on the moon and to see how it looked so close. She told us the story of the moon and how it can take us away if we look at it too long. Only look at its beauty for a short while, or it will take you away. This was her story: There was this Old Kokum (grandmother) with two of her grandchildren visiting her for a few days. One child listened very well (the girl) and the other child did not listen well and was always rebelling or opposing her words (the boy). She tried her best to teach them the way of the Anishinabekwe when they came to visit with her.

This night there was a full moon in the sky and it was a clear sky. She told the two children to go down to the lake to get her some water for the morning, but she gave them a warning not to look at the moon too long or it will take them away. The two children walked down the lake with their pails and made sure not to look at the moon. The boy, being rebellious, decided to test his grandmother's words as they were half way back up to the house (wigwam), he looked up at the moon. His sister reminded him that the moon will take him away if he does not turn his eyes down. He said he did not believe this story and the moon would not take him away. His sister begged him to please turn his eyes down, saying, "Come on, let's just take the water to Kokum." He did not listen. He kept looking up. All of the sudden, he started floating up and in a few split seconds, he disappeared. The little girl dropped her pails and went running up to tell her Kokum. She was crying and out of breath as she told her about her brother. Her Kokum just held her and said there was nothing they could do now but know that her brother was now on the moon. The little girl looked up at the moon and could see the little image of a boy on the moon with a pail.

This story is about listening to the teachings and trusting them without question. This story is about the power of the moon and to respect her. This was my teaching from my grandmother about the moon. To this day, I feel that respect for her—Dibik Giizis and the strong powerful force she carries.

500 Missing Anishinabek Women

My heart is sad when I think of these Anishinabek sisters/mothers/children that are missing or murdered. I am a woman and I have two young daughters, many nieces and granddaughters. Every time we go somewhere away from home, I keep a close eye on my children and I do not let them out of my sight. I know out there our people, the Anishinabek, are being exterminated. Such a harsh word, but a true word.

"Anishinabekwe gah minogo gedotam, ga minogo gedotam, gah kinah pi pindigak omah, wah wah ni chi neemiiak." This song says: "Anishinaabekwe you will be given your clan, you will be given your clan, all of you come in, in here, so that you can dance very well." This is the song we sang at the Take Back the Night rally. There were a lot of women there in this hall where we brought the women's drum. It was a warm feeling of women of all nations taking back the night. There was the smell of food and coffee brewing and little children laughing or crying or sleeping in their mothers' laps. We sang this song and some women cried. My older sister said, "Look behind you." I looked and there was a picture wall full of the missing and murdered Anishinabekwewag. I got the chills, and finally this song became so significant to us as singers. It was us calling all the women that had been murdered, never found to come in there with us to find their clan, to dance there with us and then to go home. It was like we were guiding them with this song to enable them to be found in spirit and to reclaim themselves from where ever they were hidden or killed.

My 11-year-old daugther asked, "Mom, why are Anishinabek women disappearing?" I did not know she was aware of this until she said it. I said to her it is because we are the carriers of our nations. She could not understand that. So I told her more straightforward. It is because we can carry life in our womb and we carry the Ancestors of our people to the children. We are always the reminder of creating life for our people. Without us, the people will vanish from this earth. Our culture will cease, our memories to this land will disappear and we will become extinct. No more Anishinabek to protect the land, air and water. This she understood and also understood why I keep her so close to me when we go to town.

I envy those non-Anishinabekwewag that can go jogging with shorts on and halter tops and go unhindered. I wish my daughters could go jogging too, but there is my fear of them disappearing, or getting assaulted by passerbys. This way of thinking is such a prison to my mind, and then I enforce that prison on my daugthers. I cannot give them the same freedom of roaming the land freely.

The enormous tragedy of missing and murdered Anishinabek women is so obscene and yet so minimized. People keep harping on the 500 Missing Anishinabek Women, but still the importance of it is on a very low scale. Posters are made, conferences are had, but still the Anishinabek Women disappear and are getting murdered. This affirms to me that Anishinabek women are totally unprotected and my daughters have an uncertain future.

Fighters

Residential school really devastated our Nationhood. It was all a plan to get the fight out of our people. I would say it mostly worked, but about 20% of our people filtered through the damage and remained fighters and passed this on to their children.

The colonizers came on our lands and extinguished some Anishinabek Nations by the Atlantic Ocean. The sweep continued, and more and more colonizers came and flooded the land. Our people fought the whole way and, no matter how hard and difficult it was, they opposed this occupation. The fight was strong in our people and nothing scared them. This is when the colonizers decided to take away our food (buffalo), but we still continued to resist. Then they gave us blankets infested with sickness (small pox), our people died and still resisted. Then they realized our children were our strength and carriers of knowledge. These were our little treasures that can carry on the people's Ode (heart). This is when residential schools were set up and there was a major sweep of children being apprehended from every community imaginable.

My aunt said the priests would travel by airplanes and go to the family's hunting grounds and, with an RCMP escort, they would grab the children. Since many of our people did not speak english, they could not understand what this black robed person was saying and why the the RCMP would be touching his gun. All they felt was a great fear of these people.

My aunt said her dad got warned by someone that there were children being apprehended. When Nowogeshig saw this plane landing, he had enough time to hide his tiny little daughter (Keegatch) but not my other aunt and my dad. They were taken away to a place unknown to their parents (McKintosh Residential School, 1930s). There my dad suffered for ten long years. My other aunt got really, really sick (she had burn marks on her neck down to her chest) and she was sent back to Hashinoqwah. Hashinoqwah had to nurse her back to health with Anishinabek medicines. There was never an explanation as to why she had these burn marks on her.

My dad came home after seeing such grotesque injustice and having the roman catholic teachings being shoved down his throat. He became a survivor and a fighter with the mind. He passed on these teachings to us, not by words but by action. It was in the things he did that gave us the mindset we now have. I am really sure there were other parents like him—the 20% that filtered through. He did not become the neocolonizer as planned. Instead he showed us how to fight back and pass that on to our children. I know in my heart this came from Hashinoqwah, his mom. There were many other Hashinoqwahs out there in the Anishinabek communities that suffered through the same cultural devastation and instead showed their children survival skills from the plan.

Drum Carriers

I have two sisters that are Anishinabek big-drum carriers and a whole bunch of nieces, granddaughters, brothers, nephews that sing Anishinabek songs. I found out Nowageshig was a great song maker in the Treaty 3 area and my dad's great grandmother was a Anishinabek big drum carrier. Since 1994, the sisters have been big-drum carriers and they learned songs. It came naturally to them and then our nieces and sisters started to participate. They started travelling to pow-wows and they had a lot of fun. People were shocked to see women hitting the drum. It was taboo according to many Anishinabek Knowledge carriers. There were frowns from the Elders and derogatory remarks from the MC's. Eventually, the women singers dismantled and now sing only in ceremonies. My sisters still carry the big drum and sing songs. If anyone questions us, our answer is that our approval comes from our dad, whose great grandmother carried a big drum. We believe women carried drums naturally and it is through colonization and the brain washing that comes from colonialism; that many foreign taboos were put on our peoples. And now through the loss of our language and old knowledge holders, we lose that assertion of old ceremonies and rituals. We need to follow our heart and spirit, as those Kanien'kehaka warriors did in 1990, to do ceremonies and have trust in them because it is the Ancestors showing us the way. We feel so strongly in our singing, but at the same time we do not force the pow-wow circle to allow us into their circle. So instead we have made our own circles and it is usually in woman circles like Take Back the Night Rally, International Women's Day, full moon ceremonies, healing songs.

The reason for writing this is to share with other women to follow their hearts. Some taboos could be from our Ancestors, and some taboos could be colonial taboos.

Blockade

The blockade against logging started in December 2002 on Asub-peeschoseewagong Anishinabek Territory. Many courageous individuals stepped up to physically stop the logging trucks. According to media, the focus was on logging. Within the inner circle of the people that stopped the trucks, the reason for this peaceful direct action was and is to protect our way of life as the Anishinabek.

We went through many of the colonial processes that the Ministry of Natural Resources set up according to their Forest Management plan and then we realized it was and is a false set up. These processes are not meant to address the concerns of the grassroots Anishinabek, but is set up just as an empty bible for industry. False processes set up by industry. So the bottom line for the blockade is to stop all industrial activity with no more resource extraction.

Our Mother Earth is tired with so many scars and her veins being cut off. She needs this extreme resource extraction to cease, and we as human beings need to look for alternative ways of surviving on her.

Healing Medicines Dreams

Dreams are a direct connection to the universe and to the Creator. Some dreams are just dreams, but some dreams are the ones that teach you directly from the spirit world. This is Creators connection to us to give messages and teachings.

One time, a friend of mine dreamt of three bannocks. She was stumped as to why she would dream of three bannocks. She said, "What does it mean, this dream?" We went to our other friend's place for a feast, and there on the counter were three bannocks cooling off. My friend said, "There are the three bannocks I dreamt of, what does it mean?" I told her, "It is just a simple dream affirming that you have the gift of dreaming and to believe in the messages you get from dreams." Before this, she was skeptical of her dreams and was not aware of them. Since that time, she has had many many dreams that have carried powerful messages and she has become an interpreter of dreams for others. I also know there are dreams that carry the turmoil of the mind, which is reflected in the dreams. If I am worried about paying my bills, I will dream of some kind of struggle.

The spiritual dream will leave you with a feeling of total and utter peace and almost a feeling of holiness and tranquility. These are the dreams that carry a message for you or for others.

I have received names from dreams too, but the Creator can only give symbols as we are such low beings of understanding to the Creator's great message that we can only understand symbols. Along with these dreams, come simple emotions to help us remember these dreams. Sometimes it is the feeling of fear, and when you wake up you remember the dream because of the emotion of fear. As the dream unfolds, fear might not even be relevant in the message of the dream. Sometimes love is the emotion. One time I dreamt of this giant bird that was floating outside my window. I was so amazed at his size and soon realized he had a man's face. All of a sudden I felt a deep love for this huge bird. I was in LOVE! I went closer to the window to get a better look at him and saw his feathers shimmered with rainbow colours. I looked so close at the huge feather, the colours were very beautiful and moving. The bird flew away and I felt a very sad longing, a feeling of lonliness and emptyness. I woke up, and the dream was so vivid I could not forget it. And the feeling of being in love stayed with me for a long time. I finally went to see a medicine man to interpret my dream. He said what I dreamt of was a thunderbird and he came and gave me a thunderbird pipe—that was the sad and longing feeling. I needed to carry that pipe. This medicine man told me to go and find a pipemaker and get a thunderbird pipe made.

So, believe in your dreams, as we are all spiritual beings.

Sacrifice

This is one very strong teaching I share with my children. I tell them stories of the our brothers and sisters that live on the streets and I call them my brother or my sister. I call them this in a true and loving way so my children will feel this authencity and be real from the heart.

I tell my children to save some money sometimes to pass it on to the squeegie kids that clean the windows and I tell my kids stories of why they could be on the streets. I try to humanize the street people as my sister Wiitahpiimahkwe (Sitting With Her) was a street person and I loved her greatly. She was my little sister. Wiitahpiimahkwe used to call to the band office on the toll-free line from California and tell me her experience of the day or the week.

Her and her partner, Ishmael, met and fell in love. He was a Mayan in Los Angeles, originally from Mexico. They both lived with Ishmael's 75-year-old mother, and she provided for them. Ishmael (Izzy) would go and look for work every day at the day-labour offices. He would find a job for a day, but could never get hired permanently anywhere. Eventually, the elderly mother, Margarita, moved in with her older son, who took care of her. Wiitahpiimahkwe and Ishmael were able to stay in the apartment for about six months, then they got evicted because they could not come up with the rent money. Their friends told them to stay in their van that was parked in a church. So Wiitahpiimahkwe and Izzy stayed there and continued looking for work. One thing lead to the next and they just started living on the streets behind garbage cans.

One time Wiitahpiimahkwe said, "I can't believe I am pushing a shopping cart with all my worldly goods in there." My message to her always was to keep a journal and to tell her, "Do not accept this as your fate, you will get out of this lifestyle and find a home someday." She would say, "Sis, I am okay as long as Izzy is with me."

Wiitahpiimahkwe would sometimes panic and call me with fear in her voice. She would tell me the police are doing a sweep of the streets. It was scarey for her, because she said sometimes the street people would never come back. She thought they would get killed somewhere. She would say, "Joe used to sit on that street and panhandle for coffee and a meal, that was his boulevard, and after the last sweep, he never came back." Then she would say, "Bill got killed last night by the street gangs, one of their initiations is to kill a street person. Poor Bill." The street people became her family and she knew which ones to stay away from as they were "bad news."

Wiitahpiimahkwe loved children and she would go and clean herself up at the library bathroom, go on the Internet and then head to the park with a good book, just to watch the little children play with their parents. The parents were okay with her for about a month, and then they reported her to the police and they told her to stay away or she would be charged with vagrancy. She was very sad when this happened. It was one of her downtimes as she was pushed further from humanity, where she became almost like an animal according to mainstream society's eyes. I kept telling her, "You know I love you and I want you home." She would say she could not leave Izzy alone.

There is more to my sister's life on the street, but one thing she told my mom is that "the only way I will come home is in a casket." Wiitahpiimahkwe's words came true. She got hit by a car August 31, 2006, at midnight. The police report says she stayed alive for six hours and had severe internal injuries. Since she had no health insurance, they just morphined her up and let her fade away. The last time I saw her, she was 130 lbs. When she came home she was 100 lbs. I know she suffered and I am frustrated with a system that alienates the street people and does not give them a break or a chance. So with every street person, I see Wiitahpiimahkwe, Lynx Clan, Anishinabekwe, my little sister, my children's aunty, Hashinoqwah's granddaughter, Nowandigo and Tahtopsipewnook's daughter—she is an honoured child and she deserves an Honour Song.

Racism Because of Land

I have lived with racism all my life and have had "head on collisions" (not literally) with rednecks and KKK mentality folks. The greatest teaching I ever received was from my dad, Nowandigo, when I was fourteen and was called an "Indian Slut who walks the street." I was alone in a bus shelter in one of Canada's most racist towns with three grown white men, and they were grumbling under their breath with those words and worse words that I cannot write in here. I kept going in front of them and saying I was not what they were saying I was. Their mouths would keep moving, but they would not give me one little inkling of an eye contact. They growled through their clenched teeth with such words of hate. I was shaking and scared, but I stood up in front of them and kept talking and tried to give them eye contact. I finally got home and told Nowandigo through my tears, and he said, "You cannot change these people, the only one you can change is yourself." As a fourteen year old, I could not figure these words. Since that time, I use these words as a source of strength when I am in a situation with racism.

I know the reason for the strong racism is because of the land. As long as we the Anishinabek are visible, we will always be the constant reminder of who truely belongs to this land of our Ancestors. I can and will say "WE WERE HERE FIRST!" This is my land, my territory, my Ancestors' land.

For this we are hated, but the teachings to their young ones are distorted messages about us being lazy or a tax load, etc. Their message should be more like "We don't like the Indians because as long as they are here we will always be reminded of who truely belongs to this land and, they will fight to protect their land and fight for their rights, and this greatly irritates us!"

I believe this is why the Anishinabekwewag are disappearing and getting murdered. The women are the carriers of the nation and hold the memories of our peoples.

Bodies and Memories

I learned from a medicine man, Martin Highbear (passed on to spirit world), that our bodies carry memories and act like a computer chip for programming. We are not robots, but we will never lose the memories of our Ancestors as it is within us. This includes songs, language, herbal medicines, land memories, how to build Anishinabek buildings. The one teaching that stays in my mind is his words "Your blood that flows through your veins is thousands of years old and is there because your mom carried you in her body, filtering all the teachings to you for ten months." This has stayed with me, and I pass this on to my children.[1]

Fasting

Fasting is one of the oldest rituals of many nations. Fasting is to go without food and water. I have learned fasting is a way of nourishing your spirit through meditation and inner reflection. It is a way of shining up your antennae to the Creator and the spirit world. The invisible antennae gets dusty from everyday interaction with other lifeforms on Earth. With the fasting, smudging, praying, meditation, the antennae gets shined up and becomes highly receptive to messages again. This is how I explain to first-time fasters. With everyday events we lose that connection to Mother Earth, Creator, spirit world, Grandmothers/Grandfathers, winged ones, thunderbeings. And fasting is the simplest and easiest way to reconnect.

Woman is Sacred/Life Givers/Mother Earth

Crazy Horse, we hear what you are saying
one Earth, one Mother,
One does not sell the Earth,
The people walk upon
We are the Land
How do we sell Our Mother
How do we sell our Mother
How do we sell the stars
How do we sell the air.

—John Trudell

These words brought tears to my eyes as I watched the images in John Trudell's video. I know and realize there are many people that feel the sacredness of woman so deeply and honour this. We must fight with all our hearts and strength to help the woman to stand up from the ground again. There are many vulnerable women being victimized right now, getting hurt, getting hit, getting abused, getting raped. This is exactly what is happening to Mother Earth. Mother Earth is so all-giving and all-sacrificing for us to live. She is kind, she is gentle, she feeds us, she overpowers us with storms, with floods. I feel once we honour Mother Earth and protect her, the women will become strong again. Women will be honoured and cherished as we are meant to be.

The women of Kanehsatà:ke, Kahnawà:ke and Akwesasne gave birth to the resistance movement that protected their land in 1990.

They made many sacrifices, and because of those sacrifices I sing this Honour Song to them. And I will also sing this Honour Song to Wiitahpiimahkwe, Hashinoqwah and all the missing Indigenous woman and children.

---

1 Editors note: For Anishinaabek people, it is our understanding that "blood and body memory" is not interpreted as a strictly genetic or biological link within our cultures and our languages. It is our understanding that these memories and this knowledge can be transmitted to any one of our citizens (as defined by our own culturally inherent citizenship laws), living in our territories regardless of blood quantum or biological ancestry. From this perspective, the genetic make up of our people is influenced by the implicate order, the landscape of our territories and our commitment to living bimaadiziwin.

Honour Songs in Multiple Harmonies

GKISEDTANAMOOGK

Introduction

To honour the People,[1] we honour all life. Indigenous theology suggests that all life is sacred; the measurement of social mores and the ethics of well being signify and characterize what it might be to honour and to be honoured. We live so that the People will live, so that the unborn generations yet to come will know the path of ancient ancestral legacies, the path of life. Honouring life commits us to remembering what is essential to the ways of life the People have always chosen to live, as must we all live. We must remember what the priorities must be, what practicalities and scenarios are necessary to engage our vast human potential. These aspects empower understanding and meaning of how to honour the integrity of being and of being in relation to all life.

At the close of September 1990, the world understood the existence of Kanehsatà:ke. Visualizing, in real-time, the incorrigible corruptibility of canadian Indian policy and the ludicrous methodology employed to repress Indigenous Peoples. In many Indigenous communities, it is only when matters become necessary to defend and protect what might be defenseless women and children from the persistently gruesome, senseless, historical dance of agency in the killing of non-combatants. As it is throughout the north american-Indigenous narrative, the People stood their ground. Were the aftermath and consequences of this particular dance of genocide meaningless and futile? I think not, as evidenced in the formidable and the indomitable legacy of Indigenous Sovereignty. Ancestral inheritance bequeaths to the People the consequential understanding that intentional massacre and wanton destruction will never conquer the heart and sacrosanctity of life and love, no matter what, how strong, and how violent, the destruction.

For me, the turbulent nineties began on July 11, 1990, with the forceful invasion of a Mohawk blockade in the community of Kanehsatà:ke, erected to keep a Mohawk burial site, the Pines, from intentional development of an additional nine-hole golf course for the city of Oka, Quebéc. Strenuous Mohawk objections could not cure the immense yearning for profits and economic wealth stemming from the westernization of Indigenous holy ground. Violence against Kanehsatà:ke continued. Since July 11, 1990, such encounters were mimicked throughout the decade up until October 5, 1999, as the Mi'kmaq Community of Burnt Church (Esgenoôpetitj) gleefully began reaping the benefits of a supreme court of canada decision recognizing and affirming their right to fish lobster for a moderate livelihood. The canadian supreme court affirmed the active validity of the 1752–1760 series of treaties with the Wabanaki, binding on the Crown. Although it was commonly understood that "illegal fishing" was the issue, as decried by the canadian government, the actual issue premised the legality of the Mi'kmaq to regulate their own fishing. Stemming from their inherent responsibilities,[2] the Mi'kmaq, in their territorial waters, which had not been ceded to canada,[3] sought to fish under a recognized, constitutional mandate to affirm Mi'kmaq aboriginal and treaty rights.

In the decade between these two events, hundreds of arrests and deaths of Indigenous persons and wanton destruction of Indigenous property culminated from various state-orchestrated incidents of violence, traumatizing Indigenous psyche and bodies. More disturbing is the tragically predictable and consistent blatant disregard by canadian federal-provincial authorities for the spirit and intent of existing treaties respecting Indigenous sovereignty. The impact for both Indigenous Nations and canadian citizen-neighbours remains to this day.

Indigenous Theory and the Persona of Inherent Responsibilities

By behaviour, innuendo, and body language, north americans have generally regulated Indigenous persona, Ad vis continuus, manipulating socio-economic, religio-ecologic, political and legal levels. Sociological pathologies apply retrograde labels to Indigenous Peoples resisting systemic integration-assimilation policies of the alternative. The Indigenous persona is never taken seriously but reacted to through hostility, derision, and various forms of violence, from the subtle to the blatant. Stereotypes and racism remain steadfastly programmatic and institutional. Despite the response, the Indigenous persona is progressively forward moving in a context aptly described as self-determined, sovereign, metaphysical. The events impacting the Communities of Kanehsatà:ke, Burnt Church, and the ongoing struggles in many First Nations such as Grassy Narrows, Akwesasne, and Sun Peaks demonstrate a growing tension and intension. The development of Indigenous responses intonates an unwillingness to be dissuaded by the ignorance and hostility of government and corporate agendas. We are going to heal ourselves, "with or without you."

It is this Honour Song I humbly give to all those who braved the impossible, who are steadfast and determined to love their People, culture, and spirit in spite of social trickery and hostility so commonly waged by north america against Indigenous Nations and their Peoples.

Personal Motivations Under Fire

I came to this state of being because I married into the community of Esgenoôpetitj (Burnt Church), intentionally founding our marriage on the value and love of our culture—to honour our Ancestors and responsibly begin to pave the way for the lives of those unborn generations yet to come. It was there, in the community, that we raised our children in the context of Wabanaki Lifeways. Doing so meant that we were placed on the "wrong side of the tracks," in the "baddest part of town"—not of our doing, but rather of the repressive, repercussive consequence of being Indigenous in the twentieth century.

The critical notion of being, in humble honour of the life of the People, is that the Sacred, which is instrumental to everything Wabanaki and all things Indigenous, persists in every aspect of life. One cannot separate from the Sacred nor ignore the inherent responsibilities involved with paying attention. North american governments are not grounded nor connected to the centre of life, amidst the sacred, but the People are. That is the difference! I honour the People and work for the sacred; I honour carrying the Fire.

Esgenoôpetitj and Wabanaki Nations

Many people in our communities are essentially convinced that the world we have come to know belongs to white anglo-saxon wealth. We have come to know this through the north american social, educational and economic institutionalization of Indigenous thought and sociality. It is an expected framework, that our communities raise our children in western colonialism, as well as socio-economic educational structures that are designed to doom Indigenous People to subservience and dependency. This institutionalization has been quite brutal. It has been exemplified by canada's *Indian Act*, the creative government of canada's play, promulgating politico-socialites of a one-man act having interpretive power over the lives of Indigenous Nations. I'll conclude the scenario in three-scene concision.

Scene one—*asserting power over Indigenous Nations, Indigenous territories, and Indigenous resources under the pretense of law.* So typical of the colonizing north american predecessors, acquiring land and territories of Indigenous Nations under the pretense of law, the *Indian Act* is founded on legal precepts of democracy—resting on democratic principles, and establishing the pretense of validating its own democratic practices. North america extends its legal systems to rob and deprive Indigenous Peoples of life, voice, and freedom—to acquire lands and resources coveted by the corporate wealth, employment, and power interests of the alternative. Acquiring jurisdiction over people, territories, and resources is prohibited in the precedence of misreading International Law (*Discovery Doctrine; Treaty Protocol; Pre-Emption Doctrine in the pre-colonial era*)[4] and calculated by north american domestic law (*British North*

American Act 1867, now the *Canada Act, 1867; the Constitution Act,* 1982; *and treaties with Indigenous Nations*). Religious law is the basis of the doctrine of discovery and early papal agency. This and the ludicrous nature of extending colonial and existing domestic law over Indigenous Nations exemplifies the eloquence of constructed racism, violence, destruction, grand theft, self-serving interests and genocidal policies. These are not attributes of democracy, social stability or genuine trust. A one-sided power hegemony warrants resistance.

Scene two—*manipulating Indigenous communities through force and termination policies designed to forcibly remove Indigenous children, create systems of economic deprivation, war and attack the centrality of Indigenous women, religiously demonizing the spirituality of Indigenous people.* There is no apparent end to the mischievous agency canada employs against Indigenous Nations. Violence is its own influential state of being, exemplified by the descriptive application of "hate-mongering" and inciting to hate, by modeling a role that socially depicts Indigenous people as a people less-valued. Emphasis should rather be that the People, whose land we live on and whose treaties we must abide by, are the law. Peace and friendship has not been the experience of Indigenous Nations with the governments of canada and its social, religious, and corporate institutions. North american societies, as a whole, know very little, if anything, factual about Indigenous people—be its history, language, treaties or realities. Very few north americans visit "the Rez,"[5] know the territories guaranteed by treaties, or understand the vital issues confronting Indigenous life head-on. Most north americans have only a sense of the part they play in the injustice done to Indigenous People. Most north americans do not rightly understand the gravity of genocide currently waged against every Indigenous nuance throughout this hemisphere whether that be ways of life, personhood, thought, home, land, economy or society.

There is the mistaken belief, inspired by deceptive public federal largess, of the federal Indian Affairs budget,[6] that Indigenous communities are well funded and "looked after' in terms of treaty commitments. To the contrary, various federally funded projects, in an explicative exposure tour, would reveal the discrepancies between the federal publicized dollar figures and the local community economies and social conditions. I believe the touring public would be hard pressed to visually validate such federal expenditures at the local level. Habitually, federal monies flowing to local First Nations communities are funded to a level of "falling short." So where is it that the feds are expending these billons of dollars if not at the local communities? Some might suggest expenditures on health, education, employment, administration, housing, for starters, and there would be reasonable certainty. Foremost, however, we are dealing with the trickle down effect. The federal Indian Affairs department is an expansive hierarchical empire, and Indigenous People have become an industry. Much of the sociological outlay of the communities is planned pathology though racist notions, manipulative, covert social public policies with very designed consequences.

Scene three—*establishing politico-legal structures designed to replicate Indigenous sovereignty under the innuendo of law and the good order of society.* What the *Indian Act,* and its cousin to the south, *the Indian Reorganization Act,* does to self-governing, self-determining Indigenous Nations is to unilaterally transform Indigenous governments into regimes that are designed to mimic north american governments. The added twist is not having full jurisdiction over their own affairs, resources, territories nor having any of their former powers. Every significant local decision is reviewed by the minister or his staff and, at times, local decisions are overturned. Perhaps it is the nature of their creation, but such community governments, commonly known as band councils, in the south, tribal councils, are easily manipulated because the ultimate authority and approval powers exist in ottawa and washington. These community regimes are not instruments of their People or of their own culture or making, but rather instruments of federal legislation. Keeping in mind, the original governing structures were completely sovereign and able to posture influence and decisions in the creation of alliances, treaties, and foreign relations, as a community or in concert with their national and confederate councils.

One word about the nature of conquest. In the present era, we are beginning to feel and witness the dangers of stronger nations and individuals, increasingly becoming the world's bullies. Bully mentality suggests those who are physically stronger will dictate to others what will be the way to live and the nature of human relations, currently exemplified by the invasion and occupation of Iraq. International law would have us believe that there is a right to respond in self-defense to an unprovoked attack from another. Customary international law equates this right with land acquisition and power over the defeated. Certain "rules" were to be followed if the right of conquest was to be upheld and recognized. No such "just war" validated any themes of "conquest" from the united states or canada over Indigenous Nations. There has never been a "just war" or the "right of conquest" against Indigenous Nations throughout this hemisphere, only blatant and barbarous acts of mass murder and the grand theft of land never belonging to any other soul but Indigenous Nations.[7] The unfolding story of Kanehsatà:ke *is* the story of this land and takes place throughout this hemisphere.

These scenes of the Indian Act provide a glimpse of the pernicious nature of puritan ethic. I cite puritan ethic as the theoretical application of theology that sets in motion the manner and thought about the deprivation of Indigenous Nations, a doctrine that continues to feed the north american post-colonial politics of hating anything Indigenous. I would submit the daily contiguous body of evidence of habitual violence to Indigenous Peoples throughout Turtle Island, including central and south america. The behaviour and attitude, the tenor of voice, is the body language of aggrieved financial commitment to the socioeconomic instability of Indian Country.

There are two relative experiences and perspectives that will always exist on this land: the view from the boat and the view from the shore. Indigenous Peoples will remain the underlying presence on this land because the land and the People are inseparable. What is done to the People and the land will eventually be the undoing of the alternative lifeways that is north america. Treaties are the likeliest possibility for relations between Indigenous Nations' citizens and north americans. The operative treaty protocols are, by definition and legal fact, part of north american political and legal reality, as in the "law of the land" having national constitutional status. It is these treaties that provide the context of a land base for north america and the forum for building trust among one another, *Universus Verum.* I believe that matters of trust will improve if the citizens of north america realize that they do have a future of peace in the Homeland territories of *Indian Country.*

These Are Not Just Indian Issues

How common we all assume to box life into categories, and to think even more that each subject is unbridgeable to other venues. In plain terms, we've come to approach most problems of human beings as sentiments of the other and have failed to feel our connections to one another. As for most Indigenous theological experiences, it is the understanding that we are all contained together in the sanctuary of the great web of life, as it is said, "What befalls one, befalls all."[8] The great oneness of being, *Naiyentaqt*,[9] expresses that we be in balance between the life above our heads and the life below our feet. The universe is one single feminine organism with deep complexities. Every fiber, structure and being is a molecular personality replete with interdependent sovereignty and rubric memory.

Every struggle in the world is a human struggle; what humans do to one another and what humans do to Earth, creation, and life. The ongoing attrition throughout this hemisphere is a human issue. As such, the solution must be achieved by, and include, all human beings. These are not "Indian issues," but the anomaly of what people do to one another. The nature of such struggles is seen and felt everywhere in the world and is of everyone's concern *and* responsibility. The profoundly simple truth is to treat every single person, every life being, as you would want to be treated. Of course, this is not similar to the self-serving, interest-layered greed responsible for much of the unrest and suffering in the world. Exemplified by the disparaging actions of municipality of Oka regarding ancient Mohawk burials and denying legitimacy to Mohawk concerns, it is what it is. Although, what is it that makes a sensible person so determined to overrule the plea of a People for the sake of extending a golf course on known burial grounds? What is it in every one of us to be capably calloused and unkind, unwilling to respond to the horror or sadness in the life of our neighbour? What is it in our nature that would strike children, women, or Elders?

The nuances of the Indigenous mind, especially from a historical context, is the collective social conscience and commitment that no one in the community would have to suffer and have to live without some necessity of life. In Wampanoag life, we reciprocally shared all that we have with one another, and those among us in better circumstances

always helped others less fortunate in the community. This remains
the continuing basis for Indigenous social wealth and values. Children,
leaders, Elders, the revered persons in Indigenous communities, would
always and at all times be highly respected and treated as such. A great
love for one another did, and does, prevail among us. Today we are
completely challenged by social alternatives not culturally based nor
valued historically by the People.

With this in mind, however, the story continues. As the aftermath of the Oka confrontation inspired widespread public awareness
and outrage, as did Wounded Knee[10] and the violence brought to Burnt
Church, the federal government undertook a complete survey of its relationship with First Nations prompted by public pressures and global
attention. The 1992–1995 *Royal Commission on Aboriginal People* produced
a solid response through conversations regarding appropriate relations
with Aboriginal Peoples. From a personal perspective, this is a good
start toward the kind of discussion needed, but as a solution to the
complexities of colonial historical patterns, the voluminous report is
not the summative solution. Many significant questions about land
tenure and the territorial integrity of Indigenous Nations, north american procedural policy development, treaty enforcement, and international law remained ominously unaddressed.

Indigenous representatives became an international voice and
presence, committed to formidable impetus for addressing long-over-
due issues of the United Nations' former lack of response to the di-
saster inflicted on Indigenous Peoples by member nation-states in
direct violation of international human rights instruments. The work
continues in the unprecedented dedication of two decades to raising
the presence and voice of Indigenity. This effort produced an enor-
mously momentous document, the *United Nations Declaration on the Rights
of Indigenous Peoples*. This document is an exceedingly positive, forward-
moving approach to peaceful relations in this world.

During the siege of Burnt Church and its aftermath, growing
public outcry culminated one morning in the summer of 2000, as department of fisheries and oceans (DFO) enforcement officers viciously
attacked and brutalized unarmed Mi'kmaq fishermen and warrior society members defending their lobster traps from unwarranted con-
fiscation. The manner and tactics used by DFO agents breached the

limits of excessive force. The community, witnesses, and churches sought to bring charges of attempted murder against these officials. Miraculously, no one was seriously injured or killed. I am mortified at the thought of what might have escalated if community members were killed by DFO agents. Tempers and the level of violence reached close to the tipping point. The foresight of community members to call human rights witness watches[11] to record the events, in video, written, and oral presentations, aided in preventing deaths in these encounters. This particular incident was recorded and aired by CBC television newscasts. The government of canada never recovered from this incident. The longest-running government offensive of the turbulent 90s, was this four continual years of unrelenting violence, ultimately traumatizing the community of Burnt Church. To this day, after ten years, community members and their canadian neighbours are not able to discuss the events of those four years. Healing for these communities remains a precarious yet vital necessity.

If We All Were True To Our Word

It was said by an Elder, how difficult it was for many of the Nations entering treaties with the united states. After a while, american officials could not be trusted. Treaties among the People were timelessly honoured, but for some of the nations entering into solemn promises with the united states, their treaties were soon after discarded by the american government, for new treaties even more favorable to the united states. Although the united states prohibited further treaty-making with the Indigenous Nations in 1871, many of the Nations stopped making treaties with the united states long before. It is the operative protocol among the People to make and hold our personal word, as well as our nation's word, a sacred matter. Rather than be based upon some particular interest or some politico-legal construct, treaties with Indigenous Nations were sacred instruments embedded in ceremony. Bringing the Creator into this world was about the making of relatives. Among the People in the western regions, treaties were promises of peace and friendship and committed to through the Sacred Pipe; in the east, many treaties were instruments of Wampum and recorded and kept in solemn regard.

Interestingly enough, these disregarded treaties have become north america's nightmare. However the careless, habitual disregard and denial, the united states and canada portray treaties with the People,[12] and although breaches are steadily made, treaties are international instruments existing only between nations and sovereigns and are never made between citizens and their governments! Treaties cannot be rescinded unilaterally and thus cannot become invalid or nullified by intentional avoidance from the actions of a single party. I would argue for this point *ad infinitus.* Simple contract law recognizes that, in this case where land cessions were part of treaty-making with Indigenous Nations, the united states and canada are legally prohibited from keeping the lands ceded by the very treaty they expect to abrogate. A treaty ends, *de facto*, only when both parties in the agreement officially and freely consent to termination.

Recently, the United Nations recognized that treaties held between the united states and canada with Indigenous Nations are treaties recognized under international law in the same regard as any existing treaty and ought to acknowledge similar benefits, responsibilities, and standards under international treaty law.[13] The circumstances of denying Indigenous Nations valid recognition of *de jure* sovereignty is a constant reflection of north american political positioning. Such is the nature of the *trust doctrine* holding control over Indigenous People, Indigenous lands and resources. This was confirmed by the recent position of canada, the united states, austrailia, and new zealand—all four being the only members of the United Nations voting against the United Nations' *Declaration on the Rights of Indigenous Peoples.*

Yet with such restrictive attempts to limit Indigenous sovereignty, it is only a matter of time before world courts will open jurisdiction to Indigenous claims against the illegitimate actions of member states. For impartial justice to prevail, Indigenous Nations and Peoples must be able to access objective third party tribunals outside of canada and the united states. Although impartial mechanisms *can* exist from north american court systems, historical patterns of incompetence and unwillingness to correctly approach Indigenous-north american conflicts as political rather than judicial demonstrate the offensive, arrogant, abusive, and unlawful nature of the issues. The actions undertaken, those of "laying charges" against Mohawk warriors, Mi'kmaq fishermen, and Indigenous community activists, are unmeritorious and unlawful if treaty protocol has not consented to extending north american jurisdiction to Indigenous Nations. It is tantamount to the united states laying charges against law-abiding canadian citizens, living in canada, for violating some american ordinance. Such activity avoids the operative treaty protocol (OPT) and subverts the integrity of both treaties and relationships. Rather than legislate according to OTP, the government of canada deceptively engages in federalizing Indigenous Nations under the *Indian Act*, claiming to be enacting treaty agreements.

The Path Before Us

Of the principles in the struggles of the People, Indigenous women have always been key, central movers and shakers. It is an acknowledgement of honour from the People that if one wants an idea to come to life, one convinces the women of its soundness and rationality. The idea will then have life and grow. The women of our nations are the life-givers, their presence and place in our families, communities, nations, and confederacies is foundational. The Cheyenne proverbial wisdom informs us of this reality; they say that when the hearts of the women are on the ground, then no matter how strong their warriors, the good fight is over. The imagery of the women of Kanehsatà:ke will always be inspiring for me—in particular, Ellen Gabriel. She stands tall among the proponents of Indigenous strength, clarity, and determination. There, with Anna Mae Aquash, Patricia Monture, Mary Ellen Turpel-Lafond, Andrea Smith, and so many more. Each of the women of Indigenous Peoples holds the nation together—I'm married to one of these profoundly powerful personalities.

Respect for women is necessary, as humanity moves into a new reality of being. This reality is a paradigm shift that quickens and harkens us all to higher consciousness. It is only a matter of time for this unfolding. Respect for life—all life—is an active movement necessitating our survival with our Great Mother, the Earth. There is no other way to this. The Great Earth Mother continues to provide humanity with life, and we must understand, respect, and work with the true sources of life. Until *we* can create air, water, and healthy earth, we must pay great attention to what we are doing, not doing, and undoing.

A Simple Matter of Choice

In the final analysis, we do what we choose to do. The Mohawk of Kanehsatà:ke and the Mi'kmaq of Burnt Church only did what they could do, out of love for their People and lifeways, given the vastness of injustice channelled toward them. Leonard Peltier once asked, "What would we do in the face of the genocide of our People?"[14] What do we do when we are confronted by a force that will not hold back from hurting and destroying the Indigenous will to persevere? Miigam'agan and I chose to raise Wabanaki Children; we chose to found our lives on the ways of our People and live that way; we chose to identify our being with those traditions and we chose these theological traditions to speak rightfully to our unborn yet to come. The Longhouse of our Ancestors, our ancestral language, the ceremonial connection to the sacred, and keeping the names of our People still profoundly remains geared and supportive to being human in a time when human life, and all life, is not valued.

What are your choices?

And so I sing this Honour Song to the courage and bravery of Kanehsatà:ke. I sing for my Family of Esgenoôpetitj and to Miigam'agan and to Miigam'agan's Longhouse. I sing to honour my clan and Ancestors and for the community of Maucipiotan[15] that gives me life and identity. I honour, with living my life according to the life plan *Ki'E'Tan* given to all living beings. I sing to honour those who understand this and become friends and allies, joining the People in this great work. I make my life an Honour Song to all who gives me sustenance, vision, inspiration, and love.

---

1   *The People* is the preferred term when speaking generally of Indigenous Peoples and Nations.

2   Inherent Responsibilities is much more appropriate terminology than the concept of "rights." The Ancestors would understand responsibility. Rights are a concept brought here by the alternative. The conceptualization of rights is one that suggests there is a higher personality that can bestow a right that one does not presently have. This authority symbol has the power to grant and remove such a right. Indigenality understands that such a concept exist by birth and can only be respected.

3 Section 25 of the Canadian Charter of Rights and Freedoms states: "The guarantee in this Charter of certain rights and freedoms shall not be construed so as to abrogate or derogate from any aboriginal, treaty or other rights or freedoms that pertain to the Aboriginal Peoples of Canada including (a) any rights or freedoms that have been recognized by the Royal Proclamation of October 7, 1763." Meaning that land tenure is an Indigenous possession until ceded to the Crown and thus, unceded territories belong exclusively to that Indigenous Nation.

4 For example, consider the BNA section 91.24 (The BNA Act of 1867 is also referred to as the Canada Act, 1867).

5 A term for the homes and reserves/reservations of Indigenous Peoples. This term is often used by youth, as slang.

6 Current federal INAC budget for Indigenous programs and People is $6.9 billion for 2009 and $7.3 billion estimate for 2010. See <www.tbs-sct.gc.ca/rpp/2009-2010/inst/ian/ian01-eng.asp#ep>.

7 Conquest is only a *right* in which the conquering nation was justified in defending itself; this differs in the light of a "just war" where a declaration of war necessitates the intentions and the conquest is limited to the actions and or duration of the war. It is understood that conquest does not afford the conquering nation any validity in possessing the territory of the defeated.

8 Chief Seathl, 1854.

9 The conceptual existential framework of Wampanoag Theology.

10 The united states embarked on a three year odyssey resulting in the voluminous report entitled *American Indian Policy Review*. Like the Royal Commission on Aboriginal People, the recommendations, as well as the report itself, remained on governmental shelves gathering dust.

11 Christian Peacemaker Teams (CPT) <www.cpt.org>, headquartered in Chicago and Toronto, sent member delegations to witness and record incidences in Burnt Church. CPT created video recordings of such incidents, filed reports, made presentations, published findings, sent, through community invitation, exposure tours to the Burnt Church Community. Aboriginal Rights Coalition Atlantic (ARCA), a maritime-based aboriginal rights and social justice advocacy organization, comprised of Indigenous and maritime canadians, also responded with trained observers. Training for observers was conducted in partnership with the Mi'kmaq Community members of Burnt Church and the Tatamagouche Center, experienced trainers in delegation and witness work among the Indigenous Peoples in Guatemala. Many other persons, Indigenous, canadian, and americans, came to visit and support Burnt Church.

12 Labelling Indigenous treaties as *sui generis* (of its own kind) and *quasi-sovereign* (meaning resembling sovereign qualities but not truly sovereign), freely translated as, not real, not the same as, primitive state of being, state of pupilage, et cetera.

13 United Nations study and report on treaties and agreements with Indigenous Nations conducted from 1992–1995.

14 Leonard Peltier is a member of the American Indian Movement, falsely accused of murdering two FBI agents on the Pine Ridge Reservation in a shoot out June 25, 1975. There is no evidence tying Leonard Peltier to these murders and yet he has been imprisoned since February 6, 1976, as a political prisoner. See <www.leonardpeltier.net/>.

15 Known commonly as Mashpee-Wampanoag horror.

Learning Relations
and Grounding Solidarity:
A Critical Approach to Honouring Struggle

SHEILA GRUNER

A Word of Introduction

To write a chapter for this particular collection commemorating the twentieth anniversary of the resistance at Kanehsatà:ke is to reflect on events that have shaped my life in multiple and profound ways. It represents a space to revisit, with others, some of the formative moments in this country's landscape of struggle against the excesses of capitalist settler society and honour those who have been at the forefront. It is a chance to gain, through dialogue and writing, deeper insight into our own formation as activists, as educators, and as common people who strive to foster relationships with the Earth, and among people based on a mutuality of existence, rather than on relationships of conquest and accumulation.

The act of bringing together diverse voices, Aboriginal and non-Aboriginal, to honour the everyday people who have rejected the impositions of development such as that proposed in Oka is in itself an act on behalf of "those not yet born," as so many Indigenous activists and scholars have taught us. It is the re-affirmation of a history of struggle for life in the face of the aggressions of capitalism that have tended to systematically undermine the integrity of ways of being and "modes of production" that represent longstanding alternatives, if only they were not denied the space flourish.

It is indeed a much needed space to reflect on the persistence of colonialist-oriented attitudes in this country, deeply rooted as they are in the social relations of capitalism, expressed through ongoing impositions of often unwanted development on the traditional territories of Indigenous people. In part, it is through the critique of capitalist social relations as crucial to the grounding of solidarity that I would like to participate in this Honour Song. These relations are what urgently need to be assessed and critiqued by Euro-descendent activists who seek to act in solidarity with the original people of these lands toward a different kind of relationality among people and within nature. The social relations of capitalism are mostly hidden to us, however, and it is not until events such as Kanehsatà:ke emerge, and emerge again and in multiple sites throughout the Americas, that we are reminded of the ongoing and urgent task before us.

Those who really contest these relations are the often unsung, everyday protagonists, the people who have tended to the physical, social and emotional well-being of entire communities with little in return but with ever-renewed belief that change is not just possible but necessary. Those who have put themselves out there out of conviction have taken on dominating interests and institutions for all of us as they face displacement, marginalization, violence and in some cases outright conflict and war. They teach us how to better celebrate life, think from within history and toward a better future, inspire youth, house and shelter people, confront aggressors and struggle for rights to live in ways that revitalize the strength and dignity of people.

My aim with this chapter is to offer a few personal reflections about learning "relations" for engaging in solidarity, as well as reciprocity, in alliance building among people and across nations. The events at Kanehsatà:ke have deeply shaped how we in Canada should perceive what is at stake for people and the planet. I hope to offer something to the discussion about how these events are related to other efforts in the Americas, and the need for developing analysis and relationships across borders imposed via capitalism and racism. I want to encourage an understanding of all of this as rooted in history, which is so often forgotten within "mainstream" Canada. History is crucial to solidarity-building, but is often an abstract notion that gets lost in the shuffle as we either focus too inwardly or become too abstract about our intentions.

It is no secret that a real understanding of history is terribly lacking in this country overall. I argue for a history that is rooted in people's relations with each other and the ground we grow from, a "felt" history that we can internalize and call our own, alive, and not alive in the past, but in relation to what we are living now, as well as what is to come. History is about how we have gone about making life happen, how life is shaped and formed through relating to others and the places we are born into, and less about the specific and chronological events that seem to lose meaning or become abstract over time. Young people are being robbed of a "felt" past as they become submerged in notions of life as purchase. In this sense, learning about the importance of Kanehsatà:ke and the struggle of Indigenous Peoples across the globe is continually stunted. Learning about Kanehsatà:ke must be about learning relations—the life giving or defying relations—that have led us to where we are today.

So I would like to explore how events such as Kanehesetà:ke are shaped and shape us, within the current context of capitalist social relations in which all of our lives are submerged. Kanehsatà:ke is important for Indigenous and non-Indigenous people alike. We are enmeshed in the relations of accumulation, and it is only through a collaborative critical approach to transforming these relations that we have a chance to build a lasting solidarity and a different eventuality for our species. We must know by now that otherwise, people and the Earth are on a losing road.

Early Years and a Cold Start to the Decade

The news of the standoff in 1990 brings me back to myself as a young person, barely twenty, wanting to participate in shaping a better world and being distressed by the costs to people really involved in doing so. It was a time of my own life, in the late Eighties and early Nineties, when I felt a deep-seated need to escape the doldrums and shallowness of suburbia that seemed to offer so little in way of meaningful, emotive and life-forging experience. I was driven to "escape," but I also wanted to actively *find* something else, or perhaps find *other people* who believed in the possibility of something more than shopping malls and a good paying job.

In the summer of 1990, I had just returned from Uruguay, South America, after a seven-month cultural exchange. It was a time when economic restructuring in Canada was taking hold, when women and "ethnic minorities" were being called "special interest groups" and then blamed for taking away jobs or for being given "special consideration" amidst cuts and the reshaping of social programming. A brief six months earlier in Canada, while I had still been away, the Montreal Massacre—a brutal killing of fourteen women—had occurred, something that was seared into the minds of most Canadians at that time. I learned of the terrible news while in a country emerging from years of a brutal dictatorship that targeted people who spoke out on behalf of the poor majorities and working people of the country. In Uruguay, there were nearly no Indigenous Peoples left, because of the aggressive and brutal European colonizing project. My mind was overwhelmed by the questions of why women, the poor and Indigenous Peoples in particular were such outward targets of unprovoked violence—questions settling into the depths of my own consciousness. Against the historical backdrop of colonialism and ongoing repression I had the beginnings of a historical backdrop to the Kanehsatà:ke uprising.

The confrontation at Kanehsatà:ke represented an era, a turning point for my own formation as activist-educator, but more importantly a decisive moment for struggle and land-based social movements in Canada, as it linked to others across the continents. It signified, among other important Indigenous confrontations to neo-colonialism in the Americas, an effort that gained enough attention to enter the psyche of a generation and moved new young people to action and critical engagement. The event of the standoff itself left a mark on the popular psyche, shook up the nice notion of a "peaceful Canada," and was the first significant happening in Canada of my early experience that explained to me that history was not a benign matter that was to be learned in textbooks. In face of otherwise skewed media biases and the many stereotyped images, the in-depth history of the standoff by Alanis Obomsawin in her 270 *Years of Resistance* focused attention on history as shaping current experience in ways far outside mainstream perception. The strong female voice of Ellen Gabriel during interviews, the presentations of many people directly affected by the confrontation in ensuing years, lead me to develop the beginnings of a critical trajectory, to put into question what was really at stake for Indigenous people and for relations between Indigenous people and "settlers" in this country.

This question of what is at stake arises time and again as we witness uprisings in Kanehsatà:ke, Ipperwash, Gufstafsen Lake, Caledonia, Grassy Narrows, Kitchenuhmaykoosib Inninuwug, and Ardoch Algonquin First Nation, to name but a recent few. It seems that Euro-descendent society has actively ignored the question for the most part. The protagonists of history in this country shift dramatically once we ask who has actually sought to redirect the rampant and seemingly unending destruction of human and ecological life on a planet we all share.

The questions have been left for all of us as to how to *opt* to proceed in face of such confrontation, for that is what decides where we are placed within history, especially when proceeding at all was such a challenge in face of social pressures to maintain the status quo. The challenge was put out there through Kanehsatà:ke to learn, to listen to what people had to say about what was really happening to their lives and lands, and to imagine actual routes out of the systematic exploitation and marginalization for trivial-seeming development projects such as a golf course.

Solidarity and Ways of Relating With(In) the World

In the following pages I want examine my understanding of two very distinct approaches to "relations" as a way of describing what binds diverse Indigenous and non-Indigenous struggles today. The first has to do with a critical reading of the dominant set of relations within which we all live; that is, the dominant economic "mode of production" that shapes our social inter-actions and indeed our relationship with the planet. We are forced to enter these relations today, and indeed, how this happens is most often outside of our view or immediate control. I think it is useful, however, to explore how we become immersed in "capital social relations" through certain arrangements, in order to understand how to better shape our solidarity as we struggle against that immersion. We need to understand how capitalist social relations shapes privilege in specific ways that creates difference as oppositional, where gender and race become abstract notions that serve to divide rather than bind.

And the second set of relations, I'll call them "life relations," are rooted in other, multiple, and "alternative" ways of knowing, thinking about, and being in the world with other people and the Earth. The idea that "life relations" is rooted in an understanding of "accumulation for profit" as leading to multiple kinds of "death" (of the planet, of cultures, of people) comes from many movements across the Americas, and is nothing new. I especially want to recognize the Nasa people in Colombia for their ongoing work about "Life Projects"—a concept shared with Indigenous, rural, African descent, women's and other groups in that country and region of the world. The Nasa have based their organizational efforts around this concept of "life" in face of the destructive relations of capitalism. Directly related to a consciousness of the relations among people and rooted in a deep sense of belonging to land, the emphasis is on privileging the interests of the community over individual interests. Perhaps the sense of "life relation" is best reflected in a phrase of the Nasa, which brings together children, adults and Elders alike. It goes like this: "Words without Actions are Empty; Actions without Words are Blind; But Words and Actions outside the Spirit of Community are Death." This saying, which encompasses so much, is a driving force of people who have gained more than 70% of their original land base back in that part of the country.[1]

Not surprisingly, there is much resonance with "life projects" among Indigenous Peoples across the Americas, and why much of the learning about alternative "ways of being" can be found in the struggles of Indigenous nations throughout the Americas.[2] These kinds of "life relations" have multiple and diverse expressions rooted in the human drive for being—being free to live in the land you are from—based on collective struggles for meaning. This has strong resonance for all people who seek to build a grounded solidarity among people, who see "relations" as needing to be rooted in respect for identity, collective struggle, family, allies, and the natural world. "Giving back" or "not taking more than one needs," and making decisions keeping in mind "those who are not yet born" are some ways these relations are maintained. Indeed it is through acts of resistance to the dominant set of capitalist social relations that those not clearly linked to a strong cultural identity, such as many Indigenous people do share, might actually be able to envision a different way of being. This is the kind of insight that the people of Kanehsatà:ke, and so many other communities in these lands and others offer to us.

By "life relations" I thus refer to relations that are about a constant and active movement toward real reciprocity among people, ever cognizant of a mutually dependent social and planetary well-being. But without a deep reading of the capitalist social relations, of what has led to the undermining of diverse ways of producing and reproducing life within history, we set ourselves up to repeat the same systematic forms of exploitation and abuse. The question about how long we are willing to allow aggressive development regimes to continue unabated remains. According to many ecologists, Elders, and people who sense the rhythms of the planet as out of whack, we are close to running out of time.

As a point of emphasis, however, I must agree with those that question the way we focus too much on hype and doom around "climate change" as a response to ecological destruction.[3] It tends to shift our minds and energies onto blaming or seeking prescriptive answers. Rather, the focus should be on the relations behind the problem. These relations are rooted in a "mode of production" that shapes our relationship with(in) nature and how that is tied to exploitation and dispossession of workers, women, the poor and, particularly, Indigenous Peoples.[4] In other words, we shouldn't be focusing so much on the crisis of the planet, which will survive beyond our species, but a crisis of relations that is leading to the destruction of our source of life. Perhaps it sounds subtle, but the nuance is of significant relevance. It has to do with how we perceive and talk about the problems at hand, and where we put our active, committed energies. Once we see these problems that are common to all of us, in terms of relations rather than abstract issues (like climate change or global poverty), we might begin to tend more closely to our own everyday actions, putting ourselves directly into the picture, toward transforming these relations.

Binding Relations Across Sites of Struggle

This reading of capitalist social relations as well as alternative life relations binds all sites of struggle throughout the Americas and beyond, as people continually seek to reorient the uprooting effects of the capitalist project. Both kinds of relations are intertwined, as capitalism sets people into specific and interdependent roles of owning, working for, or resisting, and in the case of Aboriginal people, providing territory and resources for, the accumulation of wealth. My intention is to ask how we might envision a transformation of dominant modes of being that perpetuate these kinds of roles and modalities that lead to exclusion, displacement, dispossession and ongoing devastation to the natural world, while proposing something different based on a *mutuality* among alternative modes of production and being. This implies a deep recognition of difference and the existence of multiple ways of knowing that root our everyday actions and decisions in face of pervasive impositions of a dominant kind of "relationality."

In this advanced era of capitalism, we are now driven to accumulate more than ever before, whether we think it's a good idea or not. We do this at whatever expense is allowable. And on one hand what makes it "allowable" or not is the general consensus of society, based on a *consciousness* of how our everyday, every-moment actions collectively create and re-create the world within which we live.[5] Societal consensus has been a site of much coercion, so much so that we've become blind or at the very least numb to where our actions are leading if the warming of the planet or heightening levels of poverty are any indicators.

What has essentially held us back from the total subsuming of people within a capitalist mode are the expressions of resistance that demonstrate that some people are still not willing to allow for the continued decimation of social, cultural and ecological life. When people do come to the end of their rope, they either give up, move, or refuse and stand their ground. Those fighting against the imposition of unwanted development—the warriors at Kanehsatà:ke, the Chief and Council of Kitchenuhmaykoosib Inninuwug, the Nasa people of southern Colombia—are doing so for the benefit of others who are also on the direct losing end of these relations. They have tied their own well-being to the protection of the Earth, upon which, in the end, we all depend.

Our own consciousness is tied to our understanding of how we produce and reproduce our social and material lives.[6] It is the awareness of how we produce what we need (or don't) to live on the planet, as it is deeply and completely dependent on the Earth. The notion of advanced capitalism as "relations" need not be a complicated exercise in thinking, as it is quite straightforward. We are enmeshed within the relations of capitalism which necessarily shape our activities and ways we relate to each other: it sets us up. The question is how to develop a critical consciousness about these relations in order to transform them. It is a road into history, for Indigenous-Euro descendent relations have been deeply shaped within a capitalist mode of production since contact. Indigenous scholars like Leroy Littlebear discuss the effects of European worldviews on Indigenous people in *Reclaiming Indigenous Voice and Vision.* The European worldview he discusses is rooted in a capitalist mode of production, and produces what he calls "Jagged Worldviews" among Indigenous communities.[7] This raises important issues for both Indigenous people, who can identify a kind of relationality that has survived despite colonial impositions, and for Euro-descendents who seek to reclaim a history of critique and resistance to the relations of capitalist accumulation.

The accumulation of resources and labour were driving forces behind the European colonial endeavours of the sixteenth century onward in the Americas, this we know. It is what continues to pervade most projects and notions of "development," and maintains the colonialist or neo-colonial character and ongoing paternalistic approaches by provincial and federal governments to development in First Nation communities.

While we are all implicated in capitalist relations, I am convinced that each of us has the choice to develop a consciousness about them and seek alternative pathways. The lack of opting to choose life over profit ties us implicitly to the dominant capitalist mode, whether as peons, as accomplices, or perhaps, in many cases, both. The complications arise when we cannot see clearly just what is at stake for people and the Earth, where our experience is abstracted in language that alienates us from nature, each other, and ultimately ourselves. This is how the suffering of a few—or many, for that matter—can be largely ignored or downplayed and perpetuated for people in places like Canada.

Rooting Solidarity: The Early Nineties, "Free Trade" and Expressions of Resistance

The Nineties represented an intensely dynamic and chaotic decade aimed at the re-shaping of capitalist economies throughout much of the Americas to implement a neo-liberal agenda which aims at hemispheric "integration" through the project of "free trade." Free trade has become a flag of the generation and as such is useful to root this schematic painting of how we have been bound and shaped within capitalist relations.

I also think this backdrop is an important one in reflecting on Kanehsatà:ke as the first much publicized confrontation between Indigenous people and the provincial and federal governments in this country. I don't think the role of the media can be underestimated in terms of blurring the real issues at play, and subsequently hiding the relations that led to the standoff. What it looked like to mainstream Canadian society was a group of individual "troublemakers" that had crossed the line in contesting authority, even if the situation was "somewhat justified" (after all, who can argue with people wanting to protect their burial sites)? What these events actually reflected was rendering as visible a people through their acts of resistance, whose history, identity and way of being were being submerged and hidden, to be ploughed over for a golf course.

Shortly after the events at Kahnesetà:ke, the words "free trade" began to enter public discussion in a more aggressive way. The North American Free Trade Agreement was being avidly being pushed forward by national governments and the corporate world to take the place of the Canada-U.S. free trade agreement, and people began to question what the new development might really mean for people. We were told about the trade advantages and the job opportunities. The offer of jobs has always been a justification for large-scale corporate driven developments such as free trade agreements, large extractive projects such as mining, oil and forestry and so forth. But for those who saw not trade agreements but the relations of capitalism becoming more entrenched, it became urgent to contest was on the table.

Indigenous communities in the south were actively preparing for free trade even before debates really took hold in Canada. Mayan people of Chiapas in Mexico had been training to analyze the potential impacts of free trade on their people and lands and were forming a defensive front for the likely imposition of NAFTA. In the book *The Twenty and the Ten* leaders discuss how between 1984 and 1994 the clandestine training of everyday people to analyze and act in the defense of their lands and cultural rights had taken place. On January 1, 1994, NAFTA was launched. And on January 1, 1994, the Zapatistas also came out of clandestine training to declare their defensive position against NAFTA and the excesses of capitalism. Theirs was a call and project of support to all the multiple people and communities, Indigenous and non-Indigenous alike, that were continuing to struggle to survive in face of capitalism. It was a call in defense of all those whose lives were not valued because they could not buy or sell, who lay outside of the relations of purchase and therefore did not exist.

The Zapatistas captured the imagination of much of Mexico and offered a wealth of possibilities for re-thinking what solidarity really should be about, making visible what has been rendered "invisible" through capitalism. This movement was born of people who were the most forgotten of the forgotten in Mexico, whose lands were being decimated through large-scale production for global markets, and who remained poor despite, or perhaps because of, such natural wealth. Their signatory black masks represented their systematic invisibility and served as a metaphor for so many others, Indigenous and non-Indigenous people alike, who were left out, victimized, dispossessed and abandoned by the systematic injustices perpetuated by mainstream economic relations.

Ten years later, in 2004, the Nasa people of Colombia continued at the forefront of public expression against the impositions of free trade alongside organized labour, Black, women's, peasant movements, and others. They developed perhaps the first "popular" referendums in 1995 about the proposed free trade agreement between the United States and Colombia, which brought out over 70% of the voting population in that region (many times the average turn out for national elections). Over 98% of people in the Indigenous regional communities of Northern Cauca voted against the proposed deal.[8] Subsequently, the Canadian government was to enter discussions with Colombia and offer to pave the way for the larger U.S. trade deal.

Around the same time that Prime Minister Harper and the opposition parties offered their apology to Aboriginal people in Canada, he produced the deal with the Uribe government in Colombia, against the strongly expressed will of Indigenous people in that country.

While still to be approved through parliament, the Harper government saw fit to sign this pact with a regime that had an explicit disregard for Indigenous people, workers, small-scale farmers and other organized groups who contested the impositions of development. The brutal human rights record of the Colombian ruling governments is no secret. Up to 60,000 people had been involved in marches against state violence and the proposed deal, in diverse areas of the country and on numerous occasions. This form of aggressive accumulation is considered by the Nasa as a "death project," as it will necessarily lead to the exploitation/destruction of lands and the viability of life as expressed by the Nasa, for which they have sacrificed so much to protect. As noted in a public presentation by a representative of the Nasa movement at the CINSA (Canadian Indigenous/Native Studies Association) conference in Sault Ste. Marie, the irony and injury of Harper's Apology and the signing of this agreement for the Nasa people in Colombia has been particularly harsh and contradictory. As it stands, the Canada-Colombia Free Trade Agreement is currently tabled in parliament and under review by the other parties, with the U.S.-Colombia agreement still under discussion, as of the writing of this chapter.

The fight against free trade led by Indigenous movements of the south, inspired many others to root solidarity in an understanding of alternative ways of being that contested capitalist social relations. Agreements like these represent the scripts that shape what subsequently happens in and to our lives, the ways we relate to each other and the kinds of things we do to and within the environment. It is up to us to ask how these scripts hook our individual actions within an accumulation regime that seeks labour and resources at nearly any cost, with real effects on water, animal and plant life, to the air we breathe, and ultimately ourselves.

A Final Statement on Solidarity: Honouring Teachings and Actively Being in the World

Through the writing of this chapter I hope to do justice to some of the teachings I have gained through working with Indigenous people, their movements, communities and allies. As a non-Aboriginal person, to do this means to recognize that many people are at the heart of these insights and teachings. No one can pretend any special personal insight where such concepts and teachings are born within and as a part of collective efforts, in communities shaped by relations of shared analysis, action and sacrifice, and based on a drive to protect life in the broadest of senses.

I do not propose to have answers to the deep-seated problems generated through the relations of capitalist accumulation, but rather want to emphasize a way of thinking about them that allows for deepened analysis and more meaningful solidarity. Once we acknowledge, explore and internalize the historical circumstances that shape who we are as people, we can see more clearly where our role lies in transforming the relations in a world dominated by war, drive for profit, and the exploitation of people and nature. As it becomes harder and harder to imagine a world not entrenched in the relations of capital, those who actively resist the dispossessing effects of capitalist social relations, who set the stage for those who offer a way of living "life relations," become utterly crucial.

Kanehsatà:ke remains in our minds and hearts after all these years because it inspired questioning of the deepest kind when we were young, and opened the doors to a kind of learning that invited us to imagine Canada, to imagine the Americas, differently. It invited solidarity among people throughout diverse nations then, and today brings together those who actively reject the ongoing systematic dispossession and displacement that has prevailed throughout our generation. Mostly, it continues to serve as a reminder to us all that we are ultimately bound to the Earth and each other.

It is in the spirit of honouring those who have engaged most directly in historical struggle based on a profound care for nature, identity and community, and their willingness to stick their necks out during messy, dangerous and uncertain times that this chapter is written.

1 CECIDIC (2001), *Children of Thunder: Thirty Years of Land Recovery and Resistance*, Cauca: Ethno-Education Project (CD-ROM).

2 Mario Blaser, Harvey A. Feit and Glenn McRae, eds. (2004), *In the Way of Development: Indigenous Peoples, Life Projects and Globalization*, London and Ottawa: Zed Books, and the Canadian International Development Research Center, retrieved 10 October 2009 from <web.idrc.ca/en/ev-58137-201-1-DO_TOPIC.html>).

3 James O'Connor (1998), *Natural Causes: Essays in Ecological Marxism*, New York: The Guilford Press.

4 See David Harvey (2003), *The New Imperialism*. London: Oxford University Press; Silvia Federici, (2004), *Caliban And The Witch: Women, The Body, and Primitive Accumulation*. Brooklyn, NY: Autonomedia.

5 Paulo Freire (1996), *Education for Critical Consciousness*, New York: The Continuum Publishing Company.

6 Paula Allman (1999), "Revolutionary social transformation: Democratic hopes, political possibilities and critical education," *Critical Studies in Education and Culture Series*, Westport, CT: Bergin & Garvey.

7 Leroy Little Bear (2000), "Jagged Worldviews Colliding" in *Reclaiming Indigenous Voice and Vision*, Vancouver: UBC Press.

8 Call for a Citizen's Popular Consultation Concerning the Free Trade Agreement, Pueblos en Camino, retrieved 10 October 2009 from <www.en-camino.org/node/34>.

Lessons From the Bridge:

On the Possibilities of Anti-Racist Feminist Alliances in Indigenous Spaces

ROBINDER KAUR SEHDEV

The resistance at Kanehsatà:ke[1] has many lessons to teach about power, politics and our abilities to negotiate the two in the service of justice. It has played an important part in the development of critical consciousness and political action in a number of Indigenous and non-Indigenous communities across what is now called Canada. The resistance revealed the profound problems in the relationship between the settler state and Indigenous Peoples and, as Haudenosaunee scholar Taiaiake Alfred notes, it united Indigenous Peoples and "teaches us the true nature of colonial power."[2] The resistance motivated Gerald McMaster (Plains Cree) two years later to use the gallery space as a site of anti-colonial resistance and settler education:

> That political confrontation, which left three people dead, can be seen as Canada's version of Wounded Knee. It politicized many of us. In 1992 [which marked the quincentennial of Christopher Columbus's landing in the so-called New World], we had no heart for participating in a celebration. Instead, our strategy was to make the public aware of 500 years of injustice toward indigenous [sic] peoples.[3]

More than a singular event, Haudenosaunee scholar Susan Hill observes that the Kanehsatà:ke resistance was a significant link in a chain of Haudenosaunee activism that in turn inspired Indigenous activism for land rights and sovereignty across the Canadian and u.s. settler states. "Many of these actions are unresolved leaving all parties involved unsettled."[4] Former AFN Grand Chief George Erasmus evocatively remarked that the resistance "was something everyone identified with."[5] The Kanehsatà:ke resistance reached individuals, challenging us to consider modern colonial power and our relationship to it within our communities and the settler state, and it profoundly unsettles us all. In other words, the Kanehsatà:ke resistance challenged both Indigenous Peoples and settlers to consider the possibilities and limits of resistance, renewal and common struggle. These challenges are ongoing.

Our thinking on the Kanehsatà:ke resistance speaks volumes about the lines of inclusion and exclusion implicit in the articulation of those difficult pronouns: *us, we, ours*. Throughout the resistance, and especially as the power of the state was brought to bear on those at and behind the blockades, the matter of justice gained urgency. It became clear that justice would never arrive on its own accord; justice requires work. When the news camera captured images of soldiers erecting razor wire and shooting tear gas at crowds, those of us watching the evening news could disapprove while, thanks to geographic distance, we could also remove ourselves from the state-caused state of crisis. Yet we were called upon, Haudenosaunee or not, Native or not, when negotiators and warriors reminded us that this crisis was produced by the state, and when they asked us where the honour of *our* leaders had gone. In these questions, we were challenged to consider our belonging in communities that seek justice or those that have benefitted from injustice and dispossession. For the settler, these questions unsettle the once comfortable myth of a coherent, spontaneously forming and naturally just community. That summer, "O Canada" changed from proud exclamation to shameful rebuke. For many of us on the receiving end of other forms of injustice, emancipatory politics offered a connection between our experience with oppression and the Kanehsatà:ke resistance and other Indigenous resistance movements. These politics gave us the skills to identify systems of power and structures of violence at work that summer in Québec.

As a non-Indigenous woman of colour and anti-racist feminist, I would like to explore the ways that the Kanehsatà:ke resistance challenges me to rethink my solidarity politics and the lines of inclusion and exclusion implicit in my thinking about solidarities. Counting myself among the anti-racist feminist movement, I am the beneficiary of the u.s. Third World Women's Movement, which aimed to develop coalitions in the face of multiple and overlapping systems of oppression and significant cultural and political differences among women. Women of this movement, most notably Lee Maracle (citizen of the Stó:lo Nation), ask us to consider patriarchy as operating in the service of colonialism rather than as a free-standing oppression among other free-standing oppressions.[6] Maracle explains that working with other women from different colonial and racist contexts is absolutely critical to the politics of dismantling the oppressions that she and other Indigenous women face. Such solidarity work demands "closeness." Musing on her friendship with one of the other mothers of the movement, Audre Lorde, Maracle sketches the moments of shared interest in the lives of different women and the power this gives to the Third World Women's Movement's work for justice:

> Audre Lorde [a working-class, African-American, lesbian mother and poet] and I were destined to be close. The combined knowledge of African ex-slaves and colonized Natives in North America is going to tear asunder the holy citadel of patriarchy. Who can understand the pain of this land better than a Native woman? Who can understand the oppression that capitalism metes out to working people better than a Black woman? The road to freedom is paved with the intimate knowledge of the oppressed.[7]

These shared intimate knowledges, and the mutual desire for closeness, are central to the project of social justice which contemporary anti-racist feminism pursues. Considering the colonial strategy of dehumanizing women, it becomes clear that the strategies employed and ends served are complex and powerful since women play a central role in all aspects of Indigenous spiritual, intellectual and cultural life.[8] No emancipatory politics on this land will be viable without Indigenous women active in their conception and realization. Understanding the importance of Indigenous women requires more than an understanding of the ways that patriarchy gains currency; it requires an appreciation for and intimacy with traditional politics in conjunction with an understanding of colonial power.

I must digress here to comment on the land and Indigenous diplomacy. In this chapter's title I have referenced Indigenous spaces. I mean two things by this. First, I am referencing the relationship between Indigenous Peoples and the land. This is a relationship that settlers do not have, and this is not only because our cultural, cosmological and political selves are rooted in other lands, but also because, generally speaking, we have not cultivated a relationship with this space. Secondly, by "Indigenous spaces" I am referring to spaces of meeting, or coalition spaces provided for in Indigenous diplomacy.

Anti-racist feminism counts the Third World Women's Movement as one of its Ancestors. We have inherited their analysis of the intersecting nature of oppression as well as the recognition that our different fates are interconnected. The ways that we forge those links between different women and their experiences, knowledge and skills continues to cry out for attention. Sunera Thobani articulates the need to forge those links when she says of today's women's movement,

> One of the biggest obstacles I see is articulating a vision that can inspire and bring women together. [...] we need to focus on issues of poverty, racism, indigenous [sic] rights, and anti-imperialism. This means that feminism must think of itself very differently and move away from the perspective where gender is the primary consideration. This vision, which speaks to the richness of our histories and experiences of living outside the mainstream, is one that many women of colour have been attempting to articulate.[9]

What would such a redirection look like? How might the adoption of "Indigenous rights" influence the constitution and direction of the women's movement? We walk a dangerous path, because in attempting to articulate and perform a politics of emancipation by bringing together all women, we risk simplifying the matter of Indigenous rights and homogenizing Indigenous people's experience with colonialism and patriarchy. As with other emancipatory politics, anti-racism cannot afford to settle into its methods, rather the goal of justice requires its followers to reassess its methods in light of the movement's politics. I argue that anti-racist feminism today will go nowhere if its goal is to simply incorporate Indigenous politics into its machine.

In taking up both the warriors' call to consider the constitution of *us, we, ours* and the imperative to remember and live up to treaty, this paper outlines the points of connection in the diplomatic tool of the bridge contained in Kaswentha, also known as Two Row Wampum, the formative treaty for Haudenosaunee-newcomer relations, and the figure of the bridge as enabler of coalitional politics in the Third World Women's Movement. I argue that anti-racist feminism needs to re-adopt the politics of solidarity that it inherited from the Third World Women's Movement, and also that this politics of solidarity has many lessons to learn about Haudenosaunee politics of relation and the particularity of the land that Kaswentha provides.

Resistance, Knowledge and Kaswentha

As I watched the events at Kanehsatà:ke televisually unfold, I had the vocabulary (based on experience and critical capacity) to understand the racist invectives of inferiority and non-belonging, the erasure of community histories from Canadian history and the simplification of complex knowledge systems. However, this is not enough. Having access to the vocabulary is not equivalent to having the knowledge of the ways that oppressions impact specific cultures and politics. Marginalized communities create vocabularies to understand oppression and articulate resistance. We have developed the means to identify and speak about oppression at the systemic level and the subtleties of non-verbal racism along with the paradoxes of inclusion. But these vocabularies are not uniform or universal. However, neo-liberal discourses of reverse racism evidence that such vocabularies are easily accessible and vulnerable to appropriation. Further, the assumption that access to the vocabularies of resistance offers insight into resistance struggles reduces the cultures, knowledges and traditions of the struggling community to perspective alone.

However well intentioned and critically minded I was, I did not, and truthfully cannot, understand the particular violence of colonization that the Haudenosaunee have resisted, though I do understand it as violence and as colonization. This is not to claim that Haudenosaunee experience is unknowable or inaccessible. I mean that the encounters with colonization and the resulting resistance strategies are rooted in philosophies and politics that cannot be expressed through resistance vocabularies alone. For example, during the resistance the land was referenced as mother, the encroachment of land developers as violators or rapists, and the Haudenosaunee as protectors. The relationship of the Haudenosaunee to the land is far older than the existence of Canada and colonization, and as Anishnaabek scholars John Borrows[10] and Leanne Simpson[11] both note, the relationship between people, the land and the animal world are solemnized in treaty, which ensures mutual accountability.

Treaties, Simpson reminds us, are sacred agreements, made between nations "in the presence of the spiritual world and solemnized in ceremony."[12] The Haudenosaunee imperative to protect their land from further violation is rooted in their philosophy and spirituality that teach that relatedness between human and non-human worlds, sacredness and tradition are normative principles in which Haudenosaunee political claims are rooted.[13] This is not easily translatable "into cultures that unproblematically accept the discourses of rights, sovereignty, and nationhood as the only authoritative sources of Indigenous political claims."[14]. More than a matter of appreciating perspectives or mastering vocabularies, these are philosophies of relations and politics. To recognize this means abandoning the power to simplify and subjugate knowledges. According to Haudenosaunee legal scholar Patricia Monture, "Whites can accept that Aboriginal people have politics (albeit not fully) but do not recognize that we equally have theologies, epistemologies, knowledge systems, pedagogy and history. These are all collapsed into mere 'perspective,' thus making actual the white fallacy of Aboriginal inferiority."[15] In the classification of Aboriginal political action and intellectual life as "perspective" (as in the phrase, *the Aboriginal perspective*), and political strategy as "vocabulary," the image of the settler and the well-intentioned activist/scholar as subject agent and bringer of knowledge is deployed while simultaneously othering Indigenous people, denying their wisdom and agency and enforcing the disconnection between history, mind, body and spirit.

Taiaiake Alfred is careful to note that Indigenous knowledges and traditions are not fundamentally unknowable to non-Indigenous people because to do so would be self-defeating: "Our goal should be to convince others of the wisdom of the indigenous [sic] perspective."[16]

We are challenged, then, to attune ourselves to the "gifts" of other's wisdom,[17] rather than abandoning our starting positions in appropriative gestures akin to the Indianist movements that have peppered settler history since contact. In other words, Indigenous politics are certainly not arguing for the obliteration of our different knowledges and experiences. Haudenosaunee politics, for example, manage internal diversity.[18] Why would they shrink away from diversity amongst non-Indigenous communities?[19] Failing to grasp that resistance strategies emerge not only from the existence of oppression, but also from the strength and diversity of knowledge systems, risks providing generalized and ultimately useless answers to complex problems. Indigenous politics have much more to teach anti-racist feminists than the *inclusion* of "the Aboriginal perspective" permits. The quest for inclusion also reifies the myth of the all-knowing outsider whose own subjectivity is untouchable by the very factors that alter everyone else's selfhood,[20] and the activist who can claim to be freed of the particulars of her own subjectivity in favour of chameleon-like appropriative gestures. A usable conception of solidarity must not hinge upon confusing political philosophies for perspectives, and understanding oppressions with the mastery of shared vocabularies.

The Kanehsatà:ke resistance was based in Haudenosaunee diplomacy and politics in spite of settler colonial practices to dismantle them. It relied on the guidance of Clan Mothers, without whom there would have been no negotiation or warrior action; the leadership of the Traditional Chiefs whose authority is perpetually undercut by the paternalism of the Indian Act; not to mention the work of warriors, women and children. Indeed, whole communities ensured that the barricades were maintained, the Pines protected and they held up treaty as a living document to which the state and settlers needed (and need) to recommit.

Teme-Augama Anishinaabe political philosopher Dale Turner notes that Haudenosaunee political philosophy was the normative, legitimating force in the European-Native ethical relationship and newcomers knew and accepted this.[21] Kaswentha (also called Two Row Wampum, and, in turn, the Covenant Chain of Silver are the formative treaties for Native-settler relations. Both treaties granted recognition to the Europeans. Haudenosaunee recognition legitimated

European jurisprudence in what would come to be known as Canada and the United States,[22] which upsets the settler myth of governance as a European artifact. Newcomers would not have been permitted to remain on Haudenosaunee territory had they attempted to interfere with Haudenosaunee sovereignty. Eventually, however, what was once a shared language of diplomacy came to be corrupted in spite of the many and varied efforts of Indigenous leaders to remind colonial, dominion and settler leadership of their mutual understandings and agreements which underlay those formative treaties.

Despite this disrespect to the foundational treaties, Kaswentha contains an important bridge, and it has lessons to teach anti-racist feminists. According to Kaswentha, two canoes travel parallel paths. In it, two white lines run lengthwise, three rows of purple beads are situated between the white rows and there are more purple rows still on the outside of either white row. One white line signifies the European canoe and its path; the other white line signifies the Haudenosaunee canoe and path. Dale Turner and Susan Hill[23] are careful to point out that the two rows are not separated by three rows of purple beads, they are *bridged* by the three rows. This bridge that links the two paths is comprised of peace, respect and friendship; these are the basis of all subsequent treaties, or in Métis historian David McNab's words, "This was the original meeting ground."[24] Turner explains that the exchange of wampum is a moral act, grounded in the principles of "reciprocity and renewal [...] which meant that the normative terms of a political agreement were renewed in a context of peace, respect, and friendship."[25] Wampum are not simply exchanged and abandoned, through ceremony they are returned to and reaffirmed by both sides. Treaty, then, is not something to be agreed to and forgotten about, it must be *done* and done repeatedly. In this sense, treaty is kinetic. Put another way, it is more a verb than a noun, more an action than a thing, and is always in the process of becoming.

Failure to live up to treaty means that the foundational relationship has been neglected or damaged. It does not, however, invalidate the treaty and our responsibilities to it and one another.[26] Over time, the principles of Kaswentha were violated and it became clear that the relationship between settlers and Natives needed to be reaffirmed and committed to again. The Covenant Chain of Silver was formed to reconcile the tarnished relationship between newcomers and the Haudenosaunee. Susan Hill explains its significance:

> While the ideas contained in it were not new to the Haudenosaunee, the metaphor of the Covenant Chain as representing the treaty relationship was. From that point forward, the concept of the Covenant Chain continued to develop and was eventually described as a silver chain holding both the British sailing ship and the Haudenosaunee canoe to the "Great Mountain" (Onondaga). It was described as a three-link silver chain representing "peace and friendship forever.[27]

The Covenant Chain did not replace or invalidate Kaswentha; "it used [the Kaswentha] as a basis for reconciliation and further development while acknowledging how both sides had been responsible for damaging their agreement and relationship."[28] This treaty offers an eloquent metaphor for the work of maintaining our relationship. We are charged with the responsibility to ensure that the chain is polished and its links bright. In other words, maintaining our relationship requires we relearn the diplomacy and laws that link us together and to this land. The interconnected nature of these treaties speaks to the communicative power of Haudenosaunee diplomacy: the three-linked chain and the three rows of beads retain the active and recursive component that gives them meaning. Maintaining a bridge and polishing a chain is not a linear task, but one that requires perpetual attention and care. Recovery is then built into these politics.

The Kanehsatà:ke resistance taught settlers that bridges and roads could be blocked if the foundational connective principles of peace, respect and friendship have been neglected or violated. Despite the government rhetoric of goodwill and respectful negotiations, the razor wire, tanks and machine guns belied this talk. Ellen Gabriel later spoke about July 11, the day that the Sûreté du Québec, Quebéc's provincial police force, raided the blockade in the Pines, attempting to push the warriors, leaders and children from the space, "I remember looking at the faces of the swat team and they were scared, they were like [...] young babies who had never met something so strong, who had never met a spirit, 'cause we were fighting something without a spirit. There was no thought to it. They were like robots."[29]

The concepts of obligation and protection, as Turner, Simpson and Hill have all argued, comes directly from the Haudenosaunee treaties, sacred agreements that bind all parties together. What but robotic actions can be expected from a body whose violations of its treaty responsibilities wound its own self and negate its own spirit?[30] What can we expect from a party that had an opportunity to ground itself in this land, that had the chance to forge a respectful and peaceful friendship, but opted to neglect this relationship, allowing time and arrogance to tarnish their bonds to the Haudenosaunee?

Without an understanding of the complexities of Haudenosaunee diplomacy and politics, emancipatory politics that aim to identify with the Kanehsatà:ke resistance and work toward decolonization will necessarily and perpetually miss the boat, or our (anti-racist feminist) opened arms will only tightly close around the necks of others. If our acts of solidarity are to be viable, we must recognize the ways and conditions in which we anti-racist feminists form alliances through our differences in Indigenous space.

Open Arms and Chokeholds

From my perspective, the Kanehsatà:ke resistance represented new forms of resistance. For the first time in my life, I saw people collectively resist, naming racism as racism and declaring their sovereignty from Canada. I was inspired by such strength of vision in the face of state violence. This moment was electric. For these reasons, this stood as a resistance movement with which I could identify even though I did not fully understand it. After all, my community has worked hard to be recognized as a co-creator of the Canadian nation. Ours (the Punjabi community) is a challenge to the constitution of Canadian citizenship and we have no inherent claim to this land. The concerns of First Nations vis à vis the Canadian state are fundamentally different than the concerns of, for example, my community, where one community seeks recognition for its long-ignored place within the state and the other seeks recognition of the foundational agreements between their state and Canada.

To First Nations, the gesture of inclusive citizenship does not even begin to address the fundamental problems of imposing a national structure on an existing state-to-state relationship. Legal scholar and citizen of the Chickasaw Nation James (Sakéj) Youngblood Henderson begins his critique from the fundamental position that treaties formed between Indigenous nations and the British Crown affirm the sovereignty of both. Henderson argues that the offer of Canadian citizenship to Aboriginal Peoples threatens to undermine Aboriginal sovereignty by "transform[ing] the sacred homeland of Aboriginal nations" into a parade of ethnic difference in the service of "Euro-Canadian self-congratulation and individualism."[31] Aboriginal sovereignty offers "a *sui generis* citizenship" that "accentuates relationships [and] responsibilities [between people] to a particular ecology."[32] In other words, settler sovereignty is not normative, nor does it have the authority or legitimacy to confer recognition or grant inclusion.

The recognition of the state-to-state relationship affirmed through treaty differs significantly from anti-racist politics in Canada, which hinge on the challenge to citizenship and on identifying the systems of power underlying racism. When anti-racist feminists talk of racism, we are not just indicating an event or experience, but the structures of power that produce racist acts and beliefs, that justify them, and keep them safely hidden in plain sight and everyday practice. The feminist movement has generally responded to the range of women's experiences and histories by asking how it can include these perspectives, thereby widening feminism's reach. The Third World Women's Movement casts a critical eye on such impulses, revealing the coercive potential of inclusivity that positions feminism as a movement that has only to expand its membership to increase its relevance. The Third World Women's Movement argued that inclusivity offered no healing salve for feminism's shortcomings, rather the quest for inclusivity distracted activists from attending to the particular concerns of women of colour. Feminism's objectives and methods, in short, needed to change.

The u.s. Third World Women's Movement offers insight into the complex interlockings of oppression and the ways in which such interlocking oppressions were internal to activist disciplines like second-wave feminism. It also offered insight into the formation of critical consciousness and solidarities in oppressive contexts. Women of colour poets, activists, mothers, artists and philosophers first gathered to critique the feminist movement that had excluded their interests on the grounds that the concerns of women of colour be postponed until the problem of patriarchy was resolved. Women of colour then gathered to think through the terms of and strategies for cooperation and communication in spite of their exclusion from dominant feminism and their own internal differences. This movement of women of colour was not only a movement against a common foe; it was a movement for marginalized women and the power of their coalitions. Founders of the Third World Women's Movement like Gloria Anzaldúa, Audre Lorde and Chéla Sandoval argued that women of colour were profoundly alienated from and disempowered by the structures of power within the feminist movement. Even while the feminist movement claimed to speak and work for all women, it was dominated by a narrow margin comprised of middle-class, heterosexual, white women whose ideas of womanhood flatten out women's difference, taking "womanhood" to mean *women like them* (heterosexual, middle-class white women). Such universalism, bell hooks writes, is neither fitting the matter at hand (women's conditions, if there can be said to be such a thing, are not universal) nor is it enough to unite women:

> While it is evident that many women suffer from sexist tyranny, there is little indication that this forges 'a common bond among all women.' There is much evidence substantiating the reality that race and class identity creates differences in quality of life, social status, and lifestyle that take precedence over the common experience women share—differences which are rarely transcended.[33]

The oppressions women of colour face, hooks says, are more than patriarchal, and the movement, if it is to serve women of colour, must offer an understanding and way of confronting the problems of race, class and sexuality, to name but three commonly identified matrices of power and abuse.

Instead, dominant feminism reproduced modes of oppression which decades earlier its followers condemned.[34] Once established, dominant feminists argued that Third World women's cultures were inherently oppressive and the sooner they abandoned them, the closer to emancipation they would be.[35] The reduction of Third World women's cultures and ways of knowing and doing along with the fatal postponement of their priorities not only duplicates oppressive politics, it grafts oppressive strategies onto feminist vocabularies of political struggle. If inclusivity is to be found here it is not substantive but coercive, and the arms that open to embrace difference close around the necks of others.

Bridge Work

By coming into being and community through their displacement from dominant feminist resistance, Third World women began to work through the problem of solidarity. Second wave feminists had, after all and in effect, told Third World women that solidarity through difference was neither desirable nor possible. The bridge became a powerful symbol of the work of solidarity. Not only do bridges span borders, they also connect the edges of political action and cultural recognition. Bridge crossing also lays the groundwork for the racialized subject's reckoning with her own precarious and complicit location within the settler nation, however racially and sexually marked she may be, her connection to *this* land is not spiritual, nor does it permeate her culture, knowledge systems, language or philosophies. In this regard, bridge crossing is a powerful tool for challenging settlerhood amongst *all* settlers.

The bridge, as Anzaldúa theorizes it, is a kind of suspended borderland, or a liminal pathway whose purpose it is to span an otherwise uncrossable breach. The bridge is liminal because the crosser is surrounded with its absence, and with the knowledge that liminality is necessary for any sort of political or cultural connection. The subjectivities of women of colour comprise the anchoring posts of the bridge, and their stretching bodies, its planks. This is not an apparently warm embrace or a chokehold, though it is bodily, dangerous and often painful. The bridge is a gruesome structure dependant on the labour of those stretching to create the passageway *upon the backs* of those who are liminal and so implicates the crossers in the threat of pain of those who are crossed upon. This bodily language makes it impossible to speak casually about solidarity politics as natural or spontaneously self-generative. The fact of ongoing work involved in the constancy of stretching and grasping, the threat of slipping or crossing roughly are all facts and fears crossers and bridgers must recognize and work with. The bridge of the Third World Women's Movement is also more than a passageway that links individuals; it offers a way of thinking about subjectivity within contexts of oppressive power. To address how this is so, we must first consider the shifting nature of subjectivity and relationality in turn.

As with all others, women of colour *become* through the power contexts within which we are located. For example, think of the migrant woman of colour, who, once in Canada becomes "temporary foreign worker," "underemployed," "minority," "marginal," and "settler" all at once. Not only does her sense of self shift with the shifting forces at work around her, demanding her to respond in partial and in varied ways, but in these shifting configurations of power come shifting communities, networks of knowledge, history and tradition. Sometimes these relationships are productive and help her to achieve some sense of self and justice, and sometimes they are exploitative and abusive. Regardless, layer upon layer they impinge on her sense of self in relation to others. Bridge work, as Aimee Carrillo Rowe[36] calls this labour, commits us to doing the hard work of connecting these configurations of power to the agency and selfhood of those located within them (the anchoring posts of the bridge). This is an active remembering against the general imperative to forget or disassociate. A bridge crosser would recognize that while her specific family history might not be directly implicated in the appropriation of Indigenous land, she is nevertheless the beneficiary of this appropriation even if hers is a history of marginalization. There is no room for innocence on the bridge. Because the stakes are high and the processes of re-membering and re-associating potentially open old wounds, exposing our vulnerabilities and complicities, the risk of hurting bridge crosser and bridge walker alike increases. After all, Anzaldúa writes, the labour of our bridging is commonly shouldered and the recognition that our fates are interconnected like links in a bridge does not neutralize the risk and mortal fear: "The more we have in common, including love, the greater the heartache between us, the more we hurt each other."[37] This is a "labor [sic] of [...] re-membering"[38] because it reconnects the experiences and pain of a people to their histories and stories of oppression and in doing this, actively refuses to submit to the general state of forgetting.[39] This is more than a theory of coalition; it is a theory of the ways that coalitions reconstitute the full subjectivity, the humanity of their constituents. As Aimee Carrillo Rowe eloquently puts it, "This labor of love, this bridge work, is the engaged action through which we constitute our humanity."[40] The *we* of bridgework signals a troubling of the assumption that there is a positivist *we*, a coherent community of critics, activists and committed scholars: *we* should spur questions of location and belonging, rather than settle them. The Third World Women's Movement continues, decades later, to resonate with today's political and academic environment by challenging us to acknowledge *we* as a corruptible collective where pristine beginnings and coalitions are pure fantasy. In its focus on the *becoming* of women through our relations with power, politics and one another, bridge work compels us to ask not just who are we to build these bridges, but *who do we become in desiring to build these bridges?*

First Steps Toward Transformation

How might this recognition of the ways we come into being through our politics, commitments and desires transform anti-racist feminist politics in Indigenous spaces? In an effort to recognize colonialism's role as the structuring mechanism of oppressions on this land, some anti-racist feminists have expressed accountability to Indigenous sovereignty.[41] In the context of the settler state's paternalism the identification of the sovereignty of Indigenous nations serves as a powerful reminder of the nation-to-nation relationship that is, in effect, forgotten. This recognition of the fundamental and inalienable sovereignty of Indigenous nations serves as a means of linking our work to Indigenous struggles in a way that foregrounds the imperative to decolonize and restore Indigenous nationhood. This move also points toward the strength of Indigenous leadership beyond the confines of colonization.

However, Alfred reminds us that given the historical misunderstandings of Indigenous political philosophies and the imposition of European politics and diplomacy, the notion of sovereignty is especially problematic.

'Sovereignty' implies a set of values and objectives in direct opposition to those found in traditional indigenous philosophies. Non-indigenous politicians recognize the inherent weakness of assertions of a sovereign right for peoples who have neither the cultural framework nor the institutional capacity to sustain it. The problem is that the assertion of a sovereign right for indigenous peoples continues to structure the politics of decolonization, and the state uses the theoretical inconsistencies in that position to its own advantage.[42]

When we speak of nationhood and sovereignty in the settler state, we surely do not mean the same thing. A politic of decolonization as inclusive of Indigeneity likewise carries these coercive notions of nation with it.

If we are to take the lessons of the Third World Women's Movement to heart then we cannot be convinced of the presentation of inclusivity of Aboriginal people, knowledges and politics as the missing piece of an otherwise liberating movement. After our efforts to explain the ways that oppressions cooperate, specifically the work on understanding patriarchy as a component in the colonial machine, we need a way of considering colonialism in both a particular and reflexive, as well as structural, way. However reflexive of the fluidity of identities and communities this thinking on solidarity is, it lacks an adequate accounting with the colonial problem in which such solidarity politics are based in what we now call Canada. These are failed transformations.

Taiaiake Alfred writes that settlers suffer from alienation from this land and fundamentally, their own selves; settlers have "not yet rooted themselves and been transformed into real peoples of this homeland."[43] How are we transformed through treaty? How does it call upon us and how do we then respond? The Third World Women's Movement teaches that we cannot settle into the myth of safely pre-constituted subjectivities and relationships. I have argued in this chapter that anti-racist feminists must recommit to bridge work and also that this work has much to learn from the Kanehsatà:ke resistance and Haudenosaunee politics and diplomacy. We must learn and relearn the fact that our relationship is dependant on the three-linked chain and three rows of beads. The foundational principles of peace, respect and friendship and the responsibility to ensure that these principles are forever cared for provides a space of meeting that is stable so long as it is maintained as such. For the settler, any settler, these are the grounds for our ethical belonging on this land. Without a meaningful reckoning with these politics anti-racist feminist bridges will surely collapse.

---

1   Terminology matters; in settler states, where colonization is naturalized in lived experience, terminology matters all the more. Many non-Aboriginal Canadians would know this as the "Oka Crisis." Oka is the non-Aboriginal town that claimed the area of contention as its own, therefore open to "development." By veering away from the "Oka Crisis" and toward the "Kanehsatà:ke resistance," I acknowledge the right of the Kanien'kehaka to their territories, which includes the right to resist colonial annexation of their lands. This move also seeks to denaturalize the settler's claim to Aboriginal land as well as the media's construction of Aboriginal resistance politics as disconnected moments of crisis. I warmly thank Leanne Simpson for her thoughtful insights on these important terminologies and for her and Kiera Ladner's invaluable comments and criticisms on this chapter. I thank them both for their generosity and their work. I also thank Ato Sekyi-Otu, Stacey Mayhall, Sabine Lebel, Vivian Khouw and Caitlin Don who generously read, considered and commented on various versions of this chapter.

2   Taiaiake Alfred (2005), *Wasáse: Indigenous Pathways of Action and Freedom*, Peterborough: Broadview Press, p. 65.

3   Gerald McMaster (2007), "Introductions: Mixing it up," in Joe Baker and Gerald McMaster (ed), *Remix: New Modernities in a Post-Indian World*, Washington and New York, Pheonix: Smithsonian National Museum of the American Indian and the Heard Museum, p. 56.

4   Susan M. Hill (2008), "'Travelling down the river of life together in peace and friendship, forever': Haudenosaunee land ethics and treaty agreements as the basis for restructuring the relationship with the British Crown," in Leanne Simpson (ed), *Lighting the Eighth Fire: The Liberation, Resurgence, and Protection of Indigenous Nations*, Winnipeg: Arbeiter Ring Publishing, pp. 23–45.

5   Georges Erasmus quoted in Geoffrey York and Loreen Pindera (1991), *People of the Pines: The Warriors and the Legacy of Oka*, Boston, Toronto: Little Brown, p. 273.

6   Lee Maracle (1996), *I am Woman: A Native Perspective on Sociology and Feminism*, Vancouver, British Columbia: Press Gang Publishers.

7   Ibid., p. 139.

8   For more on the importance of Haudenosaunee women to Haudenosaunee cosmology and philosophies, as well as the systemic erasure of these women from the colonial historical record see Barbara Alice Mann (2004), *Iroquoian Women: The Gantowisas*, New York: Peter Lang Publishing.

9   Sunera Thobani interviewed by Sharmeen Khan (2007), "Sunera Thobani: Anti-racism and the women's movement," *Upping the Anti: A Journal of Theory and Action*, (5), available online: <auto_sol.tao.ca/node/3013>.

10 John Borrows (2002), *Recovering Canada: The Resurgence of Indigenous Law*, Toronto: University of Toronto Press.

11 Leanne Simpson (2008), "Looking after Gdoo-naaganinaa: Precolonial Nishnaabeg Diplomatic and Treaty Relationships," *Wicazo Sa Review*, 23 (2), pp. 29–42.

12 Ibid., p. 29.

13 Dale Turner and Audra Simpson (2008), *Indigenous Leadership in a Flat World*, Ottawa: National Centre for First Nations Governance, p. 14.

14 Ibid.

15 Patricia Monture-Angus (1999), *Journeying Forward: Dreaming First Nations' independence*, Halifax: Fernwood Press, p. 28.

16 Taiaiake Alfred (2008), *Peace, Power, Righteousness: An Indigenous Manifesto*, (2nd ed.), Oxford: Oxford University Press, pp. 44–5.

17 Ibid.

18 For more on Indigenous diversity see Isabel Altamirano-Jiménez (2008), "The colonization and decolonization of Indigenous diversity," in Leanne Simpson (Ed), *Lighting the Eighth Fire: The Liberation, Resurgence and Protection of Indigenous Nations*, Winnipeg: Arbeiter Ring Publishing, pp. 175–186.

19 Andrea Smith argues for an Aboriginal understanding of sovereignty as non-statist and non-hierarchical, and takes direction from "Native women activists" who express an inclusive, relational and spiritual vision of sovereignty. She argues that the notion of sovereignty need not be shackled to European notions of sovereignty, nationalism and the corollary tactics of coercion and exclusion. Smith therefore critiques the notion that Aboriginal sovereignty and nationalism would demand the exodus of settlers today: "[sovereignty] is articulated as an open concept that suggests that a nation cannot be completely insular but must position itself in a good way with the rest of the world. It is interesting to me, for instance, how often non-Indians presume that if Native people regained their land bases they would necessarily call for the expulsion of non-Indians from them." Andrea Smith (2008), *Native Americans and the Christian Right: The Gendered Politics of Unlikely Alliances*, Durham: Duke University Press, p. 262.

20 On the researcher and the myth of her preconstituted and untouchable subjectivity see Aimee Carrillo Rowe (2008), *Power Lines: On the Subject of Feminist Alliances*, Durham and London: Duke University Press, p. 51.

21 Dale Turner (2006), *This is Not a Peace Pipe: Towards a Critical Indigenous Philosophy*, Toronto: University of Toronto Press.

22 Hill (2008), p. 32; Turner (2006), pp. 48–9.

23 Ibid.

24 David McNab (1999), *Circles of Time: Aboriginal Land Rights and Resistance in Ontario*, Waterloo: Wilfrid Laurier University Press, p. 11.

25 Turner (2006), p. 47.

26 Hill (2008). For an analysis of the foundational treaty relationship between the Wood Cree and the Crown see Harold Johnson (2007), *Two Families: Treaties and Government*, Saskatoon: Purich Publishing.

27 Ibid., p. 32.

28 Ibid.

29 Alanis Obomsawin, (Writer & Director), (1993), *Kanehsatake: 270 Years of Resistance*, Montreal: National Film Board of Canada.

30 Ke ea Hawai'i activist and attorney Mililani Trask notes that sovereignty must have a spiritual foundation if the resulting nation is to be just, "a Nation [sic] that is spiritually bankrupt is not going to be able to stand up to fight for its rights and to support its children and future generations." Cited in Andrea Smith (2008) p. 269.

31 James (Sakéj) Youngblood Henderson (2002), "*Sui generis* and treaty citizenship," *Citizenship Studies*, 6 (4), p. 416.

32 Ibid., p. 425.

33 bell hooks (1984), *Feminist Theory from Margin to Center*, Boston, MA: South End Press, p. 4.

34 See the following for more: Valerie Amos and Pratibha Parmar (1984), "Challenging imperial feminism," *Feminist Review*, 17, pp. 3–19; Gloria Anzaldúa (1990), "En rapport, in opposition: Cobrando cuentas a las nuestras" in Gloria Anzaldúa (ed), *Making Face, Making Soul: Haciendo Caras*, San Francisco: Aunt Lute Books; Audre Lorde (1984), *Sister Outsider: Essays & Speeches*, San Francisco: Aunt Lute Books; Minh-ha Trinh (1986–87), Difference: "A special Third World women issues," *Discourse*, 8, pp. 11–38.

35 Amos, (1984); hooks (1984).

36 Carrillo Rowe (2008).

37 Anzaldúa (1990), p. 144.

38 Carrillo Rowe (2008), p. 56.

39 On the active forgetting within settler historiography which enables the denial that settler states are "currently colonial" see Susan Miller (2008), "Native America writes back: The origin of the Indigenous paradigm in historiography," *Wicazo Sa Review*, 23 (2), p. 14

40 Carrillo Rowe (2008), p. 57.

41 For a two-pronged analysis of the applicability of anti-racism and anti-racist feminism and an account of the importance of rooting such scholarship and activism in the sovereignty of Indigenous nations, see Bonita Lawrence and Enakshi Dua (2005), "Decolonizing anti-racism," *Social Justice*, 32 (4), pp. 120–43. Both critique the movement's ability to represent Indigenous Peoples and perspectives though from two very different subjective and political perspectives: Lawrence as a Mi'kmaw woman who has noticed the movement's failure to explain Indigenous Peoples experiences with colonialism and patriarchy, and Dua as a woman of colour whose experiences with racism led her to perceive herself as allied with Indigenous Peoples' early in the development of her political consciousness.

42 Alfred (2008), p. 81.

43 Alfred (2005), p. 38.

The Crisis In Oka, Manitoba

DOUGLAS RAYMOND NEPINAK

Cast of Characters:

Mary: The Mother, is 49 years old. Your average North End Matriarch. Goes to the Friendship Centre for bingo, but that's about the extent of her political involvement.

Isaac: The Father, is 50 years old. He wears both suspenders and a belt. He wears baseball caps, not because they recently became fashionable again, it's a holdover from the Sixties and Seventies. He probably had involvement in the old Manitoba Indian Brotherhood. He still uses Brylcreem. He's a good storyteller.

Martha: The Daughter, is 24 years old. She knows a little about politics from her involvement in the community. Broke up with her boyfriend about a week before.

Isaiah: The Son, is 25 years old. A gas jockey. Lives at home. He's basically irresponsible and restless.

The Setting: Winnipeg, Manitoba. The home of Mary and Isaac Alexander in July 1990. The "Oka Crisis" dominates the media, and is the hottest topic around.

Saulteaux Terms:

Koo-koo-jee: A slang word we used for monsters as kids
P'cha-gush: Means "stupid"
Pa-na-juy: Means "baby bird"

Doo-doosh: Short for "doo-doosh-i-muck," which means "breasts"

Jeets: Means "asses"

The Play's History:

Crisis in Oka, Manitoba premiered on the 10th year anniversary of the "Oka Crisis" Friday, July 21, 2000, at the Winnipeg Fringe Festival with the following cast:

Directed By Tracey Nepinak (Mccorrister)

Set/Poster/Lighting Design & Stage Managed By Louis Ogemah

Marsha Knight................. Mary
Dave Mcleod .... Isaac
Mandie Seller .... Martha
Dave Boulanger............... Isaiah

ACT ONE

(Setting is the home of the Alexander's. Mary and Isaac are in the kitchen, eating neckbones. Martha is sitting in the living room in front of the television watching a soap opera.)

MAN ON TV: Brittany, I think it's time I told you something.

WOMAN ON TV: Forrest, oh Forrest, my love, whatever can it be?

MAN: Brittany, I guess there's never any easy way of saying things like this...

WOMAN: I don't like the tone of your voice.

MAN: Brittany, it's over.

WOMAN: Oh no.

MAN: Yes, Brittany. I'm sorry, but when you confessed who you truly were, I thought it wouldn't matter, but it does.

WOMAN: But I only told you I used to be a man because you confessed that you used to be a woman. I just wanted for our relationship to be one blossoming out of total honesty.

MAN: Well, in all honesty Brittany, when I was a woman I was a lesbian, I was only attracted to you because I thought you were a woman. Now that I know you used to be a man, it feels kind of, you know, icky. This relationship seems to have lost some of its sizzle.

(Martha scowls and turns off the TV, she joins her parents in the kitchen. She sits moving her food around her plate. She doesn't eat it.)

MARY: Look at Miss Misery. Nobody ever cured a broken heart by starving to death you know. There's still lots there. Eat. Eat! Ah-h, you're just moping around all the time.

MARTHA: I'm not hungry Mom. I've got no appetite. I'm sorry.

MARY: Don't be sorry. Just eat. Ooh. I told you before, I musta said a hundred times, I never liked that white boy. I said he was no good for you. An Indian boy I said. You gotta stay with your own kind.

MARTHA: Mom!

ISAAC: Yep, an Indian boy. You don't have to explain yourself all the time that way. They won't eat neckbones either, those white people.

MARTHA: I don't want to talk about it.

ISAAC: Or dried moose meat. Or muskrat. 'Specially muskrat. Only a real Indian will eat muskrat.

MARY: Oh yeah. You don't want to talk about it? But you can't sleep. You don't eat. You don't wanna come to bingo with me. You listen to sad music all night. You phone me, crying. You're tired in the morning to go to work. But you don't want to talk about it. It's not good to not talk about it my girl.

ISAAC: You got to talk about it, Martha. Pass the salt, Mary.

MARY: See. Dad knows how to eat neckbones. He keeps his strength up. Even on his most heartbroken day your Dad could eat a whole roaster pan full of neckbones. Right, Isaac? Neckbone King of Winnipeg, that old man.

ISAAC: Yeah. Good neckbones. Just about as good as boiled suckerheads and salt.

MARY: Couldn't kill that appetite, not even with a two-by-four with a poison nail in it.

MARTHA: I don't see the sense in eating, Mom. I don't even know if I really want to live.

MARY: Forgive her, Jesus! Don't say that, my girl! You're Catholic! God will hear you. You can't commit suicide unless you're Anglican.

(Looks up and makes a sign of the cross.)

Something bad luck medicine will happen to you.

ISAAC: Remember Johnny Skunk? That time he said he didn't believe in God, after he saw that movie about spaceships and aliens? Then he chopped off two of his toes with an axe? Boy, he sure became religious after that, remember? Ha-ha. All those toes in his boot.

MARTHA: You don't know how I feel, Mom. My world is over. I cry myself to sleep. I wake up feeling empty. During the day, sometimes it's like I forgot something. Like I'm missing something. And then I remember, oh yeah, I'm alone for the rest of my life.

ISAAC: Danced funny when he was drunk. Ha-ha.

MARY: Isaac, please. Holy, my girl. Like you invented and heartbreak.

ISAAC: Hank Williams invented heartbreak. And he died from a broken heart you know. Or was it from being an alcoholic?

MARY: Heartbreak doesn't change. When you get your heart broke, you sit down for a little while, but you get up and get on again. It's about time for you to get going my girl.

ISAAC: Well, I'm done. Boy, them neckbones was good. Thanks, Mom. Martha, having a broken heart is like having a boil on your bum...

MARY: Holy, don't talk like that when we're eating. And look at all the meat that's left on those neckbones!

ISAAC: What? They're clean.

MARY: Well give me them.

(Takes a butter knife and starts scraping meat off the neckbones.)

See? See all the meat that's left? Just about a whole meal here.

ISAAC: Boy you're a good scraper, old lady.

(Martha makes a feeble attempt at eating)

MARTHA: How could he dump me, Mom? Like I was nothing in his life?

MARY: Sometimes that happens, my girl. That's how life is sometimes. In a couple years you won't even remember his name.

ISAAC: What was his name again?

MARY: Ah-h-h! Shush.

ISAAC: He was funny looking anyway. Talked funny too. Big words. I never trusted him.

(Isaac begins trailing off. Mary and Martha wait for him to finish.)

Reminded me of that Ukrainian farmer with the big wart on his forehead that ran the grocery shack at the Blueberry patch where we used to go picking. Wanted all that money for Klik. For Klik! Boy that's too much, I said. You could go to town if you don't like it, he said, acting like a big white smarty pants. It's too damn far to town, I said, and you know it. That's not my problem, he said. But anyway I got a ride to town with Billy Bugger and I got a whole case of Klik. And no that farmer didn't like that! No sir (Laughs triumphantly), boy he didn't like that.

MARY: And anyway. It doesn't matter how much you starve yourself. You're not gonna feel better. You'll just be hungry too. My baby.

MARTHA: Mom. Mom.

(Starts crying. Mary embraces her)

MARY: That's okay, my girl. Get it out.

ISAAC: Martha?

MARY: That's okay, Dad. It's going to be okay.

MARTHA: His family didn't like me because I'm an Indian. I knew that right away when I first met them. They weren't comfortable. But I thought it was okay. I could live with it. That was them. I was in love with him. But our entire relationship was clouded over with bad feelings even from the very start.

MARY: You know, my girl, there's lots of times people are not going to like you cause of who and what you are. But that's just cause they got a problem. The worst thing you can do is make it your problem.

MARTHA: I love you, Mom.

MARY: I love you too, my sweetheart.

ISAAC: He was kinda stupid too, that guy. Always talking to me like I was slow or something.

MARTHA: Dad. He wasn't stupid. He had a degree in Political Science.

ISAAC: Well that don't make somebody smart. That just means he spends lots of time sitting in a school. All those big nook words. A man could sit in a university for a hundred years and still not know his head from his arse. I should have punched him in the nose. Next time he shows his stupid face around here he's gonna get it boy. I fought them farmers in Dauphin at the Kings Hotel lots of times. Their teeth were laying on the floor, those damn rednecks.

MARY: Don't get yourself worked up!

(Phone rings, Mary picks it up.)

And quit swearing. Hello. Bella!

ISAAC: I just don't like somebody thinking they're better than my family. My girl's the best.

MARY: Bingo?

MARTHA:	I love you, Dad.
MARY:	That's a possibility. I have a situation here, but I think it'll be okay.
	(Pause)
	Huh-huh. Jackpot didn't go? Holy.
ISAAC:	I'll punch him right on the nose. The Hammer they used to call me, when I worked the mines in Thompson.
MARY:	*(To Isaac)* You had such big muscles.
	(Into the phone) That big bonanza, holy!
ISAAC:	And you know I'm not someone to brag, but...
MARY:	Bye! *(Hangs up)* That's enough. Help me clear the table off, my girl. I want you to eat a little later, okay?
MARTHA:	I will, Mom.
MARY:	Make sure you put some away for your brother.
ISAAC:	Bethcha I could still place good in the flour-packing contest.
MARTHA:	He won't be back till late. He's out with those dummies again.
MARY:	Which ones?
ISAAC:	I'm not finished talking you know.
MARTHA:	You know. Koo-koo-jee, P'cha-gush and those guys.
MARY:	O-o-o, I don't like those boys.
ISAAC:	That one boy, that Koo-koo-jee, he never brushes his teeth you know. He was telling me something this one time, and he had his mouth real close to my face. And I asks him, ever heard of toothpaste? He says, what's that?
MARY:	Ah, he's gonna to get in trouble hanging out with those boys
MARTHA:	P'cha-gush got a girl pregnant, you know, and then he ran away

MARY: Oh boy, that's no good.

MARTHA: And then he said that baby wasn't even his. What a scum bag.

ISAAC: There's too much of that, kids having kids. All these young girls, pushing baby stroller, just babies themselves. They should be baby-sitters, not mothers.

MARY: What's your brother doing hanging around with those boys? They don't work, they don't go to school. I don't know what they do. Do you think they steal?

MARTHA: Probably. They're useless anyway.

ISAAC: They're good strong boys. I don't know why they're not cutting trees, or working in the mines. Betcha they could pack flour.

MARTHA: It's easier collecting welfare.

ISAAC: That's just not good. Those young guys wasting their lives. Thinking they'll win their fortunes with the 6/49.

MARY: I just hope your brother's got enough sense not to go stealing. He could get a record. He'll lose his job at the gas station. I always had to worry about that one.

MARTHA: They just like to hang around and act like they're cool or something. Just a bunch of idiots.

ISAAC: I don't know. I just don't know what's happening these days.

(sighs)

But now I'm gonna spend some quality time with my TV.

(Isaac walks into the living room and turns on the TV. You hear the voice of a TV news commentator.)

VOICE: An update on the situation at Oka, Québec. Over 100 Native leaders from across Canada have gathered in Kahnawà:ke in support of the Mohawk warriors in Oka. The Native leaders said they would not stand idly by and allow the Mohawk people to be attacked. They promised forceful action if the Federal Government didn't step in to resolve the situation peacefully. The months old situation has so far seen one death, and daily escalations in the already tense situation.

ISAAC: I just don't know. Guns. Hatred. I think it's gonna be bad for those people there.

(Mary and Martha come into the living room.)

MARY: I get so scared for those Mohawk people. Already one person shot. I pray to Jesus at night that it will turn out okay.

MARTHA: They're standing up for their rights. They're showing the rest of us what solidarity means.

MARY: Solidarity, that's a scary word. Me and Bella and Marceline been talking about this at bingo, and everyone agrees they got to negotiate. When you pick up a gun, people don't listen to you.

MARTHA: But they sure take notice. Those Mohawks have been trying to negotiate for 300 years, and where has it gotten them? Not one inch forward. They stand by their convictions. I respect that.

MARY: I just hope no one else gets hurt, that's all. I don't know why there has to be all this fighting for.

MARTHA: Mom, it's resistance against Imperialism. The oppressors never leave until they're good and bloody.

MARY: Don't say that word! Bloody. Blood scares people. It scares me for my kids.

ISAAC: It won't do nothing anyway. The white man will always have more guns.

MARTHA: But might doesn't make right, Dad.

ISAAC: Might wins wars.

MARTHA: But not moral victories.

ISAAC: Hunh?

MARTHA: Just because the oppressors have more firepower, it doesn't mean they have the right to do whatever they want. It doesn't give them free reign to deny people of their right to the land. Only the Creator can give that right.

ISAAC: O-o-o-h, I don't know what you're talking about, baby girl, but that's the way it's always been. And things got a funny way of staying the same.

MARY: It makes me afraid for the future generation.

(Just then, Isaiah walks in dressed in camouflage combat clothes, combat boots, a baseball cap and sunglasses. A bandanna is tied around his neck. He's obviously a cheap facsimile of an Oka Warrior. He stands in the living room. There is a pause of silence. Martha breaks the silence by bursting out in laughter. Mary and Isaac look at each other.)

MARTHA: Going duck hunting?

ISAIAH: Laugh if you wish, but I'm going to stand in solidarity with my people.

MARY: Who?

ISAIAH: My people. The warriors in Oka.

MARY: Holy. You're Saulteaux, not Mohawk. Your people are here, not in Quebéc.

ISAIAH: We're all the same people bound together by the chains of oppression, Mom.

MARY: Take off those sunglasses in the house, people will think you're crazy.

ISAIAH: *(Takes off shades)*

            Mom, I've made up my mind. Me and some of the guys are gonna do something about the Oka Crisis.

MARTHA: What are you going to do? Put up a roadblock in our driveway?

ISAIAH: Ha ha. Funny. No. Me, Koo-koo-jee, P'cha-gush and Morrie are going to Oka.

MARTHA: Yeah right. In what? Morrie's car? It's sitting on blocks in his back yard.

ISAIAH: We're gonna take the Greyhound bus there. I figure it will take us five days. That'll give us time to come up with our strategic plan.

MARTHA: Yeah, strategic plan. Last time you guys had a strategic plan, it was how to sneak in the movie theatre. You all got caught.

(laughs)

MARY: You guys were sneaking into the movies?

ISAIAH: It was a long time ago, Mom. Laugh if you want, Martha. We're gonna walk into glory and right into the history books, then you won't be laughing.

MARY: You're not going anywhere.

ISAIAH: But Mom, I have to. This is my big chance to be a part of history.

MARY: You mean it's your big chance to get arrested. I didn't bring you into this world to have you thrown in a cage.

ISAIAH: Mom. Choomich went to Korea.

MARY: And if I was my mom I'd have never let him go.

ISAIAH: And when Choomich went he went to defend a country that hates us. This time it's for our own people.

MARY: Mohawk people.

ISAIAH: Our people, Mom. The First Nations.

MARY: The Mohawk Nation, not us.

ISAIAH: Mom, I've got to go. This is the first time in who knows how long when things have come to a head. The planets have aligned. The nations are coming together. The Seventh Generation.

MARTHA: The Pepsi Generation?

ISAIAH: Shut up. Not you, Mom. This is my time. Native people aren't gonna take it anymore. And I'm not gonna take it anymore either. I'm going.

MARY: No you're not.

ISAIAH: Mom. It's practically my duty. It is my duty. I almost got into a fight with an apple Indian sell-out at the bus depot who said the warriors were nothing but criminals. See! That's how dedicated I am. I have to go. I have to stand with my people.

MARY: You stay here where you're needed and you're loved. Get those foolish things out of your head. You can come to bingo with me.

ISAIAH: No. I'm going and that's it!

ISAAC: You don't contradict your Mom Isaiah. She said what she said, and that's it.

(Isaiah stares for a moment, and then storms off to his room.)

MARTHA: I knew he'd get stupid hanging out with those guys

ISAAC: He's a young man. Young men just want to do important things. He just needs to cool off. He'll be okay.

(Scene shifts to Isaiah's room. He's on the extension phone.)

ISAIAH: P'cha-gush there? *(pause)* Guess what? *(pause)* Freaked out on you too, eh? What is it with these people, don't they know things are going down? Don't they care? *(pause)* This ain't the last of it. Not by a long shot. They've been treating me like a kid for too damn long. *(pause)* Gotta get off the line. I might disrupt the "bingo connection." Call Koo-koo-jee and Morrie. See you later.

(Hangs up, scene shifts back to the living room.)

MARY: What's all this all of a sudden? Where'd he get these ideas? He never had ideas before. This is bad. People are gonna get killed there. And he's the only boy I have. I won't let my boy go.

MARTHA: If anything happens to these people in Oka, this whole country is going to explode.

MARY: Don't talk like that!

MARTHA: It's true, Mom. First Nations aren't going to stand for it if those Mohawks are shot. They'll become martyrs. I can't believe the government doesn't realize that.

MARY: There's already one young man dead. That French cop. That's enough blood. Blood doesn't wash away blood.

ISAAC: He's just young. Young people find out how things are. They see things been this way so long. They say, if we don't change them now, when will things ever change? They forget that many of us before have felt and fought for these same things. Many of my old friends have died with a powerful longing in their hearts.

MARTHA: And I guess that's just it. When will things change? I don't agree with the idea of Isaiah going off to change the world. But we can't tolerate the status quo.

ISAAC: That reminds me of something. Remember Jack, last year, Mom?

MARY: You mean with Rebecca?

ISAAC: Yeah.

MARY: Holy. Yeah.

ISAAC: Well, Jack said he was walking home early in the morning, coming back from a party, six o'clock in the morning. He said these five skinny heads jumped on him.

MARTHA: Skinheads.

ISAAC: Skinheads, anyway, he said they never beat him up, they just took his clothes away from him so he was naked. And anyway, he was stuck in the bushes naked. The closest place was Rebecca and Dan's. So he ran there. And anyway, I guess Dan wasn't home, but Rebecca was. But just when he got there, Dan comes home from working night shift, and there's Jack naked in his house.

MARTHA: Dad. What does that have to do with Isaiah wanting to go to Oka?

ISAAC: Well, you just don't ever know what somebody's talking about sometimes, that's all.

MARTHA: Yeah, Dad.

ISAAC: He must have been funny naked though. Big beer-gut. Naked. *(Laughs)*

MARY: Oh Lord, I'm gonna pray to God for those people in Oka.

(Phone rings) Wait. I'm gonna answer the phone, then I'm gonna pray to God for those people in Oka.

Hello. *(Pause)* Huh-huh. *(Pause)* Yeah we heard. *(Pause)*

Well it wasn't my boy's idea. I know that cause he's a follower. *(Pause)* If anybody put anybody up to anything it was your boy. *(Pause)* Short attention span? Your boy's just a couple bricks short of a load. *(Pause)* Well I'm glad I know how you feel. Straighten out your boy first before you go trying to straighten anyone else out. *(Pause)* Bye!

(Hangs up)

That was Koo-koo-jee's mom. Thinks Isaiah is putting ideas in her boy's head about going to Oka. The Lord knows that someone oughta put something in that boy's head. Ask him anything, you draw blanks every single time.

ISAAC: Boy, I don't know what's with the kids. It'll blow over.

MARTHA: I'm going home.

MARY: Coming back?

MARTHA: Yeah. I'm just picking up some things. I'm going to spend a couple of nights here, if it's all right?

MARY: Yeah, sure it is.

MARTHA: I thought it would get better, but it seems worse now, when I'm alone.

MARY: You can stay over as long as you need, my girl.

(Isaiah comes out of his room still dressed in combat pants and a green T-shirt, looks depressed, plops himself down on the couch.)

ISAIAH: So, who was on the phone?

MARY: It was Koo-koo-jee's mom. She doesn't think it's a good idea neither, you guys going to Oka.

ISAIAH: Koo-koo-jee's mom doesn't care about anything except what time bingo starts.

ISAAC: Boy, you don't have to talk in that tone.

MARY: Isaac! Isaiah, I know you're upset, but it's only for your good. You'll get hurt. And being supportive doesn't mean travelling all the way down there.

ISAIAH: So what should I do? Stand on a street corner and carry a sign?

MARTHA: You could write a letter to the editors of the newspapers. To let people know that there are supporters of Oka here in Manitoba.

ISAIAH: The newspapers only print one side of the issue. Morrie wrote a letter to the newspaper. They never even printed it.

ISAAC: I didn't know that boy could write. For all we know he coulda stuck the letter in a garbage can instead of the mailbox.

ISAIAH: He can write, Dad. It was a good letter too. But did they print it? No. They pick and choose. The newspapers are on the same side as the SQ and the Quebéc Government.

MARTHA: Well Phil Fontaine and the Manitoba Chiefs have that Peace Village at the Legislature, why don't you go there?

ISAIAH: Where do you think I got to thinking? Me and the guys been going there. That's how we came up with this idea. We're not the only ones talking about going to Oka neither, there's a whole lot of people concerned.

MARTHA: I was wondering where you got that idea from. Well, since there's things starting to happen here, you guys could organize a march.

ISAIAH: Another march?

MARTHA: As long as the people of Canada understand that Native people won't tolerate the killing of those Mohawk people. That's the important part. And anyway, you'll get fired from your job if you try to take time off to go to Oka. What will your boss think?

ISAIAH: I don't care what he thinks. I already quit.

MARY: How come?

ISAIAH: I asked for time off to show solidarity to my people. That old fatso laughed, so I told him to shove his job up his ass.

MARY: Don't say ass, that's swearing.

ISAAC: It's in the Bible, old lady. What do you think Jesus rode on?

MARTHA: That was a smart move.

ISAIAH: Yeah, right, minimum wage. P'cha-gush quit last year because of his beliefs, and now I done the same thing.

ISAAC: He didn't quit for his beliefs, he was fired for being a dummy.

ISAIAH: No. He was standing by his rights.

ISAAC: This is what really happened. P'cha-gush was called in to work New Years Eve, pumping gas, cause someone never showed up. But he was already drunk. But he goes in anyway, About 3:00 in the morning his girlfriend Pa-na-juy calls to make sure he's alright. The phone rings and rings for a long time, and finally someone answers. It's this old lady. Pa-na-juy asks, is Norman there? The old lady says, you mean this young man sleeping on the floor here? The old lady who answered the phone was just trying to pay for her gas. Other people were

ringing theirs up, and driving off. They rung up over
$300 worth of gas. They told P'cha-gush he could keep
his job if he paid for the gas, but he wouldn't.

ISAIAH: Well, P'cha-gush was standing by his rights. He told the
supervisor that he'd been drinking, but they told him to
come in anyway. It wasn't his fault.

ISAAC: Ah-h, young people.

ISAIAH: My friends are very close to me, Dad.

ISAAC: Parasites are even closer.

MARY: You don't have to go away, my son.

ISAIAH: I guess you already told me that.

ISAAC: Isaiah!

MARY: It's okay, Dad. Isaiah. I'm afraid that people are gonna
get hurt or arrested or worse over there. This is like
the time you made the parachute and jumped off
the roof.

ISAIAH: No, Mom. Not even. Not the same. I was a boy then.
I'm a man now.

MARY: Yeah. Yeah it is. You don't think things out. You never
did. It was always one of your weaknesses. This will pass.

ISAIAH: I want to be independent.

MARTHA: Yeah, right, you still live at home.

MARY: Martha! Isaiah, this is dangerous.

ISAIAH: You just don't understand, Mom. People from across
Canada are going to Oka. It's not that I haven't thought
it out. I'm not going to sit here on my ass and watch it
on TV when I oughta be doing something about it. Now,
I know I still live at home. And I don't always chip in
for groceries. And if that's a problem, there's an answer
for that too. I may not have an education. I pump gas
for a living, or I used to pump gas, but there's at least
one thing. I will not sit here and watch those people get

killed. The time has come. No more plowed over sacred burial grounds. No more villages evacuated because of a hydro project. No more logging companies in sacred forests. No more talk, talk, talk until we're blue in the face. I'm not going to stand for it. And if I have to . . . I guess I'll have to leave home. That's it.

(Isaiah leaves the house, Mary moves towards the door. The phone rings, Mary answers.)

MARY: Hello. *(Pause)* Bella? Bella! I can't talk! I got a crisis here!

(Mary hangs up and starts crying. Isaac and Martha are silent.)

BLACKOUT.

(Scene opens with Isaac looking out the window with a pair of binoculars. Martha comes in carrying a duffle bag of things.)

MARTHA: Hi Dad.

ISAAC: *(continues looking)* Hi baby.

MARTHA: What are you looking for, Dad? Moose? Not going to see many in the North End.

ISAAC: You know. I think our neighbours are secretly nudists.

MARTHA: Dad!

ISAAC: I'm serious. I thought I saw that woman walking around with no clothes on.

MARTHA: Dad. They'll see you.

ISAAC: I didn't have my glasses on at first, so I couldn't see right. I want to make sure, so your Mom doesn't get upset. You know how sensitive she is about stuff like this. Always had to protect her in these cases.

MARTHA: If you went upstairs you could get a better view over the fence.

ISAAC: Then I'd be gawking.

MARTHA: Yeah right, Dad. Did Isaiah get tired of running away from home yet? Did he come crawling back?

ISAAC: Yeah. He's in his room. That boy won't give in. Like your Mom, you know. Feels he's being done wrong. He's always been like that. A victim that one.

MARTHA: Where is Mom?

ISAAC: Bingo. She got over her crisis finally. It would have to be a pretty big crisis to keep that woman home from bingo.

MARTHA: I saw uncle Fred at the 7-Eleven.

ISAAC: *(Puts down binoculars.)*

            What's he have to say for himself?

MARTHA: He told me to tell you that he'll be "counting" on your support at the Friendship Centre Tuesday.

ISAAC: Yeah?

MARTHA: So?

ISAAC: So what?

MARTHA: So why did uncle Fred emphasize "counting" like he did?

ISAAC: Cause he wants to drag me into one of his fights, that's what.

MARTHA: What do you mean?

ISAAC: He wants me to play Elder for him. Cause people think of me that way.

MARTHA: And are you?

ISAAC: Am I what?

MARTHA: Going to be his Elder?

ISAAC: The reason why people think of me that way is cause I'm not into political stuff like that anymore. Not like in the old days anyway.

MARTHA: Then don't, if that's not what you want.

ISAAC: He was spoiled you know. Mom and Dad always let him get his way. He always wants what he wants. And he tries pretty hard to get it.

MARTHA: He's trying to drag you into the politics?

ISAAC: He's trying to persuade people that he's right.

MARTHA: You don't think he is?

ISAAC: He's my brother, and I love him, but I see him for what he is.

MARTHA: What's that?

ISAAC: You know how some parasites live in hair? And some live in your guts? They all got their own little territory. Where they know how to live. My little brother, he's one of those parasites that live well in programs. I know that sounds awful. Don't think bad about your uncle, my girl. He's always been smart, people like him could make great changes. But in all their trying, things usually go wrong. They start working for themselves only. In their minds they think they're still working for everybody else, but they're not. And if you try to question them, they'll fight you really hard. It's sort of like they don't want to look in the mirror at themselves. They've gone away from us. That makes me sad. And I just don't want to be involved. Can you understand that?

MARTHA: Yeah.

ISAAC: I pray for him.

(Sighs, there is a slightly long pause of silence.)

MARTHA: So I guess Isaiah's got no reason to leave his room now that he doesn't have a job.

ISAAC: Yeah, he'll just stay in there playing his guitar until he cools off. That boy. He always just jumped in with both feet, ready to go. It's good in a way how he goes after life.

MARTHA: I think it's good he's starting to care about rights and stuff like that.

ISAAC: But there's no sense getting all wound up. These are all things as old as "Canada." White people and Indians, they just understand things different.

MARTHA: I think I heard this one before.

ISAAC: *(Rolls a cigarette as he's talking.)*

    But listen here for a second.

MARTHA: *(Slightly amused.)* Alright, Daddy.

ISAAC: For Indians, it was like this. They were living here for as long as anybody could remember. Then all of a sudden, boom, white people show up. At first they just wanted furs. So they formed partnerships. And who would ever want more than they could ever use? The Indians didn't know. They didn't run into real problems until the farming people got here. The fur traders didn't care much for settling the land, putting up fences, drawing invisible lines. But the farmers, they didn't want Indians walking over "their" land. That's why I figure we had the Treaties. But also, our people were powerful. We coulda just as easily sided up with the States. We coulda had a nicer looking flag here in Manitoba. And a better sounding national anthem.

MARTHA: *(Slightly giggling, obviously amused.)* I could always count on you to come up with your own angle on just about everything, Dad.

ISAAC: Oh yeah, something to think about. We were made promises, forever things. We got reserves so we didn't walk over farmer's land, or go into the cities. And they got the land. We give up a lot of those rights. For those promises we were made. So you be proud. White people are always trying to tell us that we're bumming off them. But who's really the bum? Even if I won the 6/49, I would still want my prescription for free. Our Ancestors gave up too much for me not to.

MARTHA: *(No longer giggling, more serious.)* And how do white people see it?

ISAAC: They see it like a bill of sale. Like they owe nothing more. They won't give back what they got from the deal, but they want us to let go of the commitments that were made.

MARTHA: *(Sighs)* And do you think it will ever end?

ISAAC: Everything ends, my girl. Everything that has a beginning, has an ending. That's just a fact of life as bare as your face.

(Martha puts her face in her hands and begins crying. Isaac knows he's hurt her.)

ISAAC: Martha? You know, Martha, I just go running off at the mouth most times. I don't give much thought on what I say and how it's gonna come out. And if I come barging through your heart sometimes, I want you to know I never mean to hurt you, my girl.

MARTHA: It's okay, Dad. Everything hurts me right now. It's always just below the surface.

ISAAC: He never really saw you, or us. Can you see that?

MARTHA: We always had a communication problem. We always seemed to be talking past each other. It became more and more difficult to forgive each other for even the most basic things. I came home one day and all his stuff was gone. And I don't really know if it was a white-Indian thing, a male-female thing, or a him-me thing.

ISAAC: I say white this, and Indian that, but when it's my little girl's heart on the chopping block, I just don't know.

MARTHA: We couldn't talk about treaty rights, or any other rights Indians have. He believed in equality. But his idea of equality didn't take into account history, or us. It was one of those taboo areas for us, a guaranteed fight. I used to wonder why he wanted anything to do with me, since he couldn't seem to accept me for who and what I am.

(She stops talking and puts her face in her hands again.)

I'm so heartsick, Dad, I can't even see where I'm standing.

ISAAC: I love you, my girl.

MARTHA: I love you too.

(They embrace. Mary comes into the house carrying a large conch——a large seashell to all you uncultured swine.)

MARY: Ah-h-h, no good. I think this special seashell has lost its luck. It was almost there, that good luck. I could just about taste it, but then . . . ah-h-h. I gotta get something else. My girl, if you had babies, I could take their shoes with me. Lot of luck in baby shoes.

MARTHA: I don't think that's reason enough for me to have a baby, Mom.

MARY: Well, I'd like to have grandchildren while I'm still frisky enough to take them to the park, or to the swimming pool.

ISAAC: You're frisky enough for me, old lady.

MARY: Ah-h-h you. How's Isaiah?

MARTHA: He's still pouting.

MARY: Go and talk to him, my girl. Cheer him up. I don't like it when he's like this. Pouting like a baby. He doesn't know when something is for his own good.

MARTHA: It won't work, Mom.

MARY: Well try. I don't want his lip dragging around here all day tomorrow.

ISAAC: Yeah? And that's some attitude to have.

MARY: Well, it's true.

MARTHA: I'll give it a try, but I'm not promising anything.

(Scene shifts. Martha goes into Isaiah's room. Isaiah is playing his guitar.)

ISAIAH: So you got sent in to cheer me up? The old go-between.

MARTHA: Come on Isaiah. Quit being a shit.

ISAIAH: You know I'm right. You know it. Our people are going to get killed at Oka. And here I am, just watching it on TV.

MARTHA: So quit watching the TV.

ISAIAH: Shut up.

MARTHA Well you gotta look at it from their perspective. Mom's scared you'll get killed.

ISAIAH: It's my life, Martha. Younger people than me have won wars. They're both always saying I don't do anything with my life. Think I'm happy still living at home? Bumming off Mom and Dad. But when I try to make some sort of move out, no way, you don't know what you're doing. You're too stupid, Isaiah. Fust stay in your room and play with your toys.

MARTHA: I don't think anyone said that to you.

ISAIAH: They may as well have.

MARTHA: Mom's just looking out for you.

ISAIAH: Martha, I'm a man. I want to start acting like one. I'm way past the time when I should have become a warrior.

MARTHA: Holy! Becoming traditional even.

ISAIAH: I want to bust loose. I want to be free.

(Scene shifts to the living room. Isaac and Mary are having tea.)

MARY: He's not ready to leave the nest yet. He's still a chick in the henhouse. He needs to mature a bit more.

ISAAC: You gotta let him go on his own sometime, old lady.

MARY: Ah you. You're secretly on his side. I know it. I know it. "The sins of the father..."

ISAAC: Don't try and guilt me, old lady.

MARY: But it's true.

ISAAC: *(Becomes reflective)* You know you don't have to be scared about being alone. I'll always be here for you. I always have been.

MARY: There's just never been anyway of telling what that little boy was up to, from one minute to the next.

ISAAC: But he's not a little boy, Mary. He hasn't been a little boy for a long, long time.

(They pause and look at each other for a moment.)

MARY: Did I tell you I had a sweat tonight? I just needed O-69 for the full house. They called three O's till someone else bingoed. No luck tonight. Did I tell you about Jane Turner?

ISAAC: Is she dead?

MARY: What's that?

ISAAC: Someone said once whenever you ask "did you hear about so or so" they're either pregnant, or dead. Seeing as she's sixty, I'd cross out pregnant on a easy bet.

MARY: Ah you. Remember when she was on that winning streak before?

ISAAC: No.

MARY: Well she was. People started saying she was using Indian Medicine to win bingo.

ISAAC: Holy!

MARY: Yeah, right. Anyway, Debbie Bone was sitting by the door at the Friendship Centre and when Big Jane walked in, Debbie splashed holy water on her.

ISAAC: That woman's dumb as a doorknob.

MARY: Yeah, but it worked. Big Jane didn't win that night, or since then. What do you think of that?

ISAAC: That woman's dumb as a doorknob.

MARY: Ah you.

(Scene shifts back to Isaiah's room. They light smokes.)

ISAIAH: Our people are getting together, you know. We're not going to take it anymore, and I'm going to be part of it. We're rising from the ashes. No more getting screwed in negotiations. No more caving in to outside interests. No more stabbing each other in the back. Red Power!

MARTHA: Ever going AIM.

ISAIAH: Sis, AIM always gets a bad rap. The FBI ran a good media campaign. Even Native people say, you say AIM, they get scared. Brain-washed Indians. Like Mom. Don't count on anyone to do it for you, that's AIM. Actions, not reactions. God save Leonard Peltier.

MARTHA: And you and your dum-dum buddies were going to be part of this movement?

ISAIAH: Yeah. Me and the guys were going to jump a bus this weekend.

MARTHA: Do you have money for a bus ticket?

ISAIAH: Yeah, I got enough.

MARTHA: Do you know how much a ticket costs?

ISAIAH: Not exactly.

MARTHA: Have you thought about the logistics of taking the trip?

ISAIAH: What's that?

MARTHA: Well, from my choir trip to Montreal six years ago, I know that it costs about $150 to buy a one way ticket there. It's a 35 hour bus ride. You'll need money for food. Once you get there you'll have to get to Oka. I don't figure there are too many people around there who feel like giving lifts to Indians just about now. Do you even know where Oka is in relation to Montreal?

ISAIAH: P'cha-gush was gonna take care of all that. Look for a map at the library.

MARTHA: (Laughs) That's good. Great. The dumbest one of the bunch. Taking care of the details.

ISAIAH: Shut up. Stop laughing.

MARTHA: I'm sorry. But brother, you gotta be realistic. You can't just run off and do things without giving things a second thought.

ISAIAH: I think things out. Not as good as you brainiac, but good enough. I want to do something. The world is passing me by even as we're talking. I was at the Peace Village. There was a mike set up for anyone to talk. This guy was talking. He said we're always giving way because we don't think we're good enough. He said he wasn't a violent man, but he didn't know what he'd do if those people at Oka got killed. He said he thought he'd explode. And that's what I feel like. That's me.

(The stage darkens, except Isaiah, he is at the Peace Village. He has a microphone in his hand, he nervously addresses a crowd.)

ISAIAH: Hi everybody. I guess I don't really know what to say. I think this is all cool, and you know, we got to support our brothers and sisters in Oka. Me and P'cha-gush, Koo-koo-jee and Morrie, they're my friends over there standing around, we're gonna form our own warrior society. That's right. The Oka Warriors of Manitoba. But I think maybe we gotta get endorsement from the Oka warriors first. Anyway. We're not gonna take it. We gotta stand in solidarity. And any girls that want to party with us they can. Thanks a lot for listening, Thanks.

(Isaiah smiles absently as light returns.)

MARTHA: That's not you. You're the guy who's got that 'Cuda parked in your back yard, saying you're gonna make it a mean street machine someday. You never finish anything you start. You always leave things half done. Dad's got to park his truck on the street all the time because of you.

ISAIAH: I'm not leaving things half finished this time. I've found the real Indian in me.

MARTHA: Why? Was it lost?

ISAIAH: Hey, what about you? Think about it. Out of all the boyfriends you ever had, how many of them have been Indian?

MARTHA: What does that have to do with anything?

ISAIAH: You've had four boyfriends, and they've all been white.

MARTHA: I'm trying real hard to care about what you're saying, but it's just not happening. And anyway, what about Herbie?

ISAIAH: You didn't go out with him, just hung out and let him take you to the movies. Doesn't that make you question yourself? Doesn't that make you wonder how you feel about being Anishinaabe?

MARTHA: That doesn't have anything to do with how I feel about being Indian.

ISAIAH: Yeah it does. What that tells me is you don't feel right about being Indian and you're trying to rise above being Indian by dating white.

(*Pause of silence.*)

MARTHA: You're a jerk.

ISAIAH: Think about it.

MARTHA: No.

(*Martha becomes very reflective.*)

It's easy for you to say things like that. Getting all high and mighty. That's Mom and Dad's point of view. That's their value system. It's so unfair that I was born into this Indian moral code that gives people the right to an opinion on who I date. How dare they. How dare you! I don't want the responsibility of preserving the blood of Indian people. I didn't ask for it. This is my life. I didn't ask to get caught in the middle of a race war. This is my life, I'm living it.

ISAIAH: Jeez, I didn't mean to say it that way.

MARTHA: Isaiah, right now I'm hurting. Are my feelings Indian? I am more than just the colour of my skin. My life is more than a racial issue. Everybody talks about my relationship as if it's nothing. Cheap soapbox politics. Did anyone ever stop to think that their insensitivity might be hurting me? Cause it does. My emotions are not political acts.

ISAIAH: Being born an Indian in Canada is a political act.

MARTHA: Indian people discount everything I say or do simply because of who I date. I'm automatically wrong because I date a white guy. They say I don't know a damned thing about being Indian. That I don't like being Indian. As if I ever had a choice. As if wanting something different for my life was not liking myself.

ISAIAH: We've lost just about everything Martha. The land, our language, our culture. There's practically nothing left. We keep getting pushed back, until we got our backs to the wall. Until all we got left is this one square of land. This last stand. Like Oka. Like the warriors at the treatment centre.

MARTHA: But what does that have to do with me? With my personal life? And who I love?

ISAIAH: Ever seen an Indian girl in Playboy?

MARTHA: Excuse me, but I don't read trash.

ISAIAH: I'm just trying to make a point.

MARTHA: And your point is what?

ISAIAH: In Playboy any woman with colour in her skin is "exotic," and the best piece of ass has blonde hair, white skin and blue eyes. That's the message.

MARTHA: Where the hell did that come from?

ISAIAH: Well…somebody told me. Never mind. Ever notice that if an Indian guy gets successful the first thing he does is dump the Indian girlfriend and date a blonde?

MARTHA: Yeah I guess, but I'm not famous.

ISAIAH: But that's the kind of thinking out there, over everybody. Everybody thinks like that. They don't admit it, but they do. If they had the chance they'd have that blonde too. Like Koo-koo-jee, his tongues always hanging out whenever he sees a nice looking girl go by.

MARTHA: He only gets that passed out pussy.

ISAIAH: Every one of the guys I hang out with, Koo-koo-jee, P'cha-gush, Morrie, Abey, Babey, Man-o, they stare real hard if a white girl walks by. But an Indian girl, they automatically got a bad attitude.

MARTHA: Then why do you hang around them, those losers?

ISAIAH: I don't know.

MARTHA: But look at it from my perspective, most of "the brothers" are either in jail, drying out, gay or dead. All the good ones are already taken. Most of these guys around here would just knock me up and take off with the damn family allowance check. Who in their right mind would want that? I sure as hell am not going to be sitting on a doorstep in the summertime because there's no air conditioning, overweight, three illegitimate kids from three different dads, always needing something, waiting for the damned welfare check so I can go to bingo, or maybe party one night. Or if the guy does stick around, I get a black eye cause he's so screwed up about what happened to him as a kid that I get to be his punching bag. What kind of life would that be? That's all the brothers around here have got to offer, and that's not word of a lie Isaiah, and you know it.

ISAIAH: Our people are on a healing journey Martha. It's because of all the hell we've been through. Residential schools.

MARTHA: Well I don't have time to play therapist for anyone. I'm not going to play saviour or martyr for anyone. Indian guys treat their women like shit and you're not going to convince me otherwise.

ISAIAH: You sound like such a sell-out when you say that Martha.

MARTHA:	Well, it's true.
ISAIAH:	Not all Indian guys.
MARTHA:	Most.
ISAIAH:	Not even. Sure, it happens. But white people don't understand us. White people, no matter what they tell you, they'll never trust you. Never. They always suspect you, but they don't even admit it. Probably not even to themselves. And you're not going to tell me that any white guy you date, that you being an Indian is not going to mean something to him. It does.
MARTHA:	What do you mean?
ISAIAH:	Being an Indian always means something. It means something to white buys too, no matter how liberal he thinks he is. Even his family's house, you go for turkey dinner and someone asks, "White meat or dark?" They're automatically gonna think about the two of you.
MARTHA:	*(laughs)* You are so crazy, I love you.
ISAIAH:	Your people need your support Martha. P'cha-gush always had a thing for you, you know.
MARTHA:	Believe me, I couldn't get drunk enough. I'd have to wash in Javex after.
ISAIAH:	We have come together as people. We have to be strong, That's what the people at Oka are telling us.
MARTHA:	But do you have to go to Oka? The Peace Village was set up so people here could be involved, peacefully. You don't have to go away.
ISAIAH:	A lot of times I think I do. I have to go away. I'm 25 and I've always lived with Mom and Dad.
MARTHA:	But you help them out. Doing chores, with the rent, sometimes, they need you. And I've never heard Mom say anything about wanting you to move out.
ISAIAH:	Dad has.

MARTHA: That's just when he's mad at you. Like when you eat almost all the corn flakes and leave a little at the bottom and don't tell anyone.

ISAIAH: I just don't feel like I fit anymore. And when we went to Peace Village, me and Koo-koo-jee, P'cha-gush and Morrie, we all took turns talking at the mike.

MARTHA: And you all made speeches?

ISAIAH: Well. Koo-koo-jee tried to sing and they told him to get lost. But the rest of us did. People listened to me. They heard me. It's like I was someone. A First Nation member. And we were talking about important things for once.

MARTHA: But does that mean you have to go?

ISAIAH: I've got to do something Martha, when I think that those people there might get killed, our people, I feel like my heart might break.

MARTHA: But it would be easier on Mom's nerves if you just did something here. She'll have a nervous breakdown if you go. And I'll be worried too. People might die. You're not bullet-proof brother.

ISAIAH: I'm not suicidal Martha. I'll keep my head about me.

MARTHA: We're not just trying to spoil your fun. We care.

ISAIAH: You know, I think you should start going to the Peace Village. It would be good for you. Whitey lover.

MARTHA: (laughs) Fuck you.

ISAIAH: You better not let Mom hear you swearing like that, you'll be in big shit.

MARTHA: All right, all right. You coming out of your cave?

ISAIAH: I guess so. I guess I gotta face the music sometime.

MARTHA: Holy, make it sound like a firing squad.

ISAIAH: It feels like it to me. And Martha?

MARTHA: Yeah?

ISAIAH: He didn't deserve you.

(Martha nods)

(They leave the bedroom. Scene shifts to the living room where Mary and Isaac are watching TV and drinking tea)

TVANNOUNCER: And tensions remain high, on the South Side of the Mercier Bridge, as angry residents burn the Mohawks in effigy, to protest the continued blockade of that bridge. The Mercier Bridge is a vital link for communities from the Island of Montreal to the heavenly populated suburbs on the South Shore of the St. Lawrence River.

MARY: See? See? They're burning a Mohawk scarecrow. That could be you Isaiah.

MARTHA: Mom, please.

MARY: Well, I'm just saying.

ISAAC: All that stuff you said you weren't gonna.

MARY: Supportive, old man, supportive.

ISAAC: I'm just saying, you know.

MARY: You hungry? There's stuff left in the fridge for you.

ISAIAH: No.

MARY: Isaiah. I just care.

ISAIAH: I know.

MARY: But, has your sister explained?

ISAIAH: I know what you said Mom. I haven't changed my mind. If that's what you're wondering.

MARY: So you still want to go to Oka?

ISAIAH: Yeah I do. More than ever.

MARY: *(to Martha)* What were you doing in there?

MARTHA: *(Whispering)* We talked Mom. Honest. He wouldn't budge. I told you that before I went in.

ISAIAH: This is all about making me change my mind. It's all about changing little Isaiah's mind, because he's too dumb to know what he's doing.

ISAAC: I'm glad I didn't say it.

MARY: This is about looking after your best interests. And no-one said you're dumb. My boy, you got a bad habit of stepping into things you don't...that you don't think about enough.

ISAAC: Yeah, that damn record club's still looking for him. *(laughs)*

MARY: And we love you, that's why we bring it up.

ISAAC: And that "he's dead" answer never worked. *(laughs)*

MARY: Isaac please. Can't you see that my boy?

ISAAC: I said it wouldn't work. They never believe you when you say you're dead. Too many people try that.

MARY: Old man!

ISAIAH: I might not know what I'm talking about sometimes, I might so dumb things sometimes, but that doesn't mean what I'm trying to do isn't right.

MARY: Well it sure puts questions in my mind.

ISAIAH: That's only cause you don't know me. You don't know who I am. I think I didn't know either sometimes, but I'm learning. I'm waking up. And that scares you.

MARY: What scares me is that you're stepping into a situation where you could get hurt or worse, and you think it's a game.

ISAIAH: It's not a game Mom. And I'm not playing one.

MARY: Old man, you talk to your boy. I don't know what to say anymore. Come with me Martha.

(Mary takes Martha into the kitchen, Isaiah and Isaac are left alone to talk)

ISAIAH: You're not changing my mind you know.

ISAAC: It's not about your mind. It's about me enjoying a cigarette and tea in peace.

(lights a cigarette and takes a drag)

You know Doo-Doosh?

ISAIAH: Yeah.

ISAAC: He nursed till he was seven years old you know. That's why they call him that.

ISAIAH: So what does that have to do with talking me out of going to Oka?

ISAAC: It doesn't. But anyway, one time when we were young guys, he wanted to chew snuff. It was the style then you know. Not just baseball players like now. Or like wearing bright orange hunting caps, that was the style then too, everyone was doing it. Anyway. He starts wanting to chew snuff. I never did. Your Mom wouldn't kiss me if I did, so I didn't. But you know what? After he tried it he found he didn't like it.

ISAIAH: So is that your way of saying that if I go to Oka, I'll learn it was some big mistake?

ISAAC: No. It's my way of saying that Doo-Doosh always had to have something in his mouth. All his life. And you know what? When he finally married, his wife was very well endowed. Makes you wonder about things, eh? Everybody isn't out to get you my boy. We care about you. Do what you want, but don't sell us short.

(In the Kitchen)

MARY: Don't worry Martha. Don't worry my girl. Your Dad's gonna lay down the law.

MARTHA: Mom.

MARY: That boy need a firm hand. Guidance.

MARTHA: Mom, you just don't listen.

MARY: Hunh?

ISAAC: *(from the living room)* I'm going to fill up my teacup!

(Isaac goes into the kitchen)

MARY: So has everything been resolved?

ISAIAH: *(from the living room)* I haven't changed my mind.

ISAAC: Waste of time.

(Mary starts crying, she and Martha go into the living room)

MARTHA: Mom, it's okay.

MARY: It's not okay. It feels like it won't be okay again.

ISAAC: Maybe it's time the boy stepped out.

MARY: It's easy for you to say.

ISAAC: I'm just saying that Isaiah's a young man, and a man has to decide for himself, for good or for bad sometimes.

MARY: He's just like you, what you did.

ISAAC: I done what I did, and that's just history.

MARY: But it's just like you, running off without a thought in your head.

ISAAC: Well that was a long time ago.

MARY: Your Dad abandoned us once.

ISAAC: I didn't abandon anyone. I just felt like I had to do something, and I did.

MARTHA: But what was that?

MARY: When you two were just kids, you just started school, Isaiah was in the second grade, your Dad and Dillie took off. I thought he was gone for good. I tried to stop him, but he wouldn't listen.

ISAAC: I never said I wasn't coming back. You're just jumping to conclusions all the time.

MARTHA: But where'd you take off to Dad?

MARY: Dillie got his head filled with these dreams of glory. He told your Dad that they had to go to Wounded Knee. AIM needed them. And your Dad fell for it.

ISAIAH: Wounded know? 1973? Wow Dad, you went to Wounded Knee?

ISAAC: The FBI, those bastards, oops, those sons of bitches were clobbering our people.

MARY: Not our people, the Sioux.

ISAAC: Whatever. I'm not going to argue about terms with you old woman. We went there to give support to our people.

MARY: You had no business going there.

ISAAC: My people's well-being is always my business. Right off we ran into a little trouble at the boarder. The boarder guards made us take off our shoes and empty our pockets. They searched through Dillie's big Indian car. Dillie told them we were going shopping in Fargo and if they wanted to look up our big black jeets with flashlights, they could go right ahead. We were making good time, we crossed South Dakota. Nearly got to Watertown. The state troopers stopped us. Right off I know it meant trouble. They asked Dillie, "Okay Cochise, where are you and Geronimo off to?" Dillie told him to "F" off. The trooper pulls this big horse pistol out and puts it to Dillie's head. I though he was done for. The trooper tells us to get out of the car. They took us to jail.

ISAIAH: Bastards.

ISAAC: They got is separated. It was cold in that cell. I still had my handcuffs on. From where I was I thought I could hear them working over Dillie. At first I though he shoulda just kept his mouth shut, but then I thought that it wouldn't have made a difference anyway. I just sat there waiting for my turn to come. And they came. These two big white guys wearing tight black gloves. I could tell right away that they didn't have a bit of feeling for me. I was scared but I figured I'd just try to tough it out as best as I could. One of them was talkative, the other was real quiet, with this weird kind of smile on his face. The talker asks me where we were off to. I told him that Dillie probably already told him all they needed to know, and if he was gonna beat the shit out of me he better just start, cause I wasn't giving them anything. And they started. I felt so frustrated and helpless, my fists locked in those cuffs, getting punched and kicked around. At one point there I nearly passed out, I fell down. The talker started laughing, he says, "Now that's the way I like to see Indians, on their knees." Sure enough I was on my knees. I didn't have much strength left, but with the last I had I got back on my feet, I wouldn't give those sons of bitches the satisfaction of seeing me like that. They beat me till I passed out. We got bailed out by a couple chiefs, and local Indians in South Dakota.

MARTHA: (Sobbing) Daddy.

MARY: See Isaiah, see, that's why I don't want you to go. You'll get beaten up or worse. You'll just get over whatever you're into. It'll be okay my boy. You'll be okay.

ISAIAH: Jesus. I'm not okay Mom. The world is not okay. I'm not sitting here doing nothing while those people at Oka face death. I've got to stand up and be counted. Can't you see that?

MARY: You're just a boy.

ISAIAH: I'm a man Mom. And I may not be the sharpest tack in the box, in your opinion, but I'm smart enough to know when it's time. You're scared Mom, I can understand that. I'm scared too, but I know what I have to do. I know now I'll never convince you of anything. But that's not really important. The most important thing is that I know in my heart everything I need to know. I have everything I need right here. That's it.

(Isaiah leaves and goes into his room. The remainder are silent, The TV begins another update on Oka, they all focus on the TV.)

TV ANNOUNCER: It appears that the situation in Oka, Quebéc remains unchanged. Tensions remain high without any resolution in sight. And as the military stands at the ready through the night, there are strong indications that any day now... (Fades)

(lights out)

THE END

Love and Other Resistances:

Responding to Kahnesatà:ke Through Artistic Practice

WANDA NANIBUSH

This land is ours; ours by right of possession;
ours as a heritage,
given to us as a sacred legacy.
It is the spot where our fathers lie;
beneath those trees our mothers sang our lullaby,
and you would tear it from us
and leave us wanderers at the mercy of fate.
—*Chief Joseph Onasakenarat, 1868*[1]

Love and Resistance

It was the summer of 1990, and I was experiencing the blush of first love. My world as a woman shifted. But this wasn't the only transformation for me that summer. This was also the summer when the Kanien'kehaka (Mohawk) of Kahnesatà:ke went head to head with, first, the Sûreté du Québec (SQ), and then with the Canadian military in attempt to stop an encroachment on their traditional territory. The Pines is the community's longstanding commons—a sacred space and burial ground bordering the small resort town of Oka. Oka wanted to turn the Pines into a golf course, the very place where the Kanien'kehaka buried their Ancestors and gathered for ceremony.

The events throughout the summer of 1990 shifted my sense of the world, and my place in it as an Anishinaabekwe. Forever after, my sense of politics was bound up with thoughts on love. By March 11, 1990, the Kanien'kehaka of Kahnesatà:ke had exhausted legal avenues for justice, finding themselves unable to use the Canadian courts to protect their land rights. That very day they set up a barricade to stop developers from starting work. On June 30, the town of Oka was granted a order to remove the blockade, and by July 11, Mayor Ouellette had called in the Sûreté du Québec.

Rather than concentrating on the events of the resistance, I want to explore how we as Indigenous Peoples have processed these events through our artistic practices. The event has been labelled crisis, claim, standoff, protest, blockade, standing up, revolt, and resistance depending on one's perspective, and who is doing the naming. Many ideas and concepts that were animated during the Kahnesatà:ke resistance proceeded to be processed in the production of Indigenous art across the continent. I cannot possibly reference every piece of artwork created in response to the resistance, so I like to think of this more as personal memory-work that might resonate with readers and also bring some works back into contemporary conversations.

The beginning of the Kanien'kehaka resistance imagery for me lies in the *Unity Flag*, a work of art by Louis Karoniaktojeh Hall,[2] flying high at the barricades alongside the purple and white confederacy flag and the red and white Canadian Flag. It is also referred to as the *Warrior Flag*. I can relate to it because it includes me in its interpellation of Indigenous nations working together to protect our people and land for the future generations. It is also a vision of strength as the warrior's head inside a sun marks the centre of the flag. I grew up with that flag. It always held a future promise for me, like one day we might win our claims and rights. Kanien'kehaka curator Ryan Rice rightly points to the dual meanings of the flag in his show *Oh So Iroquois*, when he states "although this assertive red and yellow flag has come to symbolize Iroquois survival, sovereignty, and presence, for some it represents defiance."[3] At the blockade in Kahnesatà:ke the future promise became the chant of "now." The waiting was over and the struggle was in the world's sight lines. It could be argued that survival and sovereignty are defiant actions on the part of Indigenous Peoples. Hall, a painter and warrior, understood the connections between cultural continuity and sovereignty that was asserted during the blockades. He saw such reconnections being made in the relationships in the Longhouse; as he stated: "Now, in 1990, the Longhouse membership is growing steadily and I think more will come to it after this crazy summer [of 1990]."[4] He wrote the warrior's handbook and interprets the meaning of the *Great Law of Peace* for his people. The flag represents for me both sovereignty and defiance but also unity. The Kahnesatà:ke resurgence united all Indigenous Peoples in our collective resistance to colonialism—specifically in our desire to keep our traditions, to write our own constitutions, to determine our own governance and in the struggle to keep our traditional territories.

Re-entering the World

Part of what the Kahnesatà:ke resistance did was increase the visibility of Indigenous Peoples. I felt we could no longer be ignored; possibly a false hope, but an experience of a necessary emotion just the same. Such emotion can renew the fight and keep you going through times when no one seems to care or notice your plight. Shows like *Okanata: An Interdisciplinary Exhibition Examining Events and Emotions of the Mohawk Summer of* 1990 tried to take advantage of the increased visibility in order to bring some critical reflection on the event. *Okanata* took place at Artspace and Workscene gallery in Toronto in 1991. It brought together a large number of non-Indigenous and Indigenous artists to reflect on the implications of Oka from a cross-cultural and international perspective. Robert Houle, Edward Poitras, and Rebecca Belmore contributed work to *Okanata.* It was curated by a team of five who selected work from 22 artists. Belmore contributed a new work, *Effigy.*

In Belmore's *Effigy,* a news article on the Oka stand off was projected onto a square of sand. There were stones placed in the sand that look liked land forms. In one corner of the sand there was a pile of smooth stones and paper burning in a fire. In a review by Carol Podedworny, it was suggested that Belmore was arguing that it does not matter to Canada what happens to Indigenous Peoples.[5]

Belmore's *Effigy* was both a tribute to land and a furious venting of the racist discourses that delegitimize Indigenous Peoples' claims. *Effigy* and *fiction* share a similar root in the word *fingere,* which means to shape, form, devise or feign. In the creation and destruction of an effigy, there is also the process of fiction. Similarity as invention. It highlights for me the way in which stereotypes can be remobilized by the community over and above their re-inscription by the press or racist comments or government policy.

Writing on Ellen Gabriel's artwork, Collette Lemmon has stated that the blockades at Kahnesatà:ke situates all events in a timeline of before and after.[6] Gabriel was a negotiator for Kahnesatà:ke during the summer of 1990. It is possible that her role as an artist gave her the skills to negotiate conflicting discourses and visions of the world. She spoke eloquently to my desire to have our vision of the world recognized and, if not understood, at least allowed space. Gabriel in 2000 painted *Grandfather Speaks* and *War Clubs*, both oil on pastel.[7] Both works can be seen as reflections ten years after the Kahnesatà:ke resistance. In *War Club* there is an arrow running from text below to a painting of a war club cut into a tree. Gabriel's text states, "I watch as the legacy of our Knowledge dwindles down to a spark ignitable only by my breath." The text captures the sense of responsibility for each of us to answer the call to action when it comes to protecting our culture and language. It also hints at the necessity for the teachings that tell us there are roles we all play—some to start the fire and some to keep it burning. How do we situate the war club in the tree, though? Gabriel seems to imply that the club makes sense only in relation to its cultural context. War without culture is just war. We must remember why we fight.

Gabriel's work reminded me of Alanis Obomsawin's insights in 270 *Years of Resistance*, another artwork that reconfigured the "Oka Standoff" from its Indigenous point of view. It placed the "conflict" in the context of a history of resistance starting with the landing of Cartier in 1535 and the standoff mounted by Chief Onasakenarat in 1868 against the Sepulchians' theft of Indian land. Many people did not (and still do not) know that Montreal was Kanien'kehaka territory until it was stolen, just as Toronto was Haudenosaunee and Missassauga Anishinabeg territories, until it was stolen. These are still our territories. Without land where things like language and culture are nourished it becomes hard to imagine cultural continuity.

In Jane Ash Poitras' OKA *Spirit Power*, 1990, acrylic, news print, photocopy on canvas mixed media work, you can see her constant and enduring questioning of who has power to define something like land.[8] She paints spiritual relationship with land in Indigenous cultures and she points out western conceptualizations of land that mark it as a surface to be owned, dissected and mined. In the same work she paints the word "Land" above a photo of a warrior, implying metonymically that Oka is a land claim and that a land claim is spiritual continuance of a people. She also implies that land theft is spiritual theft. *Okanada* is her version of a historical timeline leading from pre-contact to now whereby Canada is marked by resistance to its hegemony and rule over Indigenous Peoples.

Unity

The idea of speaking from a Kanien'kehaka perspective was a desire shared by all Indigenous Peoples. It is a radical gesture, the speaking from the margins, from the space of erasure, from the space of delegitimated knowledge. *Indigena*[9], curated by Lee-Ann Martin and Gerald McMaster, came two years after the 1990 blockades. The show was a response to the celebrations of 500 years of Columbus's legacy. It came out of a desire to show the Indigenous perspective on that "celebration" we would refer to as 500 years of colonialism. The blockade at Oka opened up this discussion by claiming that what is at stake in the resistance is a different perspective on history. If one can accept that Indigenous Peoples have legitimate historical knowledge, whether it is oral or written, then history becomes an image not of facts but of stories or narratives that compete for legitimacy and continue to change over time and with each teller.

The work that best captures this spirit is the late Joanne Cardinal Schubert's *Preservation of a Species:* DECONSTRUCTIVISTS *(This is the house that Joe Built),* 1990.[10] Schubert gives an alternative history from an Indigenous perspective, while also forcing an engagement with the history of racism against Indigenous people in Canada. One part of the work is a large blackboard with chalk writing attached to a floor display of various objects painted black. The text is headed by the words "This is My History," which is followed by "In the beginning there were Native People across the land." It is this statement the resituates the context for reading the blockades as an assertion of our understandings of the history of Canada. It immediately foregrounds Indigenous presence and title to the land as a starting point for any discussion about or with Indigenous Peoples. Unfortunately, this is what is foreclosed in the actions taken by the town of Oka and by the actions of the military on behalf of the state. Schubert proceeds to write about the displacement, dispossession, and the attempted erasure of Indigenous ways of being during the experiences of colonialism. She names and honours people who have resisted colonialism. The last title in the work, *This is the House that Joe Built*, refers to her father, Joe Cardinal, and how he shaped her sense of responsibility to change racism and colonialism in this country. Schubert honoured him by placing the words he told her on his deathbed in the work: "If I had made a stand—you wouldn't have to. You've got to stand up to them. Don't let those bastards get you. Just stand up and never give in...." Joe Cardinal's words and now Joanne's are exactly what made the resistance so much a part of my identity as an Anishnaabeg. The fact that they stood up to the town, the province, the country for all of us and we stood with them as much we could while the state undermined us. Despite the best efforts the army made to isolate the Kanien'kehaka of Kahnesatà:ke, by not allowing others to physically join them at the blockade, many blockades and sit-ins were staged across the country in solidarity. These were Joe and Joanne's words in action.

While we are specific, unique and distinct from each other as over 500 Indigenous nations, the efforts of resistance bind us. Ryan Rice, a Kanien'kehaka curator, wrote that "Iroquois artists draw upon those historical, cultural and political Haudenosaunee relationships that contribute to making sense of their contemporary identity and experience, and allow them to contribute new meanings to concepts of memory, reality and responsibility."[11] Rice's insights are guideposts to the meaning of the "Oka blockades" in our contemporary art. Artists act as interpreters for contemporary audiences and their interpretations often avoid the pitfalls of contemporary media erasures and historical stereotyping. Art brings into being the "new" through a look and excavation of the "old." Again this notion was at play in Kahnesatà:ke's resistance as being a continuance of Chief Onasakenarat's action in 1868. The new here is active interpretation of the past for the present rather than a radical break with the past. It would be useful to an Indigenous art history looking at this Indigenous conceptualization how "newness enters the world."

Memory

Colonialism is the experience that we all share, even if it has different histories. Mistakenly, unity has been struggled for in a sense of collective spirituality or culture, often referred to as pan-Indianism. Really it is the struggle against colonialism that marks a unity of all Indigenous Peoples that is more threatening to the power structures of contemporary society.

The stand that the Kanien'kehaka took in the Pines was also a traumatic event for the community and for all of us who acted in solidarity. It connects to a list of colonial traumas like "Starlight tours of Saskatoon," "Ipperwash," "Burnt Church," "500 missing and murdered Aboriginal women," "Trail of Tears," "Residential Schools," and many, many more. These specific events become part of a larger collective Indigenous history of colonialism and our resistance to it. Each new colonial event brings up a prior trauma, something almost forgotten, repressed or something that has been attempted to be erased. Dr. Bruce Granville Miller, a professor of Anthropology at UBC, speaks to the erasure of Indigenous claims through a wilful forgetting on the part of Canada.

> Ordinarily, however, I think governments change, bureaucrats retire, and public opinion simply shifts. The character in fiction, it seems to me, who best captures this mode of forgetting is Peter Pan—who, in the original book by Barrie, was a psychopathic teenage orphan, who sought out adolescent girls to engage in his fantasies. He flew with them over the open water to his Neverland, but commonly forgot about them, leaving them to crash and drown in the ocean. Wendy, in the Disney version, is but one of these girls. Peter simply doesn't remember the ones before her. It is not Peter who bears the cost of this forgetting; it is the Wendys. I recalled this idea when talking to the land claims representative for an interior tribe, who recalled, in considerable detail, community stories about the dealings with the various Crown representatives who arrived to set boundaries. These stories are now forgotten by government, which is not sure how much land was set aside. This gap between community remembering and government forgetting remains a feature of the lands claims/treaty landscape.[12]

There is a tension between remembering and forgetting that is brought into crisis when you add the fact that the Canadian government and mainstream society have very different cultural conceptions of memory when compared with Indigenous Peoples.

Robert Houle articulates the vastness of resistance when he states, "It is the project of the Enlightenment that has to be deconstructed, the autonomous, epistemological and moral subject that has to be decentred; the nostalgia for unity, totality and foundations that has to be overcome; the tyranny of representational thought and universal truth that has to be defeated; and the herculean task of self-validation within a margin created by industrial capitalism."[13] It is fitting that he articulates how anti-colonialism sits with many critics of the foundations of western philosophical traditions of the time of colonialism's beginnings when speaking about his installation, *Hochelaga. Hochelaga* interrogated the Indigenous history of Montreal, connecting its histories of oppression to the thinking that underlies them. He drew on his previous art-action during the summer of 1990 when he blocked out the sun in his studio windows with four banners with four words on them: LONGHOUSE/FALSE FACE/LAND CLAIM/SOVEREIGN, again connecting land to identity and culture. I can imagine how hard it must have been for him to paint without sun, colours struggling with the darkness. Houle has since made more work on Oka, like *Kahnesatake* and *Kanehsatake X*, which marks the event as central in his practice, where it appears in order to be remembered and honoured.

Notions of memory become tied to ideas of responsibility in Indigenous thinking. One is both responsible to remember in honour of the past but also to recreate in honour of the future. This is what Indigenous writers like Gerald Vizenor and N. Scott Momaday refer to as the imaginative underpinning of culture. When a person is asked to remember they are also being asked to create. All memory is partly an act of fiction. Our memories are not a storehouse of facts retrievable in a whole state. Instead, memory is vague, not completely retrievable and not always trustworthy. In Indigenous storytelling traditions, memory and history are conflated. The insight is that history is an interpretative event as much as memory is a story we construct. Oral history marries performativity to culture and identity. This is where art entered the everyday in our ancestral art traditions and why artists today are at the forefront of rethinking our identities and cultures. They make the connection between history-making and performative storytelling to remind, but never telling exactly what to remember.

New Realities

The new in reality is brought out by the very questioning of reality that is inherent in Indigenous work. If you have been erased from public record, if your understandings of history has been ignored, if you have been vilified and marginalized by the mainstream of a society you automatically understand reality to be in the hands of those with the power to decide what is right, normal, just and legitimate. To question what is presented as natural, normal, simply reality is to question the way power is distributed in society. To question it is to create a new reality.

Rebecca Belmore, in the sculptural performance *Ayum-ee-aawach Oomama-mowan: Speaking to Their Mother,* responded to the Kahnesatà:ke resistance by building a giant megaphone and travelling with it to different First Nation communities in order to allow people to speak to their Mother.[14] "This artwork was my response to what is now referred to in Canadian history as the 'Oka Crisis,'" says Belmore. "During the summer of 1990, many protests were mounted in support of the Kanien'kehaka Nation of Kahnesatà:ke in their struggle to maintain their territory. This object was taken into many First Nations communities — reservation, rural, and urban. I was particularly interested in locating the Aboriginal voice on the land. Asking people to address the land directly was an attempt to hear political protest as poetic action."[15] In using the megaphone in *Ayum-ee-aawach Oomama-mowan: Speaking to Their Mother,* you can feel the shift in authority. The authority to speak has been the state's but Belmore makes it clear that Indigenous Peoples answer to their mother, the Earth, and not the state. This idea could slip into unthoughtful new ageism, but Belmore restricts that reading by how the megaphone is constructed and by choosing the specific locations where the art is performed. It was evident in the Kahnesatà:ke resistance that their duty to protect their land for future generations in honour of past generations was lost on those they communicated with. The warriors and women would ask the police and the soldiers "Who is your leader? Do they have no honour?" The second point of difference highlighted in Belmore's work is the mode of speaking—soft voices need to be amplified for effect, and in the very speaking it asks, can you hear me? It seems the cultural concepts underlying the law of the Kahnesatà:ke resistance, such as The Kaianerekowa (Great Law of Peace), also could not be heard in communication with Canadian authorities.

Cowboys, Indians and Indigenous Peoples

Another aspect of Oka that became a subject of art was the reinscription or redeployment of the image of the warrior. David Neel's *Life on the 18th Hole*, 1990, and Gerald McMaster's *Oka-boy/Oh! Kowboy* use target imagery to underscore just how unfair the odds were: nine soldiers for one warrior.[16] Both artists connect stereotypic discourses of cowboys and Indians to the construction of the event, specifically how the warrior is demonized in order to justify the extreme aggression against him. It reminded me of all the stories of "Indians" where we are "wagon-burners," murderous savages and cannibals. These are stereotypes periodically deployed to justify colonial land theft, incarceration and murder.

As Houle argues in *Land Spirit Power*, another landmark exhibition of Indigenous Art, the warrior image can be manipulated by the people it is meant to contain. He states:

> For the people of Kanesatà:ke and Kahnawake it was state terrorism, the act of war without a declaration of war, so that there is no formal protection of civil rights or internationally regulated political rights.... Ironically, the warriors used the western patriarchically controlled mediascape to disseminate their own rhetoric of a democratic politics based on matriarchal principles of rule; that is, on the traditional form of the Longhouse society, which is not ruled by the technocratic specialists of the war machine. That is what made the warriors 'look' dangerous— they presented a face not recognized by or fully understandable to the non-native military machine. Again the images created by artists like Frederic Remington (1861–1909) and George Catlin (1796–1872) of 'Indian warfare' were reinforced. The electronic image continues what the hand had created.[17]

Jane Ash Poitras, *Rebirth of the Four Coyote Spirits*, 1996, mixed media on canvas, 172.8 x 111.8 cm, MacKenzie Art Gallery.

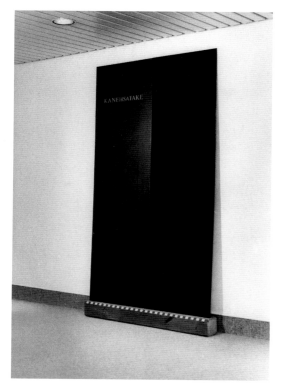

Robert Houle, *Kanehsatake*, 1990–1993, oil on
etched steel, treated wood and paint, 221 x 122 cm,
collection of the Art Gallery of Hamilton.

Robert Houle, *Kanehsatake X*, 2000, oil on paper mounted on masonite, oil on canvas, digitized photo mounted on masonite, anodized aluminum, 96 x 198 in., collection of the artist.

Robert Houle, *Mohawk Summer*, 1990, cloth banners with text installed in Houle's studio on Queen Street West, Toronto, photo credit: Mirella Mossanen, Thunder Bay Art Gallery.

Rebecca Belmore, *Ayum-ee-aawach Oomama-mowan: Speaking To Their Mother*, Fort Capelle 1992, wooden megaphone, two meters wide, Walter Phillips Gallery.

Rebecca Belmore, *Ayum-ee-aawach Oomama-mowan: Speaking To Their Mother,*
Kanehsatá:ke 1992, wooden megaphone, two meters wide, Walter
Phillips Gallery.

Rebecca Belmore, *Ayum-ee-aawach Oomama-mowan: Speaking To Their Mother,*
Ottawa 1992, wooden megaphone, two meters wide, Walter Phillips Gallery.

Gerald McMaster, *Oka-boy/Oh! Kowboy*, 1990, acrylic and oil pastel on paperboard, 94 x 114 cm. McMichael Canadian Art Collection.

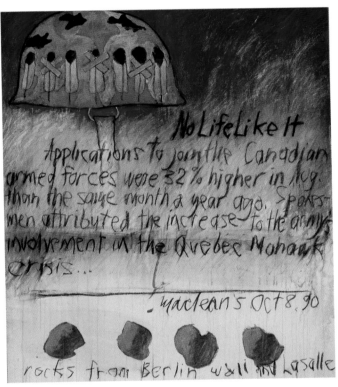

Gerald McMaster, *No Life Like It*, 1990, acrylic, oil pastel, and charcoal on board, 118.5 x 99 x 7.5 cm. Collection of The Ottawa Art Gallery. Gift of Don de Victoria Henry, 1996. Photo credit: Don Barbour.

Gerald McMaster, *Glastnost,* 1990, acrylic and oil pastel on matt board, 114 x 94 cm. Private collection.

Shelley Niro, *Red Hot*, 1992, 4' x 6', collection of the artist.

Greg Hill, *you are entering Mohawk Territory,* 1990, acrylic and latex paint, graphite, chalk, collage, aluminum and nails on plywood, 246 x 384 x 8 cm.

Greg Hill, *you are entering Mohawk Territory,* 1990 (detail).

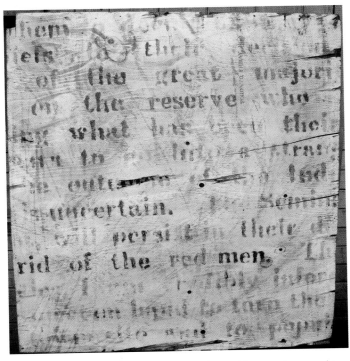

Greg Hill, *Oka History Lesson*, 1990, acrylic and latex paint, graphite on plywood, 120 x 122 x 5 cm (destroyed).

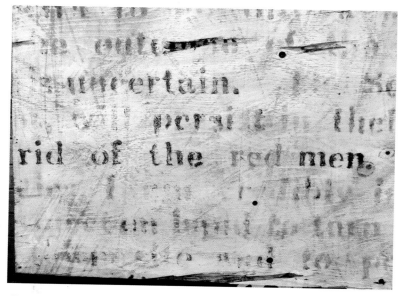

Greg Hill, *Oka History Lesson*, 1990 (detail).

Greg Hill, *Warrior*, 1990, acrylic and latex paint, graphite, collage and ⅜" hex bolts on plywood, 120 x 120 cm (destroyed).

Greg Hill, *The Lone Ranger and...*, 1990–91, acrylic and latex paint, graphite, shellac, collage and metal hinges on plywood, 310 x 122 cm (destroyed).

The warrior can also be a symbol of protection, freedom and compassion, but for that to be honoured the majority of society would have to see land claims as legitimate. Until then the warrior will read as terror(ist).

The image of the men, women and children walking out of the blockade marked me when I saw it presented in 270 *Years of Resistance* by Alanis Obomsawin. Obomsawin captured what took place behind the blockade, images not shown in the media. Despite the attempts to censor and thus shape our understanding of the events of that summer in favour of the state, artists like Obomsawin kept pushing society to understand that these were families and the fight was not a fair one. The photos of Kanien'kehaka warriors face to face with soldiers falsely presents an equality in power and might. Obomsawin shows instead the men's strength and fear. She shows how the women lead and negotiate, calm and stabilize the ferocity that comes from fear. She showed the traditional elder working with the men to help them maintain their heart in the face of death, to maintain their vulnerability in their anger. As one warrior stated in the film, behind anger there is sadness.

For Shelley Niro, after the sadness one must laugh with one's family. After images of war, both at Oka and in Iraq, and all the masculinity driving it, it's telling that she decided to do *Mohawks in Beehives*, a series of staged portraits of her and her sisters, all dolled up. The women look glamorous, fun and tough, like a lot of my Anishnaabe aunties. The portraits revel in an in-your-face flouting of societal norms and a prideful gaze of the everyday women we call mother, aunt, sister and friend. The series was shown in *Rethinking History*, a group exhibition with John Abrams, Stephen Andrews, Robert Houle, Sara Leydon, Edward Poitras, and Jane Ash Poitras, curated by Carol Podedworny in 1992. In an interview with Podedworny, Niro explained how she was driven by a feeling of taking back control:

> I'm really tired of the stereotype of Native people. I'm thinking of *Conspiracy of Silence*, the Betty Osborne story, and *Where the Spirit Lives*, about the residential schools, and that sort of thing. Although the stories need to be told and they need to be seen, as a Native person I'm sick of being the victim and being looked at as this poor person who has been manipulated and abused and

had all these terrible things done to them over the years. I think in one way it's true, but let's get on with our lives. It's making an assertive move and no longer being there—moving beyond all that. Part of it is just ignoring social good taste.[18]

Part of taking back control is an acknowledgement of where we are right now and accepting ourselves as having lived and continuing to live through traumatic experiences but not being defined by our traumas. Niro pushes us to view ourselves with pride and humour, but there is also a criticality to her work. She does not uncritically accept statements like Mohawks are matriarchal; instead her photos ask, if Mohawk society is matriarchal then the women must have decision making power and be free from being abused. She pushes us further to shed any preconception of what it is to be an Indigenous woman and actively perform it even when it does not fit or especially because it does not fit societal expectations.

The summer of 1990 transformed me and forever joined resistance to love. So what does love have to do with the Kahnesatà:ke resistance? I think of the men and women behind the blockades. They faced the strength and power of the army and the state, and ultimately faced death. It is an image of vulnerability that connects love to resistance. I think of how there were families behind the blockade who continued to laugh and learn and the image of love includes responsibility linked to resistance. If we know how to love well then we know how to see another's needs, claims, desires and demands as necessary expressions of self-determination rather than threats to our own autonomy. Rather than a struggle for power, love expresses a shared space of equality that allows us to maintain our differences from one another. Concepts like love and resistance are complex and rich and I hope I never quit trying to understand them and trying to live them.

---

1 Michael Baxendale and Craig MacLaine (1990), *This Land is Our Land: The Mohawk Revolt at Oka*, Toronto: Optimum Publishing International, p. 36.

2 Ryan Rice (2008), *Kwah Í:ken Tsi Iroquois/Oh So Iroquois*, Ottawa, *Exhibition Catalogue*, Ottawa: Ottawa Art Gallery and Aboriginal Curatorial Collective, p. 27.

3 Ibid., p. 26.

4 Baxendale (1990) p. 65.

5 Carol Podedworny (Winter 1992), "Okanata", *C Magazine*, p. 32, <ccca.finearts. yorku.ca/c/writing/p/podedworny/pode003t.html>, accessed October 1, 2009.

6 Collette Lemon, "Ellen Gabriel" in Rice, Ryan (2008), Kwah Í:ken Tsi Iroquois/ Oh So Iroquois, Exhibition Catalogue, Ottawa: Ottawa Art Gallery and Aboriginal Curatorial Collective, pp. 32–5.

7 Rice (2008), pp. 32–35.

8 Barry Ace and July Papatsie (1997), *Transitions, Exhibition Catalogue*, Ottawa, Ministry of Indian Affairs and Northern Development, pp. 20–1.

9 Lee-Ann Martin and Gerald McMaster (1992), *Indigena: Contemporary Native Perspectives, Exhibition Catalogue*, Gatineau and Vancouver: Canadian Museum of Civilization and Douglas & McIntyre,

10 Ibid, pp. 130–135.

11 Rice (2008), p. 59.

12 Bruce Granville Miller (2003), "A Short Commentary on Land Claims in BC," 11th Annual National Land Claims Workshop, <www.ubcic.bc.ca/Resources/short-commentary.htm>, accessed October 1, 2009.

13 Robert Houle (1992), "Artist Statement" in, *Hochelaga: A Multi-Media Installation by Robert Houle* and Curtis J. Collins, Exhibition Catalogue, Montreal: Galerie Articule, <www.ccca.ca/c/writing/h/houle/hou005t.html>, accessed 1 October 1, 2009.

14 For an extensive discussion of this work see Greg Hill (2009) "Caught... (Red-handed)," in Josée Drouin-Brisebois (curator), *Caught in Act* (exhibition catalogue), Ottawa: National Gallery of Canada, pp. 145–180.

15 Heather Belot (2009), *Coming Full Circle: Rebecca Belmore Brings Her Voice Back to Banff*, Banff Centre for the Arts, <www.banffcentre.ca/about/inspired/2009/winter/full_circle.asp>, accessed October 1, 2009.

16 Allan J. Ryan (1999) *The Trickster Shift: Humour and Irony in Contemporary Native Art*, Vancouver: UBC Press, pp. 233–237.

17 Robert Houle (1992), "The Spiritual Legacy of the Ancient Ones," in Diana Nemiroff, Robert Houle and Charlotte Townsend-Gault (eds), *Land Spirit Power: First Nations at the National Gallery of Canada*, Exhibition Catalogue, Ottawa: National Gallery of Canada, <www.ccca.ca/c/writing/h/houle/hou009t.html>, accessed October 1, 2009.

18 Carol Padedworny, (1992), *Rethinking History*, Group exhibition: John Abrams, Stephen Andrews, Robert Houle, Sara Leydon, Edward Poitras, Jane Ash Poitras, Exhibition Catalogue, Toronto, Mercer Union: A Centre for Contemporary Art, <www.mercerunion.org/show.asp?show_id=219>, accessed October 1, 2009.

How Golf and Lasagna Changed My Life

or

The Kanehsatà:ke Resistance of 1990

GREG HILL

Events at Kahnesatà:ke erupted July 11, 1990, during what was my summer holiday between my second and final year of a Fine Arts diploma program at Fanshawe College in London, Ontario. For me, those days mostly consisted of my summer job painting houses and riding my bike. In other words, political activism and direct action were not part of my daily routine. It is even more accurate to say that I was only beginning to deal with and understand what my Aboriginality—my Kanien'kehaka-ness—meant to me and how I related to it. It is generally known that the "Oka Crisis" was a significant moment in the history of relations between Indigenous Peoples and the people of Canada, as represented in this instance by the Canadian military. What is not understood as well is how July 11, 1990, the 78 days of standoff that followed and every day since then have been forever impacted and altered by those events and their effects on all of us. To shed a pinpoint of light on this fact, I offer my own experiences as just one example of how the courage of the men, women, and children who took a stand for our rights as Onkwehonwe (Indigenous Peoples) led to transformation and change on a personal level. Difficult to quantify, change within individuals is assessed through action and other means of outward expression. For me, the outlet and examination manifested in my artwork enabled me to learn, grow and commit to this path. I remain grateful, accountable and emboldened to this day.

I will discuss four works that I created during the period of September 1990 and through to March of 1991. There were other works created during this time but I think these are the most evocative of emotions I felt then and these are the best to explain and analyze from the perspective of today, now 20 years later.

I already mentioned I was an art student during the summer of 1990. I was learning what it meant to be an artist and going into my third and final year, I felt I was beginning to understand. I was enjoying art school so much in fact that I was grateful and even a little guilty about my privilege to be there. I did not fully understand my entitlement to educational funding as a treaty right and wondered about the apparent benevolence of the Canadian government. Why would they pay for my post-secondary education? It wasn't until later that I realized that the government had an obligation to pay according to agreements and treaties made with Onkwehonwe from sea to sea. My treaty right to educational funding was interpreted by the Canadian government and then administered by the Department of Indian and Northern Affairs through blocks of funding delivered to my recognized First Nation and divided by the Grand River Post Secondary Education Council into set amounts that would allow many of us eligible Grand River Territory band members to access it and, importantly, access a higher education. There was never enough money for everyone who wanted to go to school, and I have to add that this is funding that is still insufficient for the need and a program that is constantly under threat. I thought I was "lucky" to get to go to school. I knew that others were not getting the opportunity and I knew that without the funding I wouldn't be there. This knowledge did impart a sense of responsibility in me to do well, to make sure that the money was not wasted. The experience of travelling from my home in Fort Erie to the Six Nations reserve to meet with my education counselor and make arrangements for my funding was both a reestablishment of contact with my "home" reserve and a reminder of the separation my life and experience as an off-reserve urbanite presupposed. Even off-reserve I was subject to internalized colonial thinking that somehow erodes rights based on where one lives—whether on or off of a recognized "Indian reserve."

you are entering Mohawk Territory, 1990, acrylic and latex paint, graphite, chalk, collage, aluminum and nails on plywood, 246 x 384 x 8 cm.

The idea behind this work was that since I was not able to go to Kanehsatà:ke (or at least had decided that I would stay in school rather than go) that one thing I could do was make artworks that expressed my feelings about the events. I made several works on this theme and I believe this was one of the last, although it went through a few transformations on the way to this final (and unfinished) state. I say unfinished because the idea was that this would be a kind of travelling barricade. The idea being that it would be on wheels so that it could be towed behind a vehicle and brought to any protest site—a portable barricade ready for the next blockade. There was a lot in this work, too much probably, and that is likely why it couldn't be finished. Like earlier works I completed during this time the base imagery came from the media. There are silhouettes of the police, an image of the Mohawk Warrior flag, an AK-47, an upside-down Lone Ranger, a map painted in red of the Ontario/Québec/New York geographical area encompassing Kanehsatà:ke, phrases of text and more. The entire painting was smashed into bits and then put back together as good as possible so that the phrase "you are entering MOHAWK TERRITORY" was the most legible remnant. This for me was what the work came to be about, a double-entendre referencing one of the signs posted at the

you are entering Mohawk Territory, 1990 (detail).

blockade and an acknowledgement to myself that I too was moving into Mohawk territory with this work and that I felt a responsibility to the growing consciousness that it demanded.

As I mentioned earlier, this was one of the last works I made dealing directly with Oka and Kanehsatà:ke. One of the first paintings I did during this period I think traces my path of learning and my growing rage about the depth of injustice that was being played out in the Pines, on highway 344, in the treatment centre, at whiskey trench,[1] and on the property occupied by Joe David after the resistance movement of 1990 was "over."[2]

I began to research the events at Oka. First by collecting as many of the current articles that appeared in the media and then by looking for archival documents related to Oka. I came across a newspaper article published in Toronto in the *Globe and Mail* July 22, 1887, that was relating a dispute over the lands at Oka between Mohawks and the Sulpicians. I was shocked to find this evidence of the longstanding injustice occurring over these lands.[3] It solidified my opposition and conviction to support my Kanien'kehaka brothers and sisters in the best way I could think of. I enlarged and painted a section of this article that I think summed up the attitude of the day that continued

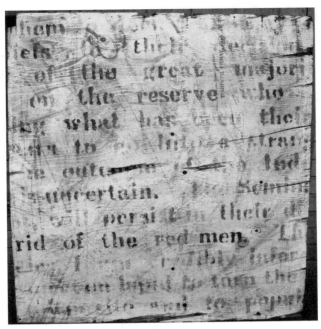

Oka History Lesson, 1990, acrylic and latex paint, graphite on plywood,
120 x 122 x 5 cm (destroyed).

to the present. The sentence "get rid of the red men" was there in black and white. I highlighted these words in my painting and I am still shocked that a mainstream print publication was able to print these inciteful words. Today, laws regulate and restrict the use of language but the attitudes that generate them still remain.

In little time I gathered an immense amount of source material garnered from all of the media attention given to the "Oka Crisis." Many of the images I collected were of special significance to me, but this image of a supporting protester with his face painted and bandana captured my attention. In this and other works from this time I used a combination of paint and drawing techniques as well as very physical engagement with the plywood itself. I nailed, screwed, routered and smashed these surfaces I think both as a physical release and to make an aesthetic connection to the ad hoc construction of the barricades and fortifications at the blockade sites.

Warrior, 1990, acrylic and latex paint, graphite, collage and ³⁄₈" hex bolts on plywood, 120 x 120 cm (destroyed).

"Warrior" of course referred to the men and women who were the defenders of the land behind the barricades. In *Warrior*, 1990, I thought of this term as also including all those who stood up and protested outside of the communities, on the city streets and outside the government buildings. Men and women who had nothing in common with Kanien'kehaka other than their disgust at the way human rights were being trampled upon and who took it upon themselves to act in support of Kanien'kehaka and all Aboriginal rights. Judging by the man's make-up and the somewhat stereotypical nature of the images he applied to his face, I thought that this was likely someone who has never really had a lot of exposure to Indigenous cultures in Canada, and still he was there.

Across the top of the painting, I placed a row of police in riot gear upside down as a kind of decorative frieze, an ominous chain of images that I think contrasted nicely with the small flower patterns that were on the man's bandana. Also painted into this work is a fragment of a message sign that the army had created as an attempted means of intimidation directed at their Warrior nemesis, code-named "Lasagne;"[4] an image of the sign for the golf course "Club de Golf" and that single word from the 1887 *Globe and Mail* article, "red," referencing the phrase "get rid of the red men" that I felt captured the essence of what was happening there. The full text of the army's sign read "LASAGNE DEAD MEAT" and was an expression of the army's contempt for one of the warriors who engaged soldiers in tests of nerve and provocation.[5]

The final work I would like to discuss here came later in the body of work that was created during this time, *The Lone Ranger and...*, 1990–91, incorporated media images and knowledge that appeared after the crisis had been defused and the specific events of the resistance at Kanehsatà:ke blended into a mélange of media reporting focused on new uprisings and the post-Oka analysis located in the pages of *Maclean's* magazine. Out of this extended journalistic interest the roles of significant players were examined, politicians were criticized, and heroes emerged; one of these was General John de Chastelain. The general was the "good guy" face of the armed forces for the media and I began to equate him with idea of the Lone Ranger. This large painting of the Lone Ranger, much larger than life at ten feet tall, was a way of equating public stature with media portrayal. I pasted a magazine image of de Chastelain to the left of the Lone Ranger. On the Lone Ranger's shoulder I pasted an image of Panama dictator Manuel Noriega as a symbol of the little devil that whispers evil suggestions into the Lone Ranger's ear. A tiny image of Tonto, the Lone Ranger's "faithful Indian companion," is upside down and defiled on the lower right of the painting and emphasizes the glorification of the Lone Ranger. The phrase "ke-mo sah-be" is between the Lone Ranger's legs and was what Tonto called the Lone Ranger (and sometimes the other way around). The meaning and origin of the phrase has been extensively debated and apparently means something akin to "Faithful Scout." Running vertically the full height of the work is the text "Nowhere in the pages of History can one find a greater champion of justice," an excerpt from the opening narration of the Lone Ranger television series.

A unique feature of this work was that it could fold in half, and the hinges that allowed this were positioned where his guns would

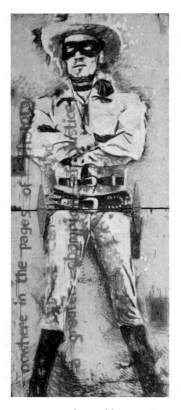

The Lone Ranger and..., 1990–91, acrylic and latex paint, graphite, shellac, collage and metal hinges on plywood, 310 x 122 cm (destroyed).

have rested on his hips. This work began to move outward from the specifics of the summer of 1990 and on to a greater awareness of how the events at Kanehsatà:ke were really a microcosm of unrest and injustice across Canada and around the world. It also began to incorporate many more personal connections. I grew up affected by my father's deep nostalgia for the Lone Ranger and Tonto. His excitement in relating the experience of seeing episodes on television and in theatres would be transferred to us whenever a rerun would come up on the television in our living room. In the myth-making mistiness of my memories of those times I began to believe that we were related to the actor that played Tonto. It was true Jay Silverheels/Harry Smith was a Mohawk from the Six Nations reserve, but he was not my uncle as I had started to wonder about. My father did know Harry Smith's brother who lived in Fort Erie, but that was about as close as we got to Jay Silverheels.

Recently, I found an old VHS compilation of the *Lone Ranger* movie and several of the television episodes and we had a great number of laughs watching these together, my parents, my children and myself. It seems that legacy will continue.

I want to thank Kiera Ladner and Leanne Simpson for inviting me to contribute to this publication. The opportunity to look back on this period is an affirmation of the path I have chosen since. It should also be noted here, and I am sure it will be elsewhere, that the so-called "Oka Crisis" is but one of a continuum of many instances of resistance to colonial impositions by Kanien'kehaka and Onkwehonwe everywhere on Turtle Island. It has now been twenty years since this particular event captured international attention, at least until it was superseded by the (first) Gulf War, and yet there are many protests that continue today, unseen and seemingly immobilized by government inaction. What does it take it take to actualize change?

Refer to colour plates, pages 195–205.

1   See Alanis Obomsawin's documentary on this particular tragic event, *Rocks at Whiskey Trench* (2000) <www.onf-nfb.gc.ca/eng/collection/film/?id=33895> accessed July 29, 2009. Alanis' award winning and powerful documentary *Kanehsatake: 270 Years of Resistance* is available online at <www.nfb.ca/film/kanehsatake_270_years_of_resistance/>.

2   Joe David was an artist who became a Warrior when he joined the group in the treatment centre. I went to visit him in 1996 with photographer Jeff Thomas who wanted to photograph him. Joe was occupying a house on the still disputed territory and related how he was constantly hassled by police. He was a really quiet and gentle man. I left there thinking that he was still very much trapped in 1990, living out a lonely siege. He was shot in the back in 1999 and died five years later. Skennen kowa Joe. For the full, sad story see <www.kahonwes.com/newyork/kanehsatake0046.htm>.

3   See also Alanis Obomsawin's documentary on the subject *Kanehsatake: 270 years of Resistance* (1993), <nfb.ca/film/kanehsatake_270_years_of_resistance> accessed July 29, 2009).

4   The bilingual spelling used in the army's signage reflected the mostly Francophone makeup of the Royal 22nd regiment "Van Doos" soldiers sent to the conflict and I think it's fair to say added the language gap added another level of distance and distrust to the tensions between the two forces.

5　One soldier, lauded for his bravery for not reacting to the taunts of "Lasagne" (it was later corrected that the Warrior in question was not "Lasagne" but another Warrior codenamed "Freddy Krueger"), had been trained as a member of the ceremonial guard—yes, the unfortunate military folk that have to stand in front of the Governor General's residence and resist the staring and teasing comments of tourists. Patrick Cloutier was charged in 1992 for drug use (cocaine) and later discharged from the army. While I was reconfirming these facts on wikipedia <en. wikipedia.org/wiki/Patrick_Cloutier> I came across a link there to a mindbogglingly inane video Clouthier apparently participated in that "spoofs" his Oka notoriety, watch it if you dare.

6　*Tonto* means dumb, stupid, or fool in Spanish.

7　Follow the link for the transcript of an email on the origin and meaning of the word between a researcher and the Fran Striker Jr., the son of the senior Striker who wrote the Lone Ranger stories at <www.old-time.com/misc/kemo.html>.

8　Gustafsen Lake Standoff, Ipperwash, and Caledonia are three that come to mind. The struggle for recognition of our land rights and sovereignty at Caledonia/ Kanonhstaton (the Protected Place) continues.

Ayum-ee-aawach Oomama-mowan:

Speaking to Their Mother

DAINA AUGAITIS AND REBECCA BELMORE IN CONVERSATION

A*yum-ee-aawach Oomama-mowan: Speaking to Their Mother* is a conceptual performance work commissioned by the Walter Phillips Gallery in 1991. Conceived by Rebecca Belmore as a way to bring First Nations protest into a new realm, the work comprises a massive, two-metre wide wooden megaphone structure that was built at the Banff Centre. On July 27, 1991, over sixty people walked in a procession to a mountain meadow in Banff National Park where Aboriginal speakers, invited by the artist, addressed the land and their relationship to it by speaking into the sculptural device and having their voices echo across the landscape. Over the following years, in 1992 and 1996, there were eleven more gatherings using the artwork.

The following is an excerpt from a conversation between Daina Augaitis and Rebecca Belmore about this work that took place on April 8, 2008.

DAINA AUGAITIS: You and I first worked together in 1990 on the megaphone project, *Ayum-ee-aawach Oomama-mowan: Speaking to Their Mother*. It was a very active time in the Canadian art world, especially with respect to issues of identity. Can we revisit that period?

REBECCA BELMORE: When I think back to the early Nineties in this country, I think "Oka Crisis." That was the burning issue for me, not as an artist but as an Anishinaabe person who was deeply affected by the fact that the Canadian government turned its military power against the Mohawk people. The question of identity in the Canadian art world was perhaps heightened by this potent political situation that challenged the notion of Canada as a peaceful, peacekeeping country. You and I first met not long after the crisis had calmed, the guns were put down and the tanks were taken away. I recall sitting across from you over coffee in a Toronto café and thinking that your invitation to make a new artwork was an opportunity for me to address this strong sense of unease and radical tension between Aboriginal people and the Canadian public.

DA: In Canadian society and also in the art world, many questions were being raised and anger was being expressed about the inequity of power. How did your work participate in those debates?

RB: It became very clear to me that my own developing notion of finding comfort in the mainstream, Canadian art world was a complicated situation. Personally, I recall realizing that racism was alive and well, definitely this was exacerbated by the inescapable media coverage of the "Oka Crisis." This image of "angry Indians" seemed to take hold of the imagination and saturate the minds of the Canadian public. I felt the sting of the anger and frustration.

Now I can see myself as that younger artist who needed to temper the personal turmoil that she felt because of what had gone down and to recognize that the political landscape in the country had shifted for Aboriginal people. This is what led me to imagine building a large megaphone with the idea of asking Aboriginal people to speak through it and directly to the earth. I recall that at one of the sites where we installed the artwork, a woman who identified herself as a young mother stated that she did not find this way of addressing the earth (speaking through a megaphone) any different than our traditional ceremonies. In retrospect, the concept for this artwork was motivated by my own need to hear our voices on the land, to recall this land as our audience—one that is listening.

DA: One of the powerful aspects of this work was how you engaged various communities across the country.

RB: I took *Ayum-ee-aawach Oomama-mowan: Speaking to Their Mother* to reserve communities, small towns and urban centres. My choice of locations itself illustrates how the Aboriginal people of this country now occupy many different realities within Canadian society.

DA: Banff was the first enactment of the work and a very special gathering.

RB: In Banff I was able to find an incredibly beautiful acoustic environment where the voice echoed up to nine times. For those who spoke, this effect conceptually integrated the sound of their own voices with the land. This magnificent experience of an echo made all who were gathered profoundly aware of the body as nature. Beyond its physicality, what was important about the megaphone was that it magnified and extended the voice through the "landscape." The art object became merely a functional tool; the essence of the piece was the voice and its reverberations across the land. Strategically, I was consciously hoping to remind listeners that our Aboriginal histories are carried by our original languages and are directly connected to the land.

DA: The procession in which everyone carried the various components of the sculpture to an alpine meadow in Banff National Park was an important ritualistic aspect of the work, where a community began to take shape through participation. This development of a "community" continued over the day as we listened to the resonance of poems, songs, laments and proclamations to Mother Earth. We were bound together in the swirling echoes of the words that spoke of riches and loss, of despair and optimism. This event encapsulated so much of the emotion and poetics of Aboriginal thought at that time. It was profoundly moving, and the feeling of political resolve was palpable. How did the work continue after Banff?

RB: The following year, in 1992, I toured the work to various sites across Canada, travelling in a van with Florene Belmore and Michael Beynon, who were as committed to the megaphone project as I. I wish to acknowledge their participation and the fact that I could not have undertaken a project of this scope without them.

To give you a sense of how the work unfolded, I will briefly describe how I recall some of the gatherings that took place. It is important to relate that events were organized by establishing a relationship with a local person who acts as our community liaison, who would choose the site and organize and promote their local gathering. Essentially, we were simply moving the art object from one site to the next. Although I was specifically interested in taking this artwork into the Aboriginal world, everyone was welcome to participate and to speak. Each gathering began with me approaching and using the megaphone. I did this as a way of showing people how the object functioned. I recall that my words always felt hesitant. I was simply there to offer the use of the artwork and then I would walk away and wait for someone to accept. In retrospect, I was impressed with the openness of the depth of what was spoken by the many people who shared their words through this visually absurd but beautiful object.

We started the 1992 tour of the work in Ottawa, on Parliament Hill, where the voice echoed off the American embassy that was located across the street. It made me think about the border between the two countries and how it divides many reserve communities located in its midst. It was significant to begin in the nation's capital, during a time when constitutional talks were well under way. In fact, during our gathering, two politicians climbed the steps and had to walk by the megaphone. I invited both to speak by asking them if they would like to speak to our Mother, gesturing toward and meaning the earth. One of the politicians, Joe Clark, who was the constitutional minister at the time, complied. The other political figure, Prime Minister Brian Mulroney, declined. It was important to start our tour on the front steps of parliament; it gave the beginning of our journey a hard edge.

We then took the megaphone to Kanesatà:ke and installed it at their second pow-wow, two summers after the armed standoff. It stood pointed toward the golf course, the very piece of land that triggered the "Oka Crisis." I felt that here the artwork was overwhelmed by the site itself. I recall how remarkable it was to just listen to the drum and the voices of the singers while watching golfers go about their game on the other side of the fence. The megaphone here became a quieted symbol, a visual reminder of all the protests that took place in this country during the hot summer of 1990.

The next site was Halifax, Nova Scotia, where the megaphone was carried from the Mi'kmaq Native Friendship Centre to the top of Citadel Hill and the voices echoed off the city below on a cool, misty morning. We returned to the Mi'kmaq Native Friendship Centre afterward for a feast of lobster and fish.

We then drove it to Thunder Bay. It was placed on Mount McKay, which is a tourist site located on the Fort William First Nation. Here it overlooked a celebrated view of Lake Superior. One of the speakers at the gathering was a six-month-old baby whose parents held the microphone mechanism to their child's mouth. To the amazement of all who were gathered, the baby made a sound, recognized its own echoing voice and then proceeded to experiment with a variety of vocal utterances. This event took a devastating turn during our time on the mountain when a man who was climbing on the rocky cliff, high above our gathering place, tragically fell to his death. This artwork was intended to create a sense of possibility, but here it was especially challenged by intervening realities—in fact, by nature itself.

In Winnipeg, the gathering was held in the downtown park where the Red and the Assiniboine Rivers meet, opposite St. Boniface Cathedral, where Louis Riel, a Métis leader accused of and executed for high treason, is laid to rest. Here, our local community organizer had arranged for a drum group to begin the gathering with an Honour Song. People began to speak, their voices aimed out and across the river. Angry passers-by actually heckled us at this particular site. It made me think about Louis Riel's much quoted words about how art has the potential to move people: "My people will sleep for 100 years and when they awake, it will be the artists who give them back their spirit."

The megaphone engaged with a real protest site that summer. This was a logging blockade north of Meadow Lake, Saskatchewan, that was organized by a group of Cree Elders to protest the clear cutting of the land in their territory. Here, the megaphone was installed for a period of four days. Because of its extended stay, people became very comfortable with this strange but familiar symbol. It was used as a means to amplify traditional fiddle music in the early evenings beside a campfire. On one afternoon during a media visit by the CBC television magazine program W5, some of the Elders in the camp who were not the official protest spokespersons chose to speak through the megaphone instead of talking directly into the cameras. For me, this was a subversive act, where the Elders spoke directly to the land that they were trying to defend. This oversized object that has the quality and beauty of a musical instrument had found its place and did its work.

I think that is where I would like to let my memory of that summer rest.

DA: What a remarkable journey. It was an extraordinary work of public art that extended far beyond the typical realm of performance art. It depended entirely on your ability to activate a variety of situations and to gain people's trust.

RB: As an artist it was a challenge taking this object into the everyday lives of Aboriginal people who experience diverse realities. I needed to go out into these communities, to find meaningful places to situate this conceptual artwork. I knew that the people would embrace the object and willingly turn their voices toward the land. This is nothing new; it is only the form that may have taken a bit of getting used to.

I asked an Oji-Cree friend what her response would be if a stranger came across one of our gatherings and asked her "What are they doing?" She said she would reply, "They are speaking to their Mother. Ayum-ee-aawach Oomama-mowan."

Refer to colour plates, pages 186–190.

This conversation was originally published in *Rebecca Belmore: Rising to the Occasion*, edited by Daina Augaitis and Kathleen Ritter, published by the Vancouver Art Gallery, and is reprinted here with permission.

Untitled

KATE MONTURE

I am only what I make myself
I can only think for myself
I am me.

Mohawk is what makes me
Strong, Independent,
Woman.
It flows through my blood
To my Heart.

Rights and Roots:

Addressing a New Wave of Colonialism

MELINA LABOUCAN-MASSIMO

Twenty years after the "Oka Crisis" we still see Indigenous Peoples on the front line protecting the sacredness of our traditional territories and the sacredness of Mother Earth. We still hear of communities all across Turtle Island trying to protect the little they have left as a result of dishonoured treaty processes and the disrespect the Canadian government has shown these sacred agreements. Agreements that our Ancestors made so we could live as equals in peace and in co-operation.

I remember learning about the "Oka Crisis" as a young person. I remember a sinking feeling when I realized the reality that exists for Indigenous Peoples in Canada. The injustices that have been perpetrated against us are all the more unsettling because Canada prides itself on being free and democratic. This has not been the case for Indigenous Peoples. It was when I first moved to the city from Lubicon territory that I began to really understand the discrepancies that existed between First Nations and urban centres, and I learned first hand that urban Canada was benefiting from our systematic oppression, the exploitation of our lands, and the extraction of our "natural resources."

The exploitation of oil, gas and logging has continued on the traditional territory of the Lubicon Cree over the past twenty years, generating 14 billion dollars in revenue for industry just since 1980. Yet to this day, my community goes without running water. In the 1980s the Lubicon received international attention for boycotting the 1988 Winter Olympics in Calgary. We erected roadblocks to prevent large-scale deforestation of our territory. We were successful in that the Japanese logging company Daishowa cancelled their contract with the government of Alberta. Yet despite these successes, oil and gas companies have continued to pillage the land without regard or remorse for its debilitating effects on wildlife or the impacts on the Lubicon people.

And now we are experiencing a new wave of colonialism, continuing the assault on our communities, our land, and our traditional and sustainable way of life. But this time, it is no longer just the government that disrespects Supreme Court rulings regarding our inherent Aboriginal Rights or the duty to consult prior to decision-making about resource extraction. It is now also multi-national corporations, eager to extract our "natural resources"—gifts that our people view as the flesh and blood of Mother Earth. Less than 100 years ago, our Mother was a healthy, living ecosystem—a beautiful majestic entity that lives and breathes just as we do. Now we are fighting against corporations and complicit governments who see our lands as a "resource" that can be torn apart, carved out, her roots ripped up to drain her life-blood. Human beings have become so disconnected from their Mother that they fail to see how truly fragile we are, how dependent we are upon her for our survival.

I was born in 1981, just after the first wave of "development" on Lubicon lands. Around that time, there were 19 stillborn babies out of 21 births over an 18-month period. This tragedy is a result of industrial contamination in and around Little Buffalo, in Lubicon territory. There have been many serious health problems in the community as a result of this contamination ranging from various forms of cancer, asthma, scarring skin rashes as well as tuberculosis affecting a third of the population.

And more development is on its way. Recently, the Alberta Utilities Commission ignored our sovereignty and our existing treaty rights by unilaterally approving the North Central Corridor (NCC) pipeline. This jumbo 42-inch-diameter natural gas pipeline is set to cross our traditional territory east to Ft. McMurray without the consent of our people. Not only will this TransCanada pipeline affect the First Nations of Alberta, but it will also extend northwest into British Columbia and the

Yukon, thus affecting many more nations as well as non-Native communities in its path.

Making matters worse, the pipeline is being built to feed tar sands extraction—the biggest and most destructive industrial project in human history. Since tar sands operations started, they have moved more earth than was moved for the Great Wall of China, the Suez Canal, the Great Pyramid of Cheops and the ten largest dams in the world combined. The targeted area of destruction will amount to the size of Florida or the country of England.

This raises the question: Where are all the people who live in this pristine boreal forest (one of the last in North America) going to go?

Each day the tar sands produce over one million barrels of oil. This is at the expense of four tons of mined earth and an average of three to five barrels of water used to make just one barrel of oil. If one million barrels of oil are produced a day that means they use at least three to five million barrels of water A DAY! To make a comparison, my family, who still does not have running water, use ONE barrel of water to drink and this can last five days to a week.

The energy used to produce the tar sands is equivalent to what it takes to heat over six million homes a day with natural gas. Some experts say we are set to run out of natural gas in ten years. How do these energy conglomerates propose to heat our homes in ten years when the known natural gas sources run out? Coal and nuclear energy is their hazardous solution.

Along with the huge water and energy consumption used by the tar sands there is also frightening amounts of toxic waste. For every barrel of oil there is 1.5 barrels of toxic biproduct produced. This toxic waste remains in holding places called "tailings ponds" that are so big they can be seen from space. Tailings ponds resemble lakes, currently spanning 130 square kilometres. Any wildlife that consumes or comes in contact with this contaminated water dies. This was seen recently in the Syncrude case where 1,606 ducks perished after landing in a tailings pond thinking it was a lake. These tailing ponds leech over 11 million litres into the Athabasca watershed every day—which raises levels of toxicity in the water and is causing elevated rates of rare forms of cancer in the area of Ft. Chipewyan (a Cree, Dene, Métis and non-Native community downstream from the tar sands). This sort of "energy development" is an insanely wasteful attempt to make Alberta a world energy power at the expense of almost a one-quarter of the province.

In the next 10 to 20 years, the exploitation of the tar sands will be one of the biggest issues and debates of how we, the human race, consume and produce energy. Working towards harnessing renewable energy and returning to our sustainable ways as Indigenous Peoples is of extreme importance if we are to live out our existence as stewards of the land, a duty given to us by the Creator. Now is the time to speak out and raise awareness for our inherent rights as Indigenous Peoples and protect the sacredness of our Mother Earth.

Oka made me acutely aware of the great lengths Indigenous Peoples have had to go to in order to make any sort of change in Canadian society. Oka encouraged me personally to be courageous and put myself on the front lines in order to protect our future and that of our children's generation. I stand up so that they will have a safe and healthy place to call home.

When I initially saw the masked warriors at Kanehsatà:ke and how the military came at them with gun fire, I was scared. As time wore on, I was enraged, but now I am inspired to be strong and un-flinching in the face of adverse conditions. This is especially true in a place like Alberta where people are willing to sacrifice their children's future by supporting the most expensive and energy intensive bottom-of-the-barrel crude oil, and the profit of big industry.

And now when we speak out, we are seen as troublemakers or "terrorists." The idea that we must agree to an imposed identity that many times contradicts the fundamental beliefs of our communities and cultures is a difficult reality many Indigenous people face. And when we choose not to perpetuate such an identity, we are looked upon as a threat. A threat that would not exists if our original treaties were respected.

The criminalization of Native Peoples who are in land struggles has to stop. Communities and individuals can no longer be terrorized for not giving into corporations and complicit governments. It is our responsibility to protect our homelands.

The "Oka Crisis" was a symbol—a symbol that we will no longer be silent while the land and Mother Earth continue to be pillaged and sold off for profit. A symbol that we must stand strong as one—mothers, fathers, sisters, brothers, Elders and young ones—we must choose to say no, no more. No more can you divide and conquer; no more will you instill fear in us. No more. We must choose to fight for the preservation of Mother Earth and a way of life that is sustainable for all.

And I for one am willing and ready to do so, and one day when I see the faces of those unborn I can say I fought for you. But if it wasn't for the women and men that stood up that day in Kanesatà:ke, I might not be here to learn from those brave ones who have come before me.

Hai hai.

-

The Seventh Generation

CLAYTON THOMAS-MULLER

One of the greatest turning points in my life was in the summer of 1990—the summer I realized how great our Indigenous nations are and, more importantly, when I realized our power as Indigenous nations. I remember being 12 years old and watching the news on TV. I remember witnessing the largest mobilization of the Canadian military since the Korean War against what looked like a group of people that could be my aunties, uncles and cousins.

Over the summer I watched along with the rest of the world the ridiculous absurdity of the Canadian government—a government stuck in the past trying to enforce racist and colonial ideologies that were just not acceptable any longer, that were never acceptable. I watch a group of Indigenous people stand up against the government and their security forces with nothing but their spirituality and hope. I watched the Grandmothers and warriors of the Mohawk nation defeat the Federal government of Canada.

From this moment something deep inside of me snapped. I quit trying to be Canadian. I just gave up. I knew from what I was watching that I was something else, something much more. That my roots to this land called Canada meant that I was born into struggle, born with responsibilities. I was Cree.

In my journey, I have confronted many challenges that have helped me come to the current understanding I have about our Indigenous struggle. I have seen how our nations' power was attacked by trying to separate our families most notably through the assimilation policy of Indian residential school.

Although I did not go to residential school, I was one of the first in my family that was integrated into Canada's public school system with no social supports to help Native children confront and over come racism in that system.

I have many fond memories of my family in the bush during the summer, picking berries watching the older boys and my Moo Shum (Grandfather) get fish from the nets. Watching my Koo Kum (Grandmother) cook bannock by our family's fire.

I have many memories of darkness in the city of Winnipeg, of our people living in the harshest of poverty. I can remember fighting my Auntie Lisa and Uncle Ovide for orange peels on Easter morning.

How did we get from such bounty to such pitiful sorrow and hunger?

Hundreds of years ago the Church and the State were inseparable, and Jesuit Priests in Black Robes came into our communities promising a solution to problems our communities faced as they confronted the violence of colonization, through embracing Christianity and changing the way we spoke with our Creator.

I know this played a part in the answer to my question.

Today, we are still confronting the violence of colonization. It has manifested in many forms that I don't care to list. One thing that is clear to me, however, is that there are still those that would enter our communities promising a quick fix to our socio-economic woes when the answer always has and continues to be sovereignty and self-determination over our lands and life.

I have observed in this time instead of Jesuit Priests in Black Robes we have corporate CEO's in Black Suits representing Toxic Waste, Timber, Mining and Energy Corporations. They come seducing our people with promises of a quick and easy solution to our poverty and sickness by entering into the industrialization game and changing our relations with the sacredness of Mother Earth, relations we've had since time immemorial.

One thing that is clear to me, is that in my life, the greatest riches I have seen have not been on 5th Avenue in New York City, nor have they been in the halls of Parliament or Congress. They were as a child with my Grandparents and my Mother reaping the riches of our loving Mother Earth.

Our greatest power as the peoples of Mother Earth is in maintaining our sacred responsibility to protect her and to speak for those animal and plant relations that cannot speak for themselves.

My human relatives, I write these words to encourage you to be strong and to continue to seek out justice in our struggle. Do not give in to the quick fix of money and political favors of the state or from the corporations that control these colonial governments, these institutions are inseparable. This can be best expressed through the recent transfer of trillions of dollars of public funds from governments of the world to the private sector to prop up a collapsing free market system.

We must continue to fight to protect the sacredness of our Mother Earth. We must remember that our sacred waters and land is forever and we must preserve their integrity to provide not just for us, but also for all life.

Today out of 1.8 million Aboriginal Peoples in Canada, 75% are under the age of 30, which means that we are in the midst of a profound generational shift of power. By 2016, one out of every four people in Canada's workforce will be a Native person. This represents a fantastic shift in economic power from the ruling class to a population that has been marginalised for some time. The shift of social, political and ecomomic power will be recieved by a highly educated and sophisticated population of Indigenous Peoples—a group has more capacity then any other generation has had before us in terms of colonial analysis and education. Many of our Indigenous prophecies speak about this time we live in, including the prophecy of my own people that speaks about a Seventh Generation that will be born free of the colonial mind. Children born in the Seventh Generation are born ready to step up and assert their right to community self-determination. Many of these Seventh Generation warriors were children when Oka happened, many of us are and will continue to hold the front line in our collective struggle in the place of our Aunties and Uncles. We have many tools to use since Oka that will help us in our rapid ascent to power in this country called Canada.

I want you to know, my relatives, that I will stand with you in this struggle, you are not alone, I will be there if you call. And to those that would sacrifice vast swaths of this land, water, air and our peoples just so that a privileged few can thrive economically know this:

We will never stop, not for one second, so you better be ready.

"We're Protecting, not Protesting":

JACOB OSTAMAN (KITCHENUHMAYKOOSIB INNINUWAUG) IN CONVERSATION WITH LEANNE SIMPSON

In early 2006, members of the community of Kitchenuhmaykoosib Inninuwug (KI), formerly known as Big Trout Lake, found a drilling crew operating on their lands without their prior consent or knowledge. The drilling crew was prospecting for platinum. Signatories of Treaty 9, the community placed a full moratorium on development within their territory until land issues were dealt with under the terms of the treaty, and Canada fully respected their land rights and responsibilities. Over the next three years (and continuing at the time this book was going to press), the community mobilized to protect their lands from Platinex, a platinum prospecting company. In attempting to protect their lands from irresponsible development, the Chief, four Band Council members, and one community member were incarcerated in the spring of 2008. They became known as the "KI 6." They were later released after a successful appeal of their sentences. To date, the land issue has not been resolved.

LEANNE: Can you introduce yourself and tell us a bit about your responsibilities to your community and to your nation?

JACOB: My name is Jacob Ostaman and I am the Director for Lands and Environment for Kitchenuhmaykoosib Inninuwaug (KI). My responsibility is to work with the lands and environmental issues in the traditional territory of KI. We are dealing with lands, resources and environmental issues. KI is located 600 kilometres north of Thunder Bay, Ontario, and has a population of 1,300 people. It is an Oji-Cree community.

LEANNE: Did your people sign a treaty?

JACOB: For KI, treaty represents a very important symbol for our ongoing relationship with the natural world. Our understanding of the treaty also includes the spirit and intent of the treaty which is being based upon as a foundation for our relationship with the white people. The treaty making with the KI is very sacred as it referenced the sun, river and grass, which further solidified an ongoing relationship with the white people and the natural world. The treaty also gave KI a way to live the "treaty way of life" or have treaty brought into KI Bimaadiziwin.

LEANNE: What is the current conflict going on in your territory?

JACOB: The issue for us is platinum exploration. Platinex was issued permits and claims to our land by the province of Ontario without our free, prior and informed consent. We said no, that they could not have access to our lands, and they took us to court and sued us for 10 billion dollars. We figure that it would take over 220 years using every cent that comes into the community to pay this off. They filed injunctions against us and contempt charges were filed and we were brought into court, and five council and one community member were sentenced to six months in jail for refusing to vacate the site. An appeal in May of 2008 released our people. The appeal court ruled that the sentencing was too harsh and that the most Indigenous Peoples should get in this sort of resistance was two days in jail and a $1,000 fine.

LEANNE: What was the impact in your community of having your Chief and Council all in jail?

JACOB: I was responsible as a KI spokesperson when our KI leaders were jailed. The impact of it all was that KI community and the people struggled in every facet of our daily lives due to severance of KI government administration and operation because of the court decision to jail our leaders. We were able to access our Chief and Council members because they were still our leaders even though they were imprisoned. They still made important decisions for all of our community issues, and our KI government was much alive then.

LEANNE: Why is it important to protect your land from industrial development?

JACOB: We believe from our Indigenous perspective that protecting our lands from the irresponsible development is important because this type of development is against the laws of Creation. Including, for example, where the lake is situated, and the relationship that it has to the smaller lakes, in this case a lake called Nemeigusabins Lake, which connects with the river system. The watershed is all connected, and we are concerned particularly about the Nuhmaykoos, the lake trout. The lake, the lake trout and the people are all connected and our identity as distinct human beings is tied to the lake and the trout.

We are following the first law as instructed by the Creator, Keeshaymanitou, to uphold our responsibilities to protect our lands. The first law must be respected by all, including all human beings, so that the earth and the things on or in the earth live in harmony according to the original creation of the earth.

An example would be our protection of our Kitchenuhmaykoosib (lake or headwater) and its special relationship with the smaller lakes and the river systems that are connect it. We refer to this as the KI Landscape, which is alive much like an organism or a spider. This is what we are trying to protect, this landscape. We have a special relationship with the Creator, the lake, and the lake trout that provides spiritual foundation. If we lose our lake the spiritual relationship will be gone forever.

LEANNE: When you came to my class to talk to the students, you told us your Creation Story. It was a beautiful and powerful story of the Spider. Can you explain just a bit of that for us here, so we can understand how your people relate to the land?

JACOB: The spider legend is our Creation Story where it tells us the first man and woman came to the lands that we presently occupy. The man and woman came to this earth as a result of spider's help of lowering them down from other dimension of life by using webbed container and cord. Once on earth, the man and woman began to multiply. The Elders interpretation with this spider legend is that of the woman having a labour: with webbed container to signify as the woman's womb and the cord to signify as an umbilical cord that is attached from the woman to the newborn baby. The Elders said that a woman made this interpretation many thousands of years ago to tell us that how we arrived to this world.

LEANNE: Chi'miigwech! How did your Ancestors live up to their responsibilities to protect KI's lands?

JACOB: Our KI Ancestors had a set of responsibilities that included leadership, protection, sustenance, learning, healing and spirituality. These responsibilities included special relationships with respect to KI law, language and land. All of these are interwoven as an overall responsibility as provided by Kichi Manitou to our KI people.

Back in the 1940s Jeremiah Sainnawap was also incarcerated by the province for breaking the harvesting rules put in place by the MNR. He taught us that we need to continue to use our resources such as beaver and other animals for our existence. Those are our rights and we have the responsibility to uphold what our Keeshaymanitou gave us.

LEANNE: In one sense, this book is about honouring all of those people that have stood up and protected their lands, in the past and in the coming generations. What would you say to Indigenous Peoples that are engaged in conflicts and mobilizations like KI?

JACOB: It is important to understand that we are *protecting* our lands, not *protesting*. We simply go to the sites, in our case Platinex site, to have in mind that we are protecting our lands and it is one of our important responsibilities that we must do.

LEANNE: What kinds of support have you received in solidarity with your nation?

JACOB: We have received support from different nations across North America including labour groups, church groups, environmentalists, social groups and other Indigenous supporters.

LEANNE: According to your own diplomatic and political traditions, how do you envision interacting with the Canadian state?

JACOB: We are looking to our traditions as part of restructuring our relationships with the land and also Canada. Including coming up with a new form of government which we call Aonuhshowanowak, meaning a place where you make decisions for your people. An example of this would be a community assembly. Hopefully in the community assembly we will find cultural ways to work with Canada. Aonuhshowanowuk also involves home visits, consulting women, Elders, youth and the clan heads staying until the decision gets made.

LEANNE: So, you're really talking here about strengthening your own Anishinaabek form of governance, with Aonuhshowanowak, the Clan system, consensus-style decision making, taking care of each other and consulting each other? It strikes me in hearing you talk that because your community has maintained a close relationship with the land, and because your Chief and Council govern using Aonuhshowanowak, that your community was able to stay strong and united during this conflict. Is that true?

JACOB: This is very true. Although we have an Indian Act system at play there is also very much of Aonuhshowanowuk at play too!

LEANNE: How has Canada responded to your actions?

JACOB: Canada has been silent.

LEANNE: Miigwech, Jacob.

Protecting Our Lands:

PAULA SHERMAN (ARDOCH ALGONQUIN FIRST NATION) IN CONVERSATION WITH LEANNE SIMPSON

In the winter of 2006–2007, Frotenac Ventures, a mineral exploration company, began exploring for uranium on the traditional territory of the Ardoch Algonquin First Nation, without their prior consent or knowledge. The community of Ardoch began asking questions in November of 2006. When no answers came over the winter, and no consultations occurred in the spring, the Ardoch community wrote to Frontenac Ventures asking them to remove their personel and equipment from their territory adjacent to the Robertsville Mine Site. Over the summer of 2007, people from the community erected a camp on the Robertsville Site to prevent access to Algonquin Land and protect their homeland. Community members Robert Lovelace and Paula Sherman were charged and Robert was sentenced to six months in jail on February 15, 2008, for refusing to obey a court ordered injunction to vacate the site and allow Frontenac Ventures access. They also received fines of $40,000. Robert was released from prison after winning an appeal on May 28, 2008, having served 104 days of the six months sentence for peacefully protecting the land and water from uranium contamination. The fines were also stayed as part of that process. At the time of writing, the land issue has still not been resolved. Even though the province has a fiduciary responsibility to consult with Ardoch Algonquin people about this project, they have consistently failed to do so.

LEANNE: Can you introduce yourself and tell us a bit about your responsibilities to your community and to your nation?

PAULA: I am Paula Sherman and I am a Family Head on Ka-pishkawandemin Family Head Council for Ardoch Algonquin First Nation. Ka-pishkawandemin Family Head's Council is the traditional governance structure of the community based upon consensus decision-making. The traditional territory of Ardoch Algonquin people is the Tay, Rideau, and Mississippi watersheds, which are tributaries of the Kiji Síbí (Ottawa River), which is the homeland of the Algonquin Nation. My responsibility as a member of the council is to up hold the Guiding Principles under which the council operates. These Guiding Principles are based upon Omamíwínini (Algonquin) Law which is still in place and in effect in the Kiji Síbí. The Omamíwínini homeland has never been surrendered or sold to the Crown and is still currently under Omamíwínini title and jurisdiction. It was our responsibility under Omamíwínini law to protect the land from irresponsible development.

LEANNE: How are your currently living up to those responsibilities as an Anishinaabekwe and as a Family Head Council?

PAULA: The current conflict we are facing in our homeland is uranium exploration. This exploration project was approved and permits issued by the province without prior consultation and informed consent. In June of 2007 we moved onto the Robertsville Site and set up a camp to prohibit access to the site by Frontenac Ventures Corporation (FVC) who planned to conduct deep drilling to obtain core samples. They took us to court and sued us for 77 million, and filed injunctions against us to have us removed from the site. We did not leave, so we were charged with civil contempt for refusing to obey and leave the site. Our lead negotiator was incarcerated and fined $25,000 while our leader was fined $15,000. An appeal in May of 2008 released our negotiator and suspended the fines. The appeal court ruled that the sentencing was too harsh and that the most Indigenous Peoples should get in this sort of resistance was two days in jail and a $1,000 fine.

LEANNE: Why is it important to protect your land from industrial development for the coming generations?

LEANNE: We need to protect our land from this development because it has the potential to impact the watershed and ground and surface water as well as the habitat of the animals that we depend upon. As well, the Mississippi contains Manoomin (wild rice) that would be destroyed from uranium contamination. We could not allow this to happen, as the Manoomin is tied to our identity as Omamíwínini people. Uranium exploration and mining was banned under Algonquin law and it is our responsibility to uphold that law.

It is important to protect our territories for a few reasons. First of all, we have a responsibility to do so under Omamíwínini law. Our identity as human beings is tied into our responsibilities and we are told by Elders such as William Commanda that this is the only place that we can call home—the Kiji Síbí. We must maintain our responsibilities in the Kiji Síbí as is mandated under the oiginal instructions that we received at the time of creation. We were given the original instructions to guide our interactions with the Natural world and we maintain them through our social and political structures within the community and the Omamíwínini Nation.

Secondly, it is also important to protect the lands and waterscapes in our homeland so that our children and grandchildren have this place to call their home as well. They also have no other place to call their home and it is up to us to protect that legacy for them and the future generations. As well, the spiritual beings in the Natural World also depend on us to maintain those original instructions and to follow the protocols and mechanisms that exist for relating to the land and waterscapes in positive ways that promote a healthy and sustainable ecosystem.

LEANNE: How have you been inspired by Indigenous Peoples in the past in terms of your living up to your responsibilities?

PAULA: On a personal level I was inspired by Harold Perry who resisted the commercial harvesting of Manoomin in the 1980s at Ardoch. He taught us that it is important to stand up and to defend the land no matter what the consequences. I have also been inspired by the direct resistance such as that at Wooded Knee, Kanehsatà:ke, and Burnt Church. There are a lot of examples of resistance that are known only by a few people that also provide guidance for how to perceive development. For example, William Commanda, the preeminent Omamíwínini Elder, shared with me that we have no other place to call our home other than the Kiji Síbí and that when we pass away our spirits go back to our homeland. If we have signed deals to extinguish our autonomy or jurisdiction through a land claims process or mineral exploration and mining, our spirits will have no place to go. This was very significant for me and was a powerful motivation to resist uranium exploration as well as participation in the claims process that is now underway. Teachings about the spiritual nature of our relationships and responsibilities within the Kiji Síbí are significant and profound mechanisms to resist.

LEANNE: What do you think the impact of the Kanien'kehaka (Mohawk) mobilization at Kanehsatà:ke resurgence at was on Indigenous Peoples?

PAULA: I think it was large and that it reminded people that we can stand up and resist bad policies and protect the land. I remember when it happened we were thinking back about the rice war that happened when the province wanted to sell commercial harvesting rights to Manoomin in the Mississippi in Ardoch. It was a wake-up call really to remember what we had accomplished as a community and to put in place practices and protocols for teaching our own people about relating to the land in positive ways that promoted a healthy and vital community.

We have learned a lot as Indigenous Peoples about resistance from the Haudenosaunee. It was the determination to protect their homeland from irresponsible development that inspired a lot of us to do the same. This is particularly significant for me considering that we have been historically portrayed as the enemies of the Mohawk people. Growing up, I heard stories about Mohawk people that were really negative because they were based upon western constructions of history. The historic record portrayed Mohawk people as demons who infested the banks of the rivers in North America. I came to understand that these images and perceptions were constructed by the French and were embedded in western constructions of history even though very little of it was true. In the same way that Haudenosaunee people inspired me to stand up for the land, the Haudenosaunee people with whom I became friends at Trent encouraged me to look beyond the historical record, to explore the true philosophical nature of

Algonquin-Mohawk relations. To me the act of defining for ourselves as Indigenous Peoples what our relationships were like within our homelands is a significant act of resistance.

LEANNE: That's a good point. The Anishinaabek and the Haudenosaunee both have responsibilities in caring for Our Dish, our shared lands. Do you see impact from the Kanien'kehaka blockades on the Canadian state?

PAULA: It caused the federal government to appoint the Royal Commission on Aboriginal Peoples. This also led the government to develop policies about dealing with Indigenous Peoples in a protest context.

LEANNE: How has Canada responded to your actions?

Paula: Canada refused to intercede or get involved because it was uranium exploration and not an actual mine. Indian Affairs told us to join the land claim process to have the issue discussed there, but we refused to do that because the claims process is corrupt and will extinguish our title and jurisdiction in the Kiji Síbí. The claims process has now endorsed the idea of uranium exploration and made a deal with the mineral exploration company to allow drilling to happen. We are still opposed to it and remain outside the claims process.

LEANNE: What kinds of support have you received in solidarity with your nation?

PAULA: We've received support from various different Indigenous nations around the world as well as many settlers or private landowners. All of the surrounding towns in eastern Ontario passed motions calling for a provincial moratorium on uranium exploration and mining.

We particularly developed an alliance with KI, who was also dealing with an issue of irresponsible development and mineral exploration. We both said no to this, but the province has not listened. We continue to work together to resist these projects.

LEANNE: According to your own diplomatic and political traditions, how do you envisioning interacting with the Canadian state?

PAULA: We would envision that it would be a nation-to-nation relationship in which people residing in our homeland would live under Omamíwínini law and would share in the responsibilities to restore the Natural World to a healthy state. In this relationship with Canada our autonomy and jurisdiction would be respected. The private land owners who supported us during our efforts to protect the land at Robertsville called themselves settlers in respect for the fact that they were living on Algonquin land and because they understood the nature of our relationships within our homeland and they wanted to also adopt this way of living and of interacting with the lands and waterscapes within the Kiji Síbí. We welcome this change in thinking and believe that they are making positive steps toward a balanced relationship between themselves and us as the original peoples of this homeland. There is still a lot of work to do in that respect, but this is at least willingness on the part of some of our neighbours.

LEANNE: Chi'miigwech for sharing your thoughts with me.

Echoes of Impermanence:

Kanehsatà:ke, Bimaadiziiwin and the Idea of Canada

DAMIEN LEE

In the summer of 1990, Kanien'kehaka (Mohawks) at Kanehsatà:ke transformed our world forever when they challenged Canada's claims to sovereignty over their land. The challenge was an expression of continued multi-generational Haudenosaunee contention with the state and its other political entities. Imbued in this mobilization was the ethic of transformation, shooting across Turtle Island and through time, echoing through all our relations. The echo was heard across Anishinabek territory, and as it travelled, it transformed and inspired. Like our Ancestors, we too believe in impermanence and in transforming our relationship with the Canadian state. Like the Onkwehonwe, we are empowered by our inherent spirit-beings to contend with the metaphorical golf courses that attempt to infringe on our territories, souls and minds. As neighbours and treaty partners with the Haudenosaunee Confederacy, the power of the echoes expressed at Kanehsatà:ke rippled across our land, and so what follows is in celebration of my Onkwehonwe sisters and brothers and their mobilization at Kanehsatà:ke.

From the perspective of the Anishinabek people, relationships are cyclical and are of the utmost importance. Our teachings tell us of an implicate order full of relationships between human societies and spiritual beings that have the power to transform our world.[1] Because of our teachings we have not acquiesced to the power of colonialism—we have resisted to ensure our identity survives the violence perpetuated by the Canadian state. We continue to survive as Anishinabek because of the power of the implicate order and its actors that continue to live and breath in our communities. Our relationships to these actors and their power continue to support our contention with the Canadian state. Even though some of our communities are more visibly colonized than others, spiritual beings of the implicate order are nonetheless alive, if only operating underground to ensure their own survival. As Anishinabek people, we continue to resist the state's violence by basing our actions in our inherent ways of being.

Our identity as Anishinabek predates the Canadian state, and so too do our intellectual traditions. Both are *sui generis*. Of primary importance to our identity as Anishinabek is our oral/aural tradition, which is used to teach culturally inherent political, economic, spiritual and cultural values to new generations. The telling and retelling of inherent sacred stories, called Aadizookaanag, disseminate our teachings. They inform all aspects of Anishinabek life because they "can be communicated in a way that reveals deeper principles of order and disorder."[2] In this sense these teachings are perpetually current to Anishinabek lives. Our Grandmothers and Grandfathers retell stories that inform new generations about Anishinabek relationships within the implicate order. These stories and relationships form the basis of our inherent forms of thought and our life context, and are embodied in our language and names for people, plants, animals and the ecology of our world. Our identity evolves and remains current because our narratives, called Dibaajimowinan, are told to describe an ever-changing reality.[3] But to call these teachings "stories" is to devalue them. Eurocentric thinkers have labelled our teachings as stories or myths because they do not resemble their own eurocentric worldviews or versions of creation stories. A more proper English term for our teachings is "echoes," whereas the proper Anishinabemowin terms are Aadizookaanag and Dibaajimowinan.[4] Our teachings are memories that echo through the generations, transmitting accumulated wisdom, reinforcing protocols and traditions, and renewing the bonds between individuals, families and Ancestors.

We echo when we speak Anishinabemowin, when we tell our inherent stories and when we call people and the world by their real names. The Onkwehonwe mobilization at Kanehsatà:ke in 1990 is echo-ing through time and space as Dibaajimowinan. These echoes link the past with the present, and the present with the future because they reso-nate through our landscapes and within the implicate order, uniting us in a common resistance, in a common world. Our Onkwehonwe sis-ters and brothers have inspired us in our own resurgence toward a re-empowered Anishinabek Nation; they continue to do so because they contended with our mutual oppressor with composure and centered their actions within inherent ways of being Onkwehonwe. We are all Onkwehonwe when we live like this. The echoes radiating like concen-tric rings through time and space, with the Onkwehonwe mobilization at Kanehsatà:ke in the centre, give us an intellectual filter for change that enables us to "evaluate meaning in truth" through our own per-spective.[5] What we learned at Kanehsatà:ke about our oppressor and about our vitality as Onkwehonwe is now being passed down through our lessons, traditions and bonds, reinforcing our oral/aural tradition and renewing our identity as Anishinabek. These echoes inform us how to live our lives and to address challenges without losing our identity; they are living memories of how to live the good life, or bimaadiziiwin.

Bimaadiziiwin is a metaphor and a performance, as it is an intel-lectual tradition and a political principle. The metaphor is performed in family life, where individuals within Anishinabek communities are expected to live balanced lives in order to maintain good relation-ships with their broader families, which in turn form the basis for healing communities and then the Nation.[6] Prior to the imposition of the *Indian Act* and its Chief and Council governance system, our Anishinabek Ancestors led their communities with a political system that was imbued with bimaadiziiwin because it was built on ties be-tween clans and families that were ultimately guided by good rela-tionships within the implicate order. Bimaadiziiwin is a performance (or a verb), and as such it perpetually creates possibilities for humans to improve their relationships among human societies and within the implicate order. In other words, in living bimaadiziiwin, one refuses to view life as permanent, as it provides humans with the space and power to transform any existing inharmonious realities into new reali-ties that are balanced within the implicate order. Thus, bimaadiziiwin is an inherent imperative to Anishinabek resistance and contention.

Bimaadiziiwin is also transformative. Living life guided in bimaadiziiwin dismantles the idea that oppressor-oppressed relationships are static, as it allows for the possibility for transformation. As a concept it is expressed in echoes that we hear and feel as Anishinabek. Youngblood-Henderson captures this inherent cultural concept when he states that "[t]o see ... things as permanent is to be confused about everything."[7] The combination of bimaadiziiwin (perpetual transformation) and impermanence are two sides of the same intellectual tradition that empowers Anishinabek and other Indigenous nations to vision and revision new futures where the imbalances caused by Canadian state oppression are corrected, leading to more harmonious relationships within the implicate order. In this sense, bimaadiziiwin is visioning and dreaming for renewal. These concepts enable us as Anishinabek to transform our world: they give us the space to dream a new reality where our traditions and identities can be expressed fully without fear of oppression, racism or violence. Within such safe spaces we are able to interact with beings of the implicate order. These beings provide the guidance and energy for us to contend with state oppression as we seek to balance the relationship.[8] The space or culturescape provided by bimaadiziiwin and impermanence, and the support given to us by beings of the implicate order in such a space, form the foundation for Anishinabek contention with the state because they are the roots of the ethic of transformation inherent to our culture.

In Anishinabek culture a key being of the implicate order that embodies transformative power is Nanabozho. Nanabozho is the being that exists between the human world and Gitchi Manitou,[9] and everything about him is transformative. Other Indigenous Nations recognize a similar being, which from a pan-Aboriginal point of view has been called the "Trickster."[10] For the Anishinabek, Nanabozho is the original man who walked the Earth; his first name was "Anishinabe" after he was nameless for some time.[11] He shows us that everything is impermanent, that everything can transform. But Nanabozho is not just a passive player in the implicate order who is affected by change, he is the very being responsible for transformations and for helping humans.[12] Nanabozho's power to transform reality is expressed to us through echoes, our Aadizookaanag. We are told that he is able to transform into different animals to transcend challenging situations, thereby showing us we have the power to transform our world too, because we are descendants of Nanabozho and thus share his power inherently. Changing into different animals is a metaphor for transforming our perspectives and ourselves to contend with situations that challenge our well-being, or to address challenges in order to help ourselves and our people.[13] For example, when Nanabozho was a baby he turned himself into a white rabbit in order to escape from under a bowl that his grandmother placed over him for protection while she grieved the loss of her daughter.[14] After his grandmother had accidentally forgotten about him, he changed his form from a trapped human into a rabbit that was able to transcend the confines of the bowl. We too can transcend our perceived confines.

Adapting this to a contemporary context, we see that changing how we perceive a problem and transforming ourselves in order to address a situation that threatens our well-being, are liberatory and empowering actions. We can change ourselves, and/or our community can play a role in changing who we are as a result of the ebbs and flows that shape us as we participate in our relationships with each other. Ultimately, Nanabozho's transformative spirit vitalizes our resistance and resurgence with Canada because he empowers us to perceive our current struggle with the state as impermanent, thereby enabling us to imagine new realities of dignified co-existence. As Henderson writes:

> The [Nanabozho] stories unravel the forces of transformation. They generate terrestrial consciousnesses in which everything is eating everything else; an ecology where all living things come into magnificent bloom and then, almost immediately, rot away [impermanence]. The stories allow people to understand what it might be like to think or behave as someone or something that they are not [e.g., empowered Nations], assisting them to understand different perspectives [filters]. ...By renouncing appearance as contrived reality, [Nanabozho] stories reveal the potential to recreate knowledge and not submit to conventional appearances [i.e., of being oppressed].[15]

Onkwehonwe in 1990 did just this. They continued to use the power within the implicate order to expose the impermanence imbued within the idea of Canada, reminding all Onkwehonwe of the presumed nature of Canadian sovereignty. They renounced the appearance of the state's sovereignty over Haudenosaunee territory as a contrived reality, almost funny in its claim were it not for the late night beatings, rocks thrown at Elders and burning effigies that accompanied the contention on the Canadian side.

But Nanabozho teaches us through echoes that have an element of humour, and so humour is important to our resurgence. We learn through his folly, and the process elicits humour. He sometimes plays jokes, which is why the term "Trickster" is sometimes applied to him. Nanabozho's jokes are important to the Anishinabek because they help us subvert the balance of power. Jokes and tricks are played by Nanabozho to transform situations—this type of transformation enables us to re-perceive allegedly "normal" or permanent patterns as arbitrary.[16] King informs us about the power of Nanabozho's humour when he writes that humour allows us to imagine "an entirely new way of structuring [society]."[17] The humour found in Nanabozho's echoes enables us to stop taking the state for granted, because it allows us to appreciate the humour in the state's ludicrous claim to sovereignty over the Anishinabek, Haudenosaunee and all other Onkwehonwe Nations on Turtle Island.

The humour generated by Nanabozho has contemporary importance too, as his echoes enable us to transform our world and to cope with stressful situations. Humour enables us to distract our minds and to get through tough times.[18] Babcock writes that "[c]omedy may be a spiritual shock therapy which breaks up the patterns of thought and rationality that hold us in bondage and in which the given established order of things is deformed, reformed and reformulated; a playful speculation on what was, is, or might be...," while Deloria writes that "[t]he more desperate the problem, the more humour is directed to describe it."[19] The attempt of a municipality to build a golf course on inherent Haudenosaunee land is ludicrous—the humour elicited by this type of misinformed political action is the enabler that allows all Onkwehonwe to see the impermanence in Canada's claim to sovereignty over our Nations. Our echoes about Nanabozho, which are often funny, empower us to re-perceive the world through playful echoes that do not incite alarmism while nonetheless empowering us to see a new reality. This is imperative to re-imagining our relationship with the Canadian state, as we cannot take the current oppressive form of the relationship for granted, and our Aadizookaanag give us the tools to dream and achieve alternate realities. When we share our echoes and when we see the humour imbued in our resistance and resurgence we transform ourselves and the world just as Nanabozho transformed himself to transcend the bowl.

As Anishinabek, we are seeking to transform our current relationship with Canada. Like our Onkwehonwe sisters and brothers, we are not seeking to defeat Canada, but instead we seek to revitalize and live in the spirit of co-existence embodied in our treaties and worldview.[20] Currently, Canada does not uphold its treaty responsibilities, opting instead to negate Onkwehonwe self-determination and to oppress Indigenous Nations with the *Indian Act*. Transformation for us means co-existing with dignity, not winning or losing. It also means re-establishing balance through healthy relationships with Canadians. Pushed underground in many Anishinabek communities, inherent leaders and teachings have had to transform appearances in order to protect inherent ceremonies and systems.[21] To exist underground in this sense is to exist in a *contending state* and ultimately ensures that inherent traditions are surviving the onslaught of violence perpetuated by the Canadian state. The mobilization at Kanehsatà:ke in 1990 showed us that though some of our inherent leaders or teachings have been pushed underground to survive, they are still alive and ready to contend for a rebalancing of relationships within the implicate order. As the state pushes harder to assimilate Onkwehonwe, our traditions still seek to balance the relationship because this is what was agreed upon in our treaties and is ultimately the inherent imperative of our worldviews.

Our resistance has enabled us to exist as Anishinabek and Haudenosaunee today. As the Canadian state continually attempts to assimilate Onkwehonwe in order to secure resources in our inherent lands, we continue to resist in various ways. By basing our resistance in inherent teachings such as bimaadiziiwin and by performing our relationships with the implicate order, we continue to empower ourselves to contend with the state as Onkwehonwe. Our view of reality does not allow for us to be colonized forever simply because we are being oppressed right now. The Onkwehonwe warriors at Kanehsatà:ke, from the communities of Kanehsatà:ke, Kahnawà:ke and Akwesasne— women, men and children—exposed the impermanence of the idea of Canada in 1990; we are more empowered today because of this. The strength of their spirit and that of their spirit-helpers has inspired us. Basing our resistance and resurgence in our inherent relationships and echoes within the implicate order, we will continue to transform ourselves and the Canadian state until we can exercise our treaties fully and in the spirit of dignified co-existence, as intended by our Ancestors.

1 The implicate order is Creation. It is "constructed on the spiraling comprehension of kinship and the implicit interpretation of the [Earth]." Comprehension of the implicate order is built into developing good relations with all of Creation, and results in codifying Indigenous inherent laws and relationships. See James (sakej) Youngblood Henderson (2006), *First Nations Jurisprudence and Aboriginal Rights: Defining a Just Society*, Saskatoon: Native Law Centre, University of Saskatchewan, pp. 122, 144–150.

2 Leanne Simpson (1999), *The Construction Of Traditional Ecological Knowledge: Issues, Implications And Insights*, unpublished doctoral thesis, Winnipeg: University of Manitoba, p. 37; John Borrows (2002), *Recovering Canada, The Resurgence of Indigenous Law*, Toronto: University of Toronto Press, p. 13.

3 More broadly, Dibaajimowinan are personal narratives, histories, observations, experiences. See Simpson, p. 37. In 2009 "new" Anishinabemowin words were recognized by Anishinabek Elders in the "Ojibwe Vocabulary Project." The Project seeks to reinvigorate and support Anishinabemowin in the face of the "language crisis." See Minnesota Humanities Centre, AANIIN EKIDONG—"HOW DO YOU SAY...." retrieved 10 August 2009 from <www.minnesotahumanities.org/resources/aaniin>.

4 McLeod informs that "Old voices [teachings] echo; the ancient poetic memory of our Ancestors finds home in our individual lives and allows us to reshape our experience so that we can interpret the world we find ourselves in." See Neal McLeod (2007), *Cree Narrative Memory*, Saskatoon: Purich Publishing, p. 11.

5 James (sakej) Youngblood Henderson (2006), p. 158.

6 The concept of performance is key to Indigenous nations in Canada generally. Being able to perform instead of "be" culture enables Indigenous people to be in flux with a changing world. It avoids permanence, which Youngblood-Henderson identifies as a Eurocentric view of the universe. Engaging with a changing world enables Indigenous people to establish and maintain a relationship with the implicate order, which creates harmony. Fluidity is achieved through performing one's culture instead of being one's culture. See Henderson (2006), pp. 153, 164–5.

7 James (sakej) Youngblood Henderson (2006), p. 155.

8 Henderson states that "[b]ecause of the embodied spirits [in the implicate order], life forms are always capable of overcoming all the conditions or determinations of their existence." See James (sakej) Youngblood Henderson (2006), p. 153.

9 The Great Mystery.

10 In this article I use Nanabozho to describe the transformative power that is common to other Nations' "Tricksters." This does not imply a pan-Aboriginal perspective, but rather I wish to prioritize Anishinabek traditions without using the term "Trickster" throughout the paper. It should also be noted that not all the traits of Nanabozho can be transposed to similar beings of other Nations. The "Tricksters" of other Nations include Raven, Glooscap, Coyote, Crow, Badger, Old Man and Elder Brother. See James (sakej) Youngblood Henderson (2006), p. 161.

11 Edward Benton-Benai (1988), *The Mishomis Book*, Hayward: Indian Country Communications Inc., pp. 3–4, 19, 31.

12 Joe McLellan and Matrine McLellan (2000), *Nanabosho Grants a Wish*, Winnipeg: Pemmican Publications, p. 7.

13 For example, Nanabozho transformed himself into a rabbit in order to steal fire from a medicine man in the east. He brought the fire back to his Nokomis and all humans thereafter had fire to keep themselves warm and healthy. See Joseph McLellan (1989), *Nanabosho Steals Fire*, Winnipeg: Pemmican Publications, pp. 5–12.

14 This story is recounted in Joseph McLellan (1989), *The Birth of Nanabosho*, Winnipeg: Pemmican Publications.

15 Henderson (2006), p. 162.

16 Mary Douglas writes that "the successful joke imagines the subversion of something formal and organized (a control) by something informal and energetic (that which is controlled) so that the balance of power is changed." See Allan Ryan (1999), *The Trickster Shift: Humour and Irony in Contemporary Native Art*, Vancouver: University of British Columbia Press, p. 5.

17 Arden King, quoted in Ryan (1999), p. 11.

18 Barry Lopez, quoted in Borrows, states that "sometimes a person needs a story more than food to stay alive." This applies here as often echoes about Nanabozho are funny. See Borrows, (2002), p. 13.

19 Barbara Babcock quoted in Ryan, p. 11; Vine Deloria, Jr., quoted in Ryan, p. 181.

20 Our treaties have always sought to promote and maintain peace, even before colonization. For example, the Anishinabek have a treaty with the Haudenosaunee called Gdoo-naaganinaa (Our Dish), a treaty that promotes peaceful co-existence by recognizing a shared territory in southern Ontario. See Leanne Simpson (2009), "Looking after Gdoo-naaganinaa: precolonial Nishnaabeg diplomatic and treaty relationships," *Wicazo Sa Review*, 23 (2), p. 29.

21 This situation of inherent leaders and teachings being pushed underground is similar to how the people who performed the Potlatch ceremony in what is now British Columbia had to change how the ceremony was performed in order to avoid being arrested and charged with a crime under the *Indian Act* in the first half of the twentieth century. See George Manuel and Michael Posluns (1974), *The Fourth World: An Indian Reality*, Don Mills: Collier-MacMillan Canada Ltd., pp. 78–9.

CÎHCAM

NEAL MCLEOD

cîhcam, mother of Gabriel
cîhcam daughter of *masâskâpaw*
"toes touching the bottom of the water"
my uncle Burton Vandall told me
water never leaving the sight of sky
cîhcam niece of *atâhk-akohp*
Star Blanket, one of the chiefs
of the *wâskahikan-iyiniwak*, House People

cîhcam, her body was our blanket
gave us life and language
brought stars from the sky
brought our souls from deep oceans
to the water of our birth
cîhcam was *mosôm*'s Gabriel's mother
cîhcam was grandmother to us all

there is a book written
blue binding and loose stiching
about her uncle *atâhk-akohp*
the northern Starblanket
from around Prince Albert
maps of kinship

connecting lines
name her as "unknown daughter"
but we know her as *kôhkom cîhcam*

cîhcam did not take Treaty
êkâ ê-âkimiht, "not counted"
not counted by Treaty

some of our relatives lived by *waskisiw*
hunting ground
place of rest in the world
lived in bush
trademarked now as a park

Grey Owl chased out Indians
to save the Beaver
movie-reel Indians
chase Real Indians
from folds of lakes
and curves of bush
land becomes heavy
with new words
old stories become distant
quiet whispers in tired mouths
new names fill the trees
game laws cut trap lines
iron tracks pass over
hunter's sleep

wind across the body
dries my cracking limbs
heavy like trees
can no longer trace the stars
nor bring the water to the sky
old names become cold whispers
our mouths
can no longer speak
old name memories

cîhcam, her words and stories
raise the earth through her lips
ancient poetic pathways
under her kitchen table
thrown blanket over
put rocks on skillet floor
improvised ceremony

cîhcam gave back air to lungs
sun back to sky
bring sanctuary of stories
and thick Cree poems
she is our blanket
of stars, takes us
to the edge of words
and the beginning of songs

we are her living body
storytellers and poets
hold traces of her
echoes and songs
give form
to the moments of our birth
warm us
with blankets of stars
wake sleeping water
to the sky

This poem was originally published in *Gabriel's Beach* (Hagios Press, 2008).

The Journalist and the Angry White Mob:

Reflections from the Field

MICHAEL ORSINI

Tell all the Truth but tell it slant—
Success in Circuit lies
Too bright for our infirm Delight
The Truth's superb surprise

As Lightning to the Children eased
With explanation kind
The Truth must dazzle gradually
Or every man be blind
—*Emily Dickinson*

I covered the "Oka Crisis," as it came to be known.

There, I said it. Well, to be precise, I did not really "cover" the "Oka Crisis" from beginning to end. I was parachuted into the story when I was needed. I walked onto the crowded Oka stage when it suited my newspaper bosses, who needed warm bodies to cover all angles of this developing story with all of its many twists and turns. My employer at the time, *The Montreal Gazette*, was not exactly seen as a champion of Aboriginal issues, which made it difficult when trying to chase down an Oka-related story. "Why should I trust you? Your newspaper ran a story that said such and such" was a common refrain. Or, my favorite: "Your newspaper ran an editorial that said such and such." Reporters will no doubt tell you how frustrating it can be when you try to be even-handed or fair in your reporting, only to wake up to an editorial in the morning paper that is full of sound and fury, and often diametrically opposed to the portrait you tried to present in your own reporting. I experienced this after writing a full-page feature story on welfare reform in the province of Québec, in which I suggested that the provincial reform was punitive for penalizing welfare recipients who were not willing to take any employment that was offered them. Following my Saturday feature article, which was illustrated with an offensive photo of a woman standing outside a shop window presumably wishing she could afford what was in the window, the newspaper ran an editorial heralding the changes as a step in the right direction! Guess they hadn't bothered to read my story, I wondered. This can set you back significantly, trying to explain that you have no control over what the editorial board writes, or the position they choose to defend on any given day. In the minds of readers, there is no separation between what reporters say and what editors say.

What follows is a series of reflections that were, up until recently, thoughts I had shared with some colleagues and friends who cared to listen. There is always a risk in sharing reflections such as these, that they lack authenticity because they are "read" through the prism of one's current experience. Hindsight is not, as is often claimed, 20/20. It is partial, deceiving. I have tried as much as possible to imagine and recreate my own thinking at the time, but leave open the possibility that my perspective is partial, as well. Embarrassingly, I am afraid, there was not much thinking going on at the time. One is always tempted to imagine outrage where none existed, to fill in the blanks with deep ruminations about the world unfolding, as it were. All I can remember is the need to file a story about what was going on, and the challenge of doing this without the benefit of a Blackberry or email. In my case, it meant finding a payphone and literally calling in the story to an anxious, deadline-weary editor typing faster than I could speak or think.

Indeed, one of the most regretful aspects of these reflections relates to how journalists can become unthinking and unwilling participants in history, not because they are unfeeling or uncaring but because journalistic culture, or at least the culture that is projected to budding journalists in journalism school, presents a romanticized view of the journalistic craft and rarely pauses to ask journalists to reflect on their own reporting and the impact it might have on others.

At the end of the day, the story is all that matters. People only matter in so far as they provide "colour" or context. Sometimes, when under intense deadline pressure, you write the story and fill in the appropriate blanks—in most cases, quotes from a source here and there—to buttress the perspective you hope to get across. People—so desperately needed to grab the throat of the media consumer who is suffering from a bout of "compassion fatigue"—illustrate something that might be difficult to get across in an abstract way. This helps to explain why the media reinforce stereotypical images of marginalized groups in the society. It is easier to stick to the script, to take comfort in the images we know and understand, and to use these filters to make sense of the world. In the case of Aboriginal people, as Harding has explained with reference to the final report of the Royal Commission on Aboriginal Peoples, the media take refuge in three comfortable stereotypes of Aboriginal people: as villains, as victims or as noble environmentalists.[1]

While graduate school provided me with the necessary tools in social construction to appreciate the role of discourse and images in shaping how we think about the social and political world, there was little talk of anything discursive in journalism school. As a journalist-in-waiting, the world is presented in black and white, point, counter-point. Get both sides of the story, one is counselled. What if there are more than two perspectives? Little attention is paid to the pivotal role the media play in producing particular stereotypes or characterizations of individuals and groups. Ian Hacking, the renowned philosopher of science, has used the term "interactive kind" to refer to how characterizations or labels can have a "looping effect" on the way groups or individuals view themselves, not to mention the range of societal or political responses to issues affecting these groups:

> We are especially concerned with classifications that, when known by people or by those around them, and put to work in institutions, change the ways in which individuals experience themselves—and may even lead people to evolve their feelings and behaviour in part because they are so classified. Such kinds [of people and their behavior] are interactive kinds. This ugly

phrase has the merit of recalling actors, agency and action. The inter may suggest the way in which the classification and the individual classified may interact, the way in which the actors may become self-aware as being of a kind, if only because of being treated or institutionalized as of that kind, and so experiences themselves in that way.[2]

It was interesting to discover in the course of researching this chapter that *The Gazette*'s coverage of Oka was viewed as more sympathetic than that of its rival francophone daily newspaper, *La Presse*.[3] One wonders if the same could be said today were the two media outlets compared with respect to their coverage of Aboriginal issues. Neither newspaper, to my knowledge, has a reporter devoted to covering Aboriginal affairs, which is not surprising given the tendency of many news outlets to discourage beat reporting. The message is simple: as a journalist, you need to specialize in everything. Aboriginal politics is just another thing to add to that long list. This is selective, of course. One would not argue that just anyone could cover Parliament Hill. Some background knowledge of or interest in politics is necessary.

Many of us who covered Oka were thrust into these events with little in the way of background knowledge about Aboriginal people, which is not suggested as a way to excuse the coverage. Imagine a time that was pre-Google, when research meant visiting the library and reading newspaper clippings. And the summer of 1990 was a particularly busy one for Montreal's journalists. Apart from what would come to be known as the "Oka Crisis" or "Oka Standoff," Montreal's police force became implicated in the shooting of an unarmed black man, Marcellus François. For members of the city's Black community, that incident bore a striking resemblance to the shooting death of another unarmed black man, Anthony Griffin, in Montreal's Notre Dame de Grâce community years earlier.

I had just landed a much coveted position as a summer intern/reporter at *The Gazette*, the city's only English-language daily. For someone just about to complete a journalism degree, the thought of full-time employment sure beat the prospect of life as a dreaded freelance reporter. It was expected, however, that as the "cub" reporter, one would cover those less glamorous stories from which any self-respecting reporter would scurry. Press conferences at which nothing was announced were assigned to the junior folks like me, garden-variety fires, and the occasional murder. In the case of the latter, a junior reporter eager to please his or her bosses would trip over themselves to one up the tabloids like the *Journal de Montreal,* which covered crime stories like they owned them. So it was entirely surprising to find myself covering one of the defining moments in the history of Canadian-Aboriginal relations.

So what did I know about Aboriginal issues? About enough to fill a paragraph in a story, and that was a stretch. It was up to reporters to fill in the story with some background, which usually meant searching through the database of previous articles and, time permitting, perusing a few books or reports in the media library at the newspaper. I do not recall doing much of either.

The media deserve a fair helping of criticism for their coverage of Aboriginal issues in general. But it is too facile to lay all of the blame at the media's door. One especially unnerving criticism relates to how the profit motive dictates what is and is not covered. While one should not dismiss outright claims about how the profit motive has sullied the world of journalism and distracted the media from its public interest mission, it would inaccurate to suggest that in the "Oka Crisis" many reporters saw simply another opportunity to sell more newspapers. Indeed, there was intense public interest in this story, but as I recall it, *The Gazette's* wall-to-wall coverage was motivated not by a desire to ramp up sales, but by a desire to do the story justice, even if there were several screw ups along the way. Reporters do not really give much thought to the product when they are putting together or researching a story. Some reporters might thrive on ego gratification—getting a story on the front page or, even better, "above the fold" was and is highly coveted. But the bulk of reporters were simply trying to get as comprehensive a story as was humanly possible in a day.

Only a handful of reporters are permitted to spend day upon day researching a story. Normally, the types of stories they were investigating were full-scale investigations of scandals. This was, for many, the golden age of journalism, when media outlets invested resources in investigative reporters who did not have to worry about the daily grind, a period when newspapers felt a commitment to journalism that was squarely in the public interest. The rest of us were not so lucky; we were filing at least one story per day, sometimes two and three depending on whether the office was short staffed.

The defining moment for me in the Oka saga was a story I covered on August 28, 1990. My assignment editor, unaware what was really going on or he would have probably sent a more experienced reporter to cover the story, told me to travel to the Mercier Bridge, which connects the reserve with the city of Montreal. Residents had been angry for some time that the bridge had been blocked for several weeks by Mohawk protesters. There were rumblings that something might be happening there. "Go check it out," I recall the assignment editor telling me. On many occasions, "go check it out" turned into the proverbial dud, a non-story.

The incident involved a crowd of angry residents of the neighbouring town of Chateauguay who had assembled on the Mercier Bridge to confront the Mohawk families who were being escorted off the reserve by car for their own safety. Cars were filled with frightened children staring out at the small crowd shouting obscenities as their cars sped by.

Then came the rocks. I was standing a short distance from the crowds with my notebook and pen jotting everything down that I could, and doing what had been drummed into me in journalism school: capture the mood, get the local flavour for the reader who can not be there to witness the event and must rely on your portrait of the event.

What was the mood like?

Harrowing. It was clear that tensions had reached a boiling point among Mohawk spokespeople and government negotiators, and among citizens inconvenienced by traffic delays and the like. But rocks? Was there no other way to release one's frustration than to hurl rocks at cars? I just kept taking notes, and more notes, not fully aware of what had indeed transpired. There was a deep sense that I was standing apart from the event, possibly because it was the only way I could imagine stomaching this. Distancing myself was a way to separate myself from this ugly expression of violence by white people like me. I recall a man in his 50s, beads of sweat streaming down the side of his face, ambling toward a small hill to collect some rocks suitably big enough to smash a few windshields. Each time a rock was met with the sound of broken glass, a small group watching on the sidelines cheered on the rock throwers.

Being asked to reflect on an experience that has affected me so deeply, but in unexpected ways, is challenging to say the least. At the time, I was a lowly reporter who had visited the Kahnawà:ke reserve a few times, but with little knowledge of Aboriginal politics and culture. Growing up in Montreal in a disadvantaged southwest region of the city does not prepare you for the experience of being a foreigner on Native land. It did not help that many of the Mohawk were not particularly fond of *The Gazette* or its coverage of Native issues. And why should they? *The Gazette* had paid scant attention to Aboriginal issues, and only covered issues related to Aboriginal people when it affected non-Aboriginal people. Come to think of it, this sounds very much like how my own discipline of Canadian Politics has treated Aboriginal Politics up until recently. The debates currently raging in the field of Canadian Politics following an exchange involving a scholar who has been highly critical of Indigenous perspectives would be laughable were they not so depressing. To suggest the existence of an Aboriginal orthodoxy overstates the influence of these perspectives in the discipline and cuts to the heart of what is essentially a dispute about the policing of boundaries. The implicit message is that Indigenous perspectives are less scholarly, less worthy of academic attention, especially in a field such as political "science." Never mind that some of these claims are coming from scholars whose own perspectives—political economy or neo-Marxist analysis—fought for a space in the field. There is nothing like the previously excluded standing at the gates refusing entry to potential newcomers!

If you're non-Aboriginal and interested in Aboriginal issues, if you are too sympathetic, you run the risk of being dismissed as yet another bleeding heart or someone with niche interests, the ultimate put down. My primary interest is in health, which would also be written off as a niche interest, I suppose. If you're Aboriginal, you cannot win either. Either you are too Aboriginal and therefore dismissed as a proselytizer lacking rigour or objectivity or you're not Aboriginal enough, you have sold out your people. Non-Aboriginals like me do not need to speak on behalf of Aboriginal people; as these pages illustrate in great detail, Indigenous folks do not require our help in articulating or expressing themselves. As non-Aboriginal scholars, we can, in our own fields of inquiry, engage in meaningful dialogue that cuts across these divides. This does not mean accepting all Aboriginal points of view *tout court*, but sharing the public space in which ideas are debated and recognizing that these spaces are not simply open to anyone. They are political spaces in which power struggles are played out.

The problem with the mainstream media's coverage of Aboriginal issues, in general, might be better termed a bad case of "Johnny come lately." The media only seem to shuttle into communities when they are at their most vulnerable. And when they do, in an effort to illustrate some of the problems in "Indian Country," they leave the reader or viewer with the impression that there is something inherently wrong with Aboriginal people themselves. The real "Aboriginal orthodoxy," to correct Tom Flanagan, is the one perpetuated in media circles and transmitted outward to popular culture that there is an Aboriginal pathology. Proponents of this orthodoxy argue that Aboriginal people do not fare as well in society because a) they are unable to govern themselves, b) they are unable to take care of their families, c) they are unable to take care of their own health, and the list goes on. The images of reserves replete with inadequate housing, poor sanitation, and the like are reframed as problems created by and supported by Aboriginal people. The fact that some reserves have resources and, horror of horrors, an adequate infrastructure is used to buttress the claim that some Aboriginals are basking in the glow of affluence. And the idea that some Aboriginals are well off and do not share their wealth with others is also part of the pathology, as if non-Aboriginals are keen to share their wealth with those who are less fortunate.

The experience of covering Aboriginal issues in a sympathetic manner immediately branded you an apologist for the factions within some Mohawk communities. The image of the violent warrior was a potent symbol on the media landscape, to be sure. It galvanized the naysayers who thought we had given away too much to the Aboriginals, implicitly supporting the development of rogue militants in our midst. The idea that there were radical and moderate voices within Aboriginal communities was also used to demonstrate that there were deep divisions in the community, with some voices being frozen out of debates. Again, there is nothing particularly shocking in discovering that everyone does not agree all of the time. Indeed, it would be surprising to find common ground on all of the issues. Still, black and white characterizations of polarized opinion served as de facto proof that something was seriously amiss in Indian Country.

Lessons Learned? Whose Lessons? Whose Learning?

It is common almost 20 years later to reflect on ugly incidents such as these and ask, what are the lessons learned? I am afraid that as far as the media are concerned, not very much. Aboriginal issues are covered, with few exceptions, in much the same way they have been for years. We recoil in horror at the legacy of the residential school system, and wash our hands of the collective blame with a cheque and a contrite apology. The media speak to survivors, who share their unimaginable pain and then it's back to business as usual. The media speculate about whether it is wise to write such a big cheque to survivors lest they spend it irresponsibly. Can they really be trusted to invest the money in a GIC, they ask?

As I write this, the front page of *The Globe and Mail* has reported that First Nations communities in Manitoba had been sent body bags in response to their pleas for help in fighting a potential outbreak of the HINI virus. To suggest that Health Canada's offer of assistance was insensitive is an understatement. This came on the heels of an initial reluctance on the part of public health authorities to send hand sanitizer to reserves for fear that community members might use the sanitizer to get their alcohol fix! What does the Oka conflict have to do with public health disasters? Everything. The way in which we collectively structure responses to problems affecting Aboriginal people remain stuck in a particular mindset, what Ladner and I referred to as "paradigm paralysis."[4] It doesn't matter if it's a land dispute regarding ceremonial lands, or a potential flu outbreak. The difference today, one might argue, is that there may be a greater willingness in the media to call out governments for such wrong-headed decisions or approaches.

Aboriginal people, whether it concerns their health and well-being or experiences with the legal system, continue to be constructed as pathologically inferior to whites. When tragedies occur on reserves, the reporters (and academic researchers for that matter) descend like vultures, train their camera on grief-stricken families, document the misery, and drive off, never to be seen again. A few reporters will dare to challenge the status quo, probing deeper. But media resources being what they are, there is scarce support for journalists who want to stick with stories, who want to dig deeper. Besides, there are other stories, literally bursting with pathos and misery, waiting to be told.

I left journalism—or maybe journalism left me—partly because I grew disenchanted with the increasing inability to tell stories in their full, rich complexity. Oka was the start of my slide into existential angst about my role as a journalist. I had always hoped that an Aboriginal person would emerge fresh out of journalism school with the balls to "tell the truth, but tell it slant," to quote the late poet Emily Dickinson. Media consumers cannot handle all of the truth at once. It needs to be told to them in bits and pieces, in digestible, bite-sized chunks.

Readers would benefit from hearing the story as told by a different narrator. No matter how much white journalists tried to explain what was going on, we were always limited by a perspective that was shaped by our inability to fully gets our heads around the Aboriginal experience in its many forms. I remember first hearing about National Film Board filmmaker Alanis Obomsawin as a student journalist in the 1980s and was immediately drawn to her and her work precisely because of her uncanny knack for storytelling. She had produced one of the most compelling accounts of the "Oka Crisis," *Kahnesatake: 270 Years of Resistance*. I met her pre-Oka, as it were, when I interviewed her for *The Link* student newspaper at Concordia University about a film she had released titled *No Address*, about Montreal's homeless population. Obomsawin is not only a gifted filmmaker, but also a captivating presence. Anyone who has met her is not likely to forget her. When I ran into her at Oka with a film crew—she stuck it out there for the duration of the conflict—I took comfort in the fact that despite the surreal experience that was unfolding, we could rest assured that the Oka story would be given its proper due. The story of Oka, as I understood it and as the Obomsawin documentary would go to pains to explain, did not begin in 1990, but media narratives leave little room for complex backgrounders. That was the kind of thing people in the newspaper business crammed into sidebars, background that was relevant but limited in terms of space.

With the benefit of years studying social movements and other civil society actors, I wonder if that perspective has allowed us to imagine the resistance at Oka differently. As a young reporter, I did not have the vocabulary to express what I was witnessing. In the rough and tumble world of daily journalism, it was much more comforting to slide into those well-worn stereotypes of good and evil. It didn't help, of course, that some of the key dramatis personae in this unfolding story stuck faithfully to the script. The provincial police force, the Sûreté du Quebéc, believed everyone was the enemy, journalists among them. I recall when I tried to inquire one day in Oka as to why the officers were not wearing name badges to easily identify them as there had been rumblings about officers roughing up some of the Mohawk residents, they refused to answer. When I pressed further, as I had been taught to do in journalism school, the officer turned away, stepped into his cruiser and drove off. I was asking for a reason: several Mohawks had complained of maltreatment at the hands of police, but had no recourse without being able to identify the officer in question.

The "Oka Crisis" sparked my interest in Aboriginal issues, an issue I continue to address today in my own research, albeit from a different perspective. I am particularly drawn to Aboriginal politics because I am interested in how knowledge claims are made in the policy process, and how situated or experiential knowledge might figure in the political realm. I also tackle Aboriginal issues from the lens of health and social justice because it is striking how little we have actually learned when it comes to the link between poverty and poor health. Instead of connecting the necessary dots, there is a dogged insistence on putting Aboriginal people in charge of their own misery. I recognize, of course, that I am travelling down a very slippery slope here but we need to speak truth to power when we see instances in which others are appropriating the discourse of self determination to justify standing by idly and not doing anything. In my own work, I have seen this in the field of TB, where there is a clear recognition in study after study that housing density affects the possibility of contracting TB—this is not rocket science—but very little in the way of political will to address the horrific housing conditions on many reserves. What's more, basic necessities such as clean water, which are taken for granted in many communities, can affect health in myriad ways. For instance, when public health officials urged resident on the Garden Lake Reserve in Manitoba to wash their hands frequently to lower the risk of acquiring TB, the chief had to step in to explain that less that only a quarter of residents had access to running water.

To suggest there are lessons learned from Oka would be to trivialize the importance of this event in the public imagination. Oka's lessons cannot be reduced to an executive summary, or Power Point slide. For those who lived it and through it, it is almost cruel to ask them to imagine a series of lessons or take-home messages. For others, including myself, the "Oka Crisis" remains a focusing event, a reminder, a call to question our own assumptions. Oka's lessons are ours for the taking, if only we have the guts to listen.

---

1 Robert Harding (2005), "The Media, Aboriginal People and Common Sense," *The Canadian Journal of Native Studies* XXV:1, p. 111.

2 Ian Hacking (2000), *The Social Construction of What?* Cambridge and London: Harvard University Press, p. 104.

3 See Elizabeth Andrea Keller (1996), "Anglos With Feathers: A Content Analysis of French and English Media Coverage in Quebéc on the Oka Crisis of 1990," unpublished Master's thesis, Department of Political Science, Vancouver: University of British Columbia. On general issues of bias in the media vis-à-vis minority populations, see Frances Henry and Carol Taylor (2002), *Discourses of Domination: Racial Bias in the Canadian English-Language Press*, Toronto, Buffalo, and London: University of Toronto Press.

4 See Kiera Ladner and Michael Orsini (2005), "The Persistence of Paradigm Paralysis: The First Nations Governance Act as the Continuation of Colonial Policy" in Michael Murphy ed., *Reconfiguring Aboriginal-State Relations. Canada: The State of the Federation 2003*, Montreal and Kingston: McGill-Queen's University Press, pp. 185–203.

Angry Indians, Settler Guilt, and the Challenges of Decolonization and Resurgence

RICHARD J.F. DAY

I would like to introduce myself as a settler of "mixed European descent," and to say that I am honoured to be included in this volume, which contains the words of many powerful writers and activists whom I deeply respect. I am myself a theorist-practitioner, by which I mean I do things, as well as write and talk about them. What I'm most interested in, lately, is the creation of sustainable alternatives to the dominant global order. Although I understand from the Maya people that 2012 is nothing as special as Hollywood is making it out to be, I do feel a sense of urgency brought about by knowing, and feeling, that western civilization is a dying, panicky, raging beast lashing about with its sharp claws and agile tail. I see my work, for the remainder of my life, as helping to lower this dying beast into the ground, in a way that will minimize the damage it does, while simultaneously building other ways of living, being, thinking, acting. I have only failures, so far, to speak of in this regard. Yet, from each failure I learn more, and at any rate, I see this work as taking many generations. My contributions are small, only a start, or better yet, eddies in a current that never quite goes away, although it often subsides, and for a time lives only as memory and potentiality.

I am not an Indigenous person. Yet I feel a strong connection to the land where I was born—Coast Salish territory on the west coast of the territories claimed by the Canadian state. Although I have lived away from my home for many years, at many different times, it remains the most powerful place there is, for me. In fact, even as the people and places I knew when I was young are uprooted and paved over, even as they and the land cry out, this feeling only increases. As so many Indigenous people have said and written, as I have been taught by loyal friends and strong allies, I know that the best chance any of us has at living a life that is honourable, sustainable, joyful, and peaceful is through reconnecting to the land, our Mother, and listening to what she has to say.

I feel equally strongly that we must, somehow, creatively recover the spirit in which my people were welcomed to this land. A spirit that most of us, sadly, are barely aware exists, and when we do acknowledge it, when we feel its tug, it is almost always as nostalgia, longing, sadness for something apparently irretrievable. We have this crazy origin myth, for which the ancient Greeks must be blamed, that locates all good things in the past (the Golden Age). At the same time, through our (post)modern technological gadgets, we strive toward a future in which we might recreate that time of joy and plenty. More craziness. What we have a hard time doing, we settlers, is living, here and now, as though we know where we are, where we have come from, and where we might be going— or at least wanting to go. We have, quite simply, lost our way.

Yet, while we are like city-born children alone in the forest, we are, unfortunately, far from defenseless. We have our gadgets and we know how to use them to get things done, to express (what we think is) our will in actions. As Leroy Little Bear has pointed out, this seems to be our gift. And a frightening, difficult gift it is, for as the last few hundred years of colonialism have shown, it all too often leads us to hurt, control, destroy, and dominate.

The ongoing history of Canadian colonialism is obviously deeply important for what for what I want to talk about here. But I also want to touch upon something less commonly discussed: the ability of settlers to hurt, control, dominate, and destroy *ourselves*. I want to reflect upon what we can learn, what we must unlearn, as we come to orient differently to our relations with ourselves, Indigenous Peoples, and the land. Most particularly, what does the resurgence of Indigenous individuals, cultures, and powers, their recovery of their lands, traditions, and powers mean to and for us as we struggle to decolonize ourselves?

Angry Indians and Settler Guilt

For me the connection of all of this to Oka is obvious. But that's only because I'm getting to be an old guy. Most of the undergraduate students I teach at Queen's University, for example, know nothing about it. They are in their teens or early twenties, and were either unconscious or non-existent when it all went down. Teaching at Queen's is challenging in all of the ways that have become normal for the neoliberal university. The students are wildly stressed, pushed for time, money, and emotional energy, and worried—already, incessantly—about what they will do after they graduate—that is, about *getting a job*. This, of course, is for the most part why they're in the classroom at all. Listening to someone like me go on and on about all of the problems in the world is just one more thing they have to do in order to get that all-important certification, that stamp on the forehead: something to prove that they have been there, done that, that they are ready to become, as the university letterhead exhorts, "global leaders for the twenty-first century."

But in addition to these many distractions, there's another set of factors that make the work of encouraging critical reading, writing, thinking and acting even more difficult. Almost all of the students in the social sciences and humanities at Queen's are straight, white, middle/upper class, young, and beautiful in a uniform, mallish sort of way. They have no experience with what it feels like to be on the "wrong" side of racist colonialism, they know nothing about poverty, the women reject feminism as something archaic and unnecessary, and so on. Yet, and perhaps because of this protective distance from the downsides of structural inequality, they are filled with a deep-seated desire to "help" those whom (they think) are less fortunate than themselves ... without, of course, giving up any of their own privilege while going about it. This is to say that the charity model reigns supreme, as the dominant mode of "activism," i.e., of caring about anyone or anything other than oneself.

While I'm obviously blowing off steam and sounding quite harsh, I've tried hard, in the last two paragraphs, to indicate that I'm not talking about *all* Queen's students, that I'm aware of the perils of reducing any complex set of identities and forces to a monolithic sameness. In this case, what needs to be marked is that in the eight years I have been there,

there has always been some kind of critical-radical formation, whether at the graduate or undergraduate level, working on issues relevant to the university in general and Queen's in particular, and also involved with various individuals and communities outside the campus. I've worked often with such folks, I learn from them and am inspired by them, and don't want ever to be read as pretending they don't exist, or as minimizing their importance. This having been said, the radical contingent at Queen's generally comprises no more than 50 or so out of 10,000 students, or 0.5% of the population. They mostly get it. They wouldn't need to read this article. And because of that, they're not who I'm trying to talk to or about here. Rather, I'm aiming at the 99.5%, those normal Queen's students who are on the way to becoming superior Canadians. Because it's those normal-superior Canadians—myself among them— who keep colonialism going, who always have and always will, be absolutely necessary to this particular form of *governmentality*.[1]

As a teacher, and as a public intellectual often called upon to "educate" settlers about Indigenous issues, I'm constantly struggling to find ways to slip past the many layers of protection I've just mentioned. I learned long ago that a full-frontal attack—using logic, reason, analysis— simply strengthens the colonial *habitus*, as Pierre Bourdieu has called it.[2] One must be more subtle than this. I have found, for example, that working at an unconscious, emotional level can momentarily dissolve the settler's shield in a way that no argument ever could. And here is one direct link to Oka, as a mimetic resource, a jog to the settler (un)*conscience collective* that, while it remains dormant under the cover of an ever-shifting mass-media landscape, can be called to the surface again. I have found Alanis Obomsawin's film *Kanehsatake: 270 Years of Resistance* to be particularly effective in this way. Just as few people these days can find the beat in music without a drum kit and electric bass subwoofing it into their bodies, it seems that masked warriors, gunshots, tear gas, and running soldiers are necessary to get them to pay attention to the steady rhythm of Canadian colonialism.

So, what does a normal Canadian liberal-settler child do when sat down in front of a film like *Kanehsatake* for a couple of hours? Generally, they are totally enveloped, carried along by the action and the narrative, silent in a way that is completely new for them, and for me. They are listening, learning, getting some inkling of what it might be like to be behind the lines, scared, yet defiant, ready to fight, perhaps to die. Fighting Canadian soldiers, the good guys! As the film ends, they sit stunned, some wiping their eyes as the lights come on, with nothing at all to say. I let the silence play itself out. This creates a certain sort of tension, which mounts until someone who is feeling particularly uncomfortable, or wishes to relieve the discomfort of others, finally speaks.

Then comes an outpouring of guilt and sadness, rage at the army, the government, the settlers throwing stones. Rage all around, directed everywhere, except at us sitting there, in that room. As Sarita Srivastava has pointed out, strategies of anti-oppressive education can easily reproduce dominant relations of power. In this case, it might be that the only Indigenous person in the class, who may or may not be "out," takes on the role of educator and cultural translator, thereby setting him or herself up as a target for various forms of resistance and aggression from those among the class who would rather not have to think of themselves in complicit in all of this. That was then, this is now . . . that was there, this is here. . . .

Also, what Srivastava calls "let's talk" techniques can "encourage a focus on the emotions and moral deliberations of some white participants, rather than on measures for organizational change."[3] Again, although Srivastava is talking primarily about anti-racist workshops in social movements, these same symptoms emerge in the university classroom. The guilt, the sadness, whose are they? Those of the settlers. Who will benefit from the lifting of these emotions? The settlers. And so, eventually, someone will ask, what can we do about it? Someone else who is in the know will point out that, right now, just down the road, the Mohawks of Tyendinaga are in a similar state of siege. Also nearby, the Ardoch Algonquin are fighting the building of a uranium mine on their territory. There are protests at the courthouse in Kingston, blockades to support with food, clothing, and one's own presence, and a Facebook group where you can learn how to get involved. Most people in the room will nod, write down the info, feeling better about themselves, thinking they just might do something!

At this point, I feel very confused, my own feelings getting the better of me. I am happy they've learned something, been moved, at least heard about what's going on around them with respect to

Indigenous struggles and settler solidarity. But I also feel deeply frustrated by the limits of the emotional approach. There has been a revolution of sorts, but mostly in the original sense of the term, as involving a departure from, and return to, a long-standing norm, rather than the permanent replacement of the status quo by something new and somehow superior. At this point I will make some pithy, obscure remark about my own complicity as a settler. Returning to the word, where I am most comfortable, I will ruin things a little bit, cast doubt on what we might have achieved today. I will become, again, that crazy old guy who can't leave well enough alone, who always seems to be unhappy. This usually leads absolutely nowhere, and we're near the end of the class, so the books and computers start getting closed up and conversation returns to safer topics. The students have ended the class.

Settler Decolonization and Resurgence

While all of this can be quite frustrating, the biggest problem I have with the kind of settler education work I find myself doing in the university is that just as it focuses our attention on the situation of Indigenous Peoples, it necessarily brackets the question of our own decolonization. This is, for me, the second important and very direct link to Oka in my life. I find myself forced to ask, again and again: Where do I stand? What will I risk? And who will be standing beside me?

I know there are a few things I can and will do to fight Canadian colonialism, because I already do them. The most important of these is to help undermine the global system of states and corporations whenever and wherever I can. Every impediment to this system is an impediment to Canadian colonialism and its domination and exploitation of people and the land. In this work, I stand beside many other people struggling against the existing order, in many ways, all over the world. I can also use my privilege to support Indigenous nations in their struggles, in whatever ways are possible for me and desirable for those with whom I'm working. This may include strategies and tactics aimed at reforming the status quo. I know that it's possible to reduce misery for many people, here and now, and even achieve positive effects of empowerment, via the state form. I admit that I'm ambivalent about this approach, as I've said elsewhere many times. But I increasingly feel that it is primarily my own position in the structures of power that allows me to posit a certain sort of purity in this regard.[4] At any rate, there's no doubt that, however I might be thinking, what I actually *do* is take up reformist tasks when they are sufficiently close to my own life (i.e., not universalizing/hegemonic) and support others in their own work of this sort.

All of these acts can contribute to decolonization in that they can help to lead settler societies away from tactics of genocide, theft, and dishonesty in our relations with Indigenous Peoples. But there's a harder question that is raised by a tactic I haven't yet mentioned in this regard. It seems increasingly clear to me that we will never beat this monster at its own game. It will always be more willing than us to lie, cheat, steal, destroy, dominate, and so on, and so we will lose if we try to play things this way. And if we do not resist these temptations, we simply become the monster ourselves, which means that it wins again. There is no choice but to do what the state form, what capitalism, have done—that is, to slowly seep into our lives over a very long period of time, suffering many setbacks, but always staying "on task" and "on message," as they themselves like to say. To do the same thing, but in a different way (non-violently), and with different guiding values (mutual respect and aid, harmony, lack of hierarchy, love for the land). To renew the spirit, that is, with which my people were originally welcomed to this land, and which, sadly, we have shown that we mostly do not comprehend.

This raises the question then of settler resurgence through withdrawal from the dominant order, and the construction of alternatives to it. Something that is bound up with decolonization, but is, at least for me, much more difficult to think through, to act upon. For despite what I said above about my home, I know I am not really *of* the land, anywhere. Just as I am landless, it is also very unclear who are my people, other than, as I've already mentioned, that I am some kind of European settler. In addition to this confusion of ethnic identity, as I am finding out to my increasing perplexity, while I am politically too militant for the mainstream, I am also too mainstream for the militant. Too impure, too much in-between, on the margins. A nomad, wanderer, with fragments of a family, a few friends widely dispersed, many contacts, but no real community, no one, other than my two boys, whose fate I share, whether I like it or not. Will that 0.5% really be of any use, since we have in common only the fact that we have so little in common? Can there be a true community of the homeless and landless?

Not only this, but it is clear that anywhere we nomads might try to find a home, we will be on indigenous land. We can't "move in" to a reserve, as I've heard recently suggested in what seemed to be a serious tone, since most are already very much over-burdened, and there would be insurmountable cultural and political barriers to our "integration" (it could be called "cultimulturalism," perhaps?). If we buy land to "do our own thing" in an insular way, we are no better than, no different from, any other colonizers. Thus it would appear that the resurgence of settler autonomy, our escape from the tyrannies we have foisted on ourselves, once again can only come on the backs of Indigenous People. The best idea I've heard so far, which came up at a recent gathering of settlers and Indigenous People, is to buy land from the Canadians and offer a substantial, non-swampy chunk to the Indigenous nation(s) from whom it was taken, no strings attached. I know that this would be a tough thing to set up, given the state of relations between our peoples. However, it seems like the only way to do anything differently for now. And perhaps, over many generations of living beside each other respectfully, peacefully, and sustainably, after weathering some tough times together, such an approach might eventually lead to a recovery of the Two Row Wampum ideal and practice through a process of mutual resurgence in which the means are the end and we are able to play a non-zero-sum game.

Conclusion

While the horrors of several hundred years of colonialism in the Americas must never be forgotten, we must also remember that before the white Man could colonize anyone else, he had to colonize himself. And so, before he can truly stand beside anyone else to confront the tasks of decolonization and resurgence, within, against, or outside of the dominant order, he must attend to his own decolonization at the level of both the individual and the community, however the latter might be understood. The courage of every person who stands up to the soldiers and cops and politicians, the sacrifices of every kind of warrior, such as those at Oka and their many supporters, motivate us all to take up this difficult, unending, but very necessary task.

---

1 Michel Foucault (1991) "Governmentality," trans. Rosi Braidotti and revised by Colin Gordon, in Graham Burchell, Colin Gordon and Peter Miller (eds) *The Foucault Effect: Studies in Governmentality*, Chicago, Il.: University of Chicago Press, pp. 87–104.

2 Pierre Bourdieu (1999) "Structures, Habitus, Practices" in Anthony Elliott (ed) *The Blackwell Reader in Contemporary Social Theory*, Malden: Blackwell Press, pp. 107–118.

3 Sarita Srivastava (2007), "'Let's Talk': The Pedagogy and Politics of Anti-racist Change" in Mark Coté et. al. (ed.) *Utopian Pedagogy: Radical Experiments Against Neoliberal Globalization*, Toronto: University of Toronto Press, pp. 294–313.

4 White middle class anarchists (like me, but also unlike me) seem to take this stance quite often.

The Mohawk Refusal

ARTHUR KROKER

It is appropriate to reflect on Paul Virilio's theory of "pure war" in the context of Montreal, a city which in the early 1990s was the scene of the violent application of the Canadian war machine against its Aboriginal population, the Mohawks. A city, that is, which in the summer of 1990 experienced as part of its cultural politics the invasion of the Mohawk reserves surrounding Montreal by all the policing strategies that could be produced by the state: 6000 soldiers of the Canadian army, complete with tanks, armoured personal carriers, and even TOW missiles, the greater part of the Quebéc provincial police, and the RCMP. All of this power belonging to the state was set against, in the end, less than 50 Mohawks who only wished to prevent the destruction of a sacred pine grove of their Ancestors by developers intent on extending a golf course to eighteen holes. (In a perfect symbolic gesture, the Mohawks not only reclaimed the sacred pine grove at Kanehsatà:ke, but also took physical control of the Mercier bridge—one of the main traffic arteries between the south shore suburbs and the island of Montreal.) If in cultural politics we should be able to read the universal in the particular, to decipher a larger war logic in local applications, then Kanehsatà:ke is a scene of what the cultural theorist, Paul Virilio, describes as "pure war."[1]

First, it is about an urban space, not as a site of commerce, but as defined in relation to war. That is Montreal, which has always been a site of war first and of commerce second. A city of two founding extremisms: the original genocide of Indigenous peoples by French colonizers who, speaking the language of Christian salvation, imposed the spatial logic of "enlightenment" on the northern tier of North America and then the attempted exterminism of the local French population by English colonizers, for whom the "conquest of Québéc" was most of all about the suppression of a Catholic French America by a Protestant mercantilist logic. Montreal, then as always a site of pure war—an intensely urban zone as a spatial vector for the war machine— a site of maneuver, negotiation and conquest—a violent scene of sacrificial power.

Second, in the summer of 1990 Kanehsatà:ke is a matter of tactics, strategy and, most of all, logistics. Just as Virilio has theorized in *Pure War*, it is about an indefinite preparation for war involving the colonization ("endocolonization") of local populations. Thus, for example, the Canadian military stated at the time that this "conflict" could be over in two or three minutes, but the real war was a media war to win over the consciousness of the civilian population. Here, logistics could be an endless preparation for war: control of food, communication, space. And all of this accompanied by constant helicopter flights over Montreal as if to demonstrate symbolically the state's control of the local population. Is this not what Virilio has described as "state terrorism"—the act of war without a declaration of war, so that there is no formal protection of civil rights and no political rights for international agencies to intervene on behalf of the Mohawks? And is the indefinite occupation of Kanehsatà:ke and the ceaseless police raids into other indigenous territories not an indefinite preparation for war in another way: not really only about Mohawks at all, but a violent warning to all Indigenous Peoples, most of all to the Cree in northern Québéc, not to intervene physically (by blocking roads) or legally (by court actions) in the future construction of James Bay II, the Great Whale project (the state-driven project for a vast extension of hydro-electric development on Indigenous lands in northern Québéc). Kanehsatà:ke, then, as a pure technological war between the energy requirements of the high-intensity market society and the irrepressible demands of Indigenous peoples for control of their territories and cultures. A technological war, that is, where the war machine comes inside us and takes possession of our identity. Virilio is correct: "All of us are already civilian soldiers. We don't recognize the militarized part of (our) identity, (our) consciousness?"[2] And anyway, what is so dangerous about the Mohawks, about the sovereignty claims of the First Nations? Virilio states that the war machine is the crystallization of science as the language of power, of the depletion of the energies of society and their draining away into the war machine. Maybe this is what is so threatening about the struggles of the First Nations. It violates and refuses the genetic logic of the technological dynamo.

Consequently, a politics of remembrance of twenty-five thousand years of Indigenous history versus what Virilio has described as the extermination of time (in favour of spatialized power) in technological societies. Here, tribal consciousness and real grounded sovereignty—duration and a vital sense of sedentariness—militate against the pure mobility of the war machine. And not just memory, but the cultivation of a dynamic ecological relationship with land, economy, and culture on the part of the abstract vectors of speed of consumer society. This is perfectly captured by the bitter political struggles between the peoples of the First Nations of Labrador and NATO low-level training flights by fighter jets. In the war machine, it is always land without history, people without remembrance, space without a sense of duration, the abstract control of territory against the loss of the history of territory.

Finally, what makes the Mohawks really dangerous for the Canadian state is their creation of a model of democratic politics based on matriarchal principles of rule. Here, the traditional form of the Longhouse society militates against rule by technocratic specialists of the war machine. Virilio says that in the war machine there are no longer priests who can mediate death. Now, the leaders of the war machine can speak triumphantly of mega-deaths, because death is also a release from the earthly constraints of gravitation. In this sense, the Mohawks are like gravity, a fall into real time, whose very communal existence militates against the pure speed, the will to endless circulation, of the war machine. If the peoples of the First Nations can be so oppressed, not only in Montreal but also in all of the Americas, from the United States to South America, maybe that is because they are the bad conscience of what we have become in the society of speed and war: perfect sacrificial scapegoats for feelings of anxiety and doubt about that which has been lost in the coming to be of the technological dynamo.

A previous version of this paper was originally published in A. Kroker, *The Possessed Individual*, New World Perspectives, 1992. Reprinted here with permission.

1 Paul Virilio (1983), *Pure War*, trans. Mark. Polizotti, New York: Semotext(e), p.18.
2 Virilio (1983), p.18.

you're enemy tongue

CHARLIE GREG SARK

your enemy tongue
is forked and strewn.
twitching in and out
of life's twilight.
darting and striking
with quick ease
in shadow truth,
always retreating.

your enemy tongues,
moist and practiced
in the sidewalk
chatter that slaps
and sucks the life
out of true love
strong, north and free.

your enemy tongues,
developed a taste
for the rough side
of marginal existence.
it's the monger
that greases the

glide of death
blood on its tip.

your enemy tongues,
asleep in the dark
corners of your
reality, but within
the reach of our
desire to be free;
reaching into our
dreams inherent
star-truths.

your enemy tongues,
a lie.
it lies to the many,
but even more
it lies to
you.

your enemy tongue
rejects talking respect,
and prefers talk
that tastes of blood.

your enemy tongues,
talk pounds flesh raw.
the pooling blood quenches
enemy tongues' thirst.

your enemy tongues,
are forked and strewn,
twitching in and out
of lifes' twilight.
darting and striking
with quick ease
in shadow truth,
always retreating.

your enemy tongues,
moist and practiced
in the sidewalk
chatter that slaps
and sucks the life
out of true love
strong, north and free.

your enemy tongues,
developed a taste
for the rough side
of marginal existence,
it's the mongers' justification
that greases the
glide of death
blood on its tip.

your enemy tongues,
sleep in the dark
corners of your
reality, but within
the reach of our
desire to be free;
reaching into our
dreams inherent
star-truths.

your enemy tongues,
lie.
lies to the many,
but even more
it lies to
you.

your enemy tongues,
reject talking respect,
preferring talk
that tastes of blood.

your enemy tongues'
talk pounds flesh raw,
the pooling blood quenches
enemy tongues' thirst.

Gratitude and Inspiration:

An Honour Song about Kanehsatà:ke

JUNE MCCUE

The summer of 1990 was when I woke up. Only 20 years old, with three years of undergraduate training behind me, I secured summer student employment at the Native Council of Canada (NCC) in Ottawa. During the hot summer days, we worked on bringing in Elders to speak to leaders about health issues from traditional perspectives. I remember meeting Albert Lightning and his son Rick Lightening from Hobema that summer. NCC had supported Aboriginal youth initiatives across Canada too. Through the Aboriginal Youth Council of Canada, I began to learn about politics at the national political organizational level. Then in July, Kanehsatà:ke happened.

The events I witnessed during the summer of 1990 changed my life forever. After work, I would rush back to the flat I shared with non-Aboriginal students to watch news updates about the Kanehsatà:ke crisis (we did not have email or the internet yet). I remember seeing a young spokesperson, Ellen Gabriel, speaking to media, warriors, rock throwing, a fatal gun shot, the SQ and the Canadian army. I knew there was an injustice taking place regarding the attempt to extend a golf course on Haudenosaunee lands, but I did not know about the complex issues that Kanehsatà:ke would raise for all of us (whether you were Indigenous or Canadian) as well. The deep current of political and racial tensions, which are always swirling between Canadian society and Indigenous Peoples, came to a head that summer. I had yet to develop an understanding about the nature of colonization, imperialism, racism, and land dispossession against Indigenous Peoples by colonial states like Canada. Nor did I have the legal training to understand the constitutional developments regarding Aboriginal peoples that had taken place over a decade before that summer in 1990. Kanehsatà:ke began my path to learning about issues like sovereignty, self-determination, and the inherent powers and rights of Indigenous Peoples. These are issues that I work on today and which I now have a responsibility to address. To achieve justice, we still need constitutional reform, legal pluralism, decolonization and the recognition of our inherent, international, and constitutional rights as Indigenous Peoples. Kanehsatà:ke was a pivotal moment in my life. Kanehsatà:ke woke me up to this reality.

A new generation of Indigenous leaders were born during that summer of 1990. Leaders who are now continuing the work of all those Elders, warriors, peacemakers, women, healers and braves ones that woke up, and began to teach the youth about our responsibilities. My political consciousness grew in the eastern direction from all those connections to Indigenous Peoples that I met in Ottawa since 1990. At a global level, I was part of an awaking by many Indigenous Peoples who also witnessed the human rights violations taking place during that summer. Almost 20 years later, I now see the magnitude of impact that Kanehsatà:ke had on me when I was an Indigenous youth. My Honour Song about Kanehsatà:ke is one of gratitude to the Haudenosaunee for standing up for their land and peoples, carrying on the legacy of their Ancestors and showing the rest of the world that we have come to a point of no return. For there to be peace, there must be justice.

It was pure serendipity to find myself working as a summer student at a national Aboriginal political organization when Kanehsatà:ke happened. Efforts were underway to mobilize support for the community members behind the barricades by actually going to them. Indigenous Peoples all across Canada and the United States organized solidarity gatherings to support the Mohawks that were behind the barricades too. On a very hot Saturday I went with friends from work to Kanehsatà:ke. We found out when we got near Kanehsatà:ke that the SQ and Canadian army had created a zone for protestors and that was the only place we would be allowed to go. I remember those black SQ uniforms vividly. Speeches were made by leaders, songs were sung, drummers beat their drums, people were dressed in beautiful regalia announcing to one another their identities. Although we knew about the hardships behind the barricades, on that hot summer day, I wondered if the families behind the barricades knew how much support they had from us. I picked up a Canadian flag with an Indian portrayed on top of the maple leaf, you know, the one that you get at pow-wows.

Back at my apartment, I told my roommates about the gathering. They just could not relate. I decided to use my Indian-Canadian flag as a curtain in my bedroom. I proclaimed that I would not take down this flag until the Haudenosaunee took down their barricades and there was peace. My roommates, all non-Aboriginal women from eastern/central Canada did not agree and told me to take it down. Their reason: it did not represent the views of everyone in the townhouse, yet it sent a message to anyone that walked by about support for the Haudenosaunee. This was the first time politics framed my relations with my roommates. Tension grew each day until I found myself getting a lock for my bedroom and not talking to my roommates much thereafter. It was like I was in my own little barricade. I continued to go to rallies and gatherings on Parliament Hill. Eventually, I moved out of the townhouse, but my flag did not come down until September 27, 1990.

I decided to apply to law school. I also continued my activism with the Aboriginal Youth Council of Canada regarding the United Nations Conference on Environment and Development (UNCED) and Rio.

To make sure Kanehsatà:ke did not happen again and to improve Canada's tarnished international face on human rights, a political will was manifested to create the Royal Commission on Aboriginal Peoples in 1991. I was fortunate to work as a summer student at the Commission researching on Aboriginal youth issues and participating in the First World Indigenous Youth Conference in Quebéc City. I met so many Elders and people from different nations around the world that summer. I will never forget that solidarity amongst Indigenous youth, nor the nights we slept out in tipiis on the Plains of Abraham, and waking to Hopi Elders conducting ceremonies and telling us about prophecies. We shared our similar stories and histories about crises, like Kanehsatà:ke.

Kanehsatà:ke was a catalyst for the constitutional talks regarding the Charlottetown Accord. Again, I worked with the Aboriginal Youth Council of Canada to mobilize aboriginal youth from across the country to participate in super quick consultations about the aboriginal package. My nascent legal training being in first year law school at that time assisted me to understand the amendments being sought by Aboriginal Peoples. But the problems in the package being proposed seemed to be at odds with the self-determining message that the Haudenosaunee and other Indigenous Peoples had rallied behind in 1990. The limits set out by Canadian governments were too great in my view and our peoples did not have enough time to review the proposal to consider the pros and cons. I was concerned about the Peace, Order and Good Government (POGG) clause limiting s. 35 rights and powers and that each Indigenous People or Nation in Canada was not at the table representing their respective peoples through their own agency. Learning from Kanehsatà:ke, I was particularly concerned that Canada could use its law enforcement power against Indigenous Peoples that were protecting their respective territories and peoples just as the Haudenosaunee did in 1990. I could anticipate that we would be back to the same problem all over again, except Canada could justify such coercive state control over our Peoples through their security or military apparatuses based on an unqualified POGG power. The peace and security of Indigenous Peoples in Canada remains a live issue to this day. I have come to learn about my own People's traditions about peace-making. And I have an elementary understanding of the Haudenosaunee's Great Law of Peace, which remains one of the very important teachings by Indigenous Peoples for the world.

Kanehsatà:ke also led to changes regarding specific claims. The Indian Claims Commission was set up to address outstanding treaty issues and outstanding crown obligations to aboriginal peoples. In British Columbia, a new treaty process was created. In the courts, more Indigenous Peoples were standing up for their rights, and some of the key Supreme Court of Canada decisions came out during this time to interpret the aboriginal and treaty rights s. 35 of the Canadian constitution. An elder's Kumick was set up at the Department of Indian and Northern Affairs. While I went to law school, I went to the Kumick to visit with Elders from all over the world as much as I could so I could get my "Indian education—Indigenous traditions" to balance out what I was learning about Canadian law and how Canada uses its laws to control our Peoples and lands. Without that training, I would have found it difficult to get through law school. All of these movements would not have taken place if the Haudenosaunee had not taken a stand in 1990.

During my time back east in the 1990s and since then, I met many inspirational teachers, Elders and people from the Haudenosaunee Confederacy. Elders like Ernie Benedict spoke often about constitutional reform, the peace treaties, and the Two Row Wampum relations with Canada and the United States and how these states continue to violate that relationship. Janice Longboat taught us about herbs and healing properties of the earth. I also remember listening to Sylvia Maracle talk about the clan mothers' role amongst her people. Patricia Monture was teaching at Ottawa Law School when I was there and has had a huge impact on Indigenous law students and women through her expressions about law, society, justice and her people, as a Mohawk woman. She continues to be an inspiration for me. Roberta Jaimeson is another strong leader from Six Nations that I have heard eloquently speak many times about our common issues, and some of the issues her people face now. At the international level, I have watched John Mohawk, Tom Porter, Mike Mitchell, Tonya Gonnella Frichner, Kenneth Deer and Beverly Jacobs advocate for Indigenous Peoples' rights. They have continued the work of their Ancestors that have been seeking equality for all nations of the world since World War I. I enjoy the writings of Taiaiake Alfred and the important messages he brings to colonial settler society and all Indigenous Peoples, especially youth. Olympians Alwyn Morris and Waneek Horn Miller have inspired many Indigenous youth in sports. These people love their lacrosse. The Haudenosaunee have a strong determination to lead, are proud of their heritage and identity and exercise their sovereignty. They have similar challenges as other Indigenous Peoples in the world who face poverty, but their belief in their inherent rights and power is irrepressible. This is evidenced in how they are handling recent disputes such as

Caledonia, as well as their ongoing border crossings and jurisdictional issues with states. In March 2009, I had the pleasure of meeting Ellen Gabriel for the first time in Ottawa. We talked about those prophecies and our collective responsibilities as Indigenous Peoples in this world. The message is the same as it was in 1990, our peoples need to get ready for the changes in the world—climate change and toxic pollution being front and centre. Ellen now takes leadership to advocate for Indigenous women in Quebéc, nationally and internationally. All of these Haudenosaunee people have assisted me to understand more about myself since Kanehsatà:ke happened. I learned this by observing their actions, hearing their voices and witnessing their expressions of self-determination, sovereignty, justice and peace.

After 10 years of teaching at a Canadian law school as an indigenous law teacher, I have picked up some legal tools to research and understand the legal dimensions to the land dispute that lead to Kanehsatà:ke, about human rights, and peace and security. Almost 20 years after Kanehsatà:ke, I continue to see the same unilateral, unlawful and unauthorized use of force deployed against Indigenous Peoples in Canada and in other states. Despite the fact that we have recommendations from inquiries and commissions, Indigenous human rights standard-setting, and court decisions that provide us with some tools to resolve land and jurisdiction questions in Canada, Indigenous Peoples and their lands continue to be under threat. Indigenous human rights defenders have been criminalized. The international Committee on the Elimination of Racial Discrimination has asked Canada this past summer to report on this matter. Some activists have been labelled and treated as "internal terrorists" or "domestic terrorists"—the perpetual enemy. Indigenous Peoples continue to experience the full force of Canada's (and the u.s.) law enforcement without scrutiny. This is unacceptable.

Indigenous Peoples have successfully convinced the world that our peace and security are fundamental universal human rights of collective and individual nature that states must respect and are obligated to adhere to. In my view, these standards limit state sovereignty and territorial integrity in relation to our Peoples and territories. We are continuing to press for international oversight, monitoring, protection in special times of conflict if necessary. The 2007 *United Nations*

Declaration on the Rights of Indigenous Peoples sets out the following standards that could have assisted the Haudenosaunee in 1990, and which can now be used to deal with the aftermath of Kanehsatà:ke. For example,

Emphasizing the contribution of the demilitiarization of the lands and territories of Indigenous peoples to peace, economic and social progress and development, understanding and friendly relations among nations and peoples of the world,

Art 3: Indigenous Peoples have the right to self-determination. By virtue of that right they freely determine their political status and freely pursue their economic, social and cultural development.

Art 7: 1. Indigenous individuals have the rights to life, physical and mental integrity, liberty and security of the person. 2. Indigenous peoples have the collective right to live in freedom, peace and security as distinct peoples and shall not be subjected to any act of genocide or any other act of violence, including forcibly removing children of the group to another group.

Art 8: 2 States shall provide effective mechanisms for prevention of, and redress for:

(b) Any action which has the aim or effect of dispossessing them on their lands, territories or resources;

Art 25: Indigenous peoples have the right to maintain and strengthen their distinctive spiritual relationship with their traditionally owned or otherwise occupied and used lands, territories, waters and coastal seas and other resources to uphold their responsibilities to future generations in this regard.

Art. 28: 1. Indigenous peoples have the right to redress, by means that can include restitution or, when this is not possible, just, fair and equitable compensation, for the lands, territories and resources which they have traditionally owned or otherwise occupied or used, and which have been consfiscated, taken, occupied, used or damaged without their free, prior and informed consent.

Art. 30: 1. Military activities shall not take place in the lands or territories of indigenous peoples, unless justified by a relevant public interest or otherwise freely agreed with or requested by the indigenous peoples concerned. 2. States shall undertake effective consultations with the indigenous peoples concerned, through appropriate procedures and in particular through their representative institutions, prior to using their lands or territories for military activities.

Art. 36: 1. Indigenous Peoples, in particular those divided by international borders, have the right to maintain and develop contacts, relations and cooperation, including activities for spiritual, cultural, political, economic and social purposes, with their own members as well as other peoples across borders. 2. States, in consultation and cooperation with indigenous Indigenous people, shall take effective measures to facilitate the exercise and ensure the implementation of this right.

Art. 37: 1. Indigenous peoples have the right to the recognition, observance and enforcement of treaties, agreements and other constructive arrangement concluded with States or their successors, and to have States honour and respect such treaties, agreements and other constructive arrangements.

Art 40: Indigenous peoples have the right to access to and prompt decision through just and fair procedures for the resolution of conflicts and disputes with States or other parties, as well as to effective remedies for all infringements of their individual and collective rights. Such a decision shall give due consideration to the customs, traditions, rules and legal systems of the indigenous peoples concerned and international human rights.[1]

By analyzing the story of Kanehsatà:ke at the intersection of the land dispute, peace and security and protection of human rights, and applying the aforementioned standards listed above, we can provide a fundamental check on state power through a mechanism to assess:

1. The status of Haudenosaunee Sacred and burial sites;

2. Outstanding land claim;

3. Municipal (city) powers to call on provincial police powers and army;

4. Role of SQ, RCMP, Canadian Armed Forces;

5. Review of Anti-Terrorist legislation, if applied to Indigenous Peoples including the Haudenosaunee;

6. Border issues;

7. Review of 2005 Canadian Forces Counter-Insurgency Manual that may treat Indigenous Peoples, but specifically the Mohawk Warrior Society as a domestic group that could use terrorist tactics in the future. This review should be set in historical context of how Haudenosaunee Ancestors were also treated like terrorists when they stood up to the world to have their political status recognized;

8. Use and impact of military activities, equipment, reconnaissance, aircraft over Haudenosaunee territory;

9. Review of those Haudenosaunee detained and arrested after Kanehsatà:ke

10. Reconciliation for lives lost, affected by PTSD, or on-going racial discrimination as a result of Kanehsatà:ke;

11. Review of the lack of federal obligations to protect constitutional status of Haudenosaunee, including their treaty rights;

12. Implementation of free, prior informed consent of Haudenosaunee re: lands and consultation regarding military matters;

13. Impact on Haudenosaunee self-determination including the role of Haudenosaunee women in decision-making about land and the people;

14. How to renew and implement treaties between Canada, U.S, and the Haudenosaunee; and

15. Haudenosaunee's laws of peace.

Some of this work could be done at the international level as well as with Canada at the state level. But what the Haudenosaunee have taught me is that their answers (and Canada's too) are set out in how their Ancestors related to each other, the covenants and promises they made to each centuries ago marked by the Two Row Wampum; the Great Law of Peace and their treaties. In other words, the Indigenous legal, political, social, cultural and economic traditions of the Haudeosaunee need to be respected with any diplomatic engagement with Canada. Finally, I firmly believe that it will be the Haudenosaunee women directing their men, guided by their Elders and inspired by their youth, that will lead to a restoring of balance in their relationship both internally amongst their citizens, and externally with Canada and the U.S. and other peoples around the world.

To the Haudenosaunee, you have taught me, along with my people and others, that

> *All peoples have the right to defend themselves.*
> *All peoples have the right to self-determination.*
> *All peoples have the right to peace.*
> *Including Indigenous Peoples.*

It is important that the compilation of stories in this book be told to the world. Even though Kanehsatà:ke happened almost 20 years ago, we now have a generation (both Indigenous and not) that is unaware of the huge impact Kanehsatà:ke had in our lives. By telling them these stories, I hope they can learn from this recent history and become aware or awake to our connection to these people and their courageous spirit to stand up to and challenge colonization in the name of peace.

---

1 *United Nations Declaration on the Rights of Indigenous Peoples* (2007), G.A. Res.61/295, U.N. Doc. A/RES/61/295 (2007).

The Human Right to Celebrate:

Achieving Justice for Aboriginal Peoples

PATRICIA A. MONTURE

It is despair with the way that the present system operates in practice that has led Aboriginal people to call for change. An Aboriginal system could fall well short of perfection and still respond to the needs of Aboriginal persons more effectively than the present justice system. As Donald Marshall, Jr., knows only too well, sometimes the police arrest innocent people, prosecutors purse them and courts convict them. We do not conclude that our system is unworkable; we strive to improve it. Let us approach Aboriginal justice systems in the same spirit.[1]

—*Law Reform Commission of Canada*, 1991

When I originally agreed to write this paper, I thought the focus would be on the 1991 report of the Law Reform Commission of Canada titled "Aboriginal Peoples and Criminal Justice: Equality, Respect and the Search for Justice" (Report 34). The Minister of Justice, Kim Campbell, requested this report under section 12(2) of the *Law Reform Commission Act* shortly after the "crisis" at Oka. But because of certain sudden and unexpected events in my life, my focus shifted.[2] I do wish to acknowledge the importance of the Commission's report because it advocated for the first time in a federal report the need to establish Aboriginal justice systems.[3]

A few months ago, my daughter and I were sitting in the living room watching the local news. There was another story about

Aboriginal Peoples that was negative. I do not even remember what the story was, largely because such a story is a frequent occurrence on the local Saskatchewan news, but I suspect it was the release of more criminal justice statistics. My girl, Kate, was very upset with this story. She asked me why do they always report the "bad" things about Aboriginal people. Then she started listing off a number of the Aboriginal youth she knew and what they had accomplished. It was a long list of accomplishment. All of my children have often participated with me on many protest walks often about the rights of women to be safe. Thinking about her friends and their accomplishments, she asked me: "why don't we have a human right to celebrate, rather than just be safe?" She stunned me that day with wisdom more profound than is expected of a sixteen year old. And I have returned to her question many times in the following months, recognizing the distance that spaces the demand to be "safe" from the one that recognizes we live lives that must be celebrated.

Recognizing that Aboriginal women (and men), do not yet have a right of safety, demonstrates to me just how far the journey ahead of us is. It also demonstrates to me that for a long time now I have been setting my standards far too low. Acknowledging this distance is an excellent way to begin a consideration of the gains that have been made since the "standoff"[4] at the Pines with regard to the achievement of justice for Aboriginal Peoples. It is my conclusion that we can no longer be satisfied with the demand to be safe, as this is a minimalist position.

There are many different ways that concepts of justice, including the right to be safe, are wound through what many know as the "Oka Crisis." The first stems from the reference that the Kanehsatà:ke's stand for their land at the Pines has become commonly known. Many an Aboriginal person recognizes the irony that the "crisis" is referenced to the white town and not some Kanien'kehaka[5] point of reference. The word "crisis" is also interesting to me as it infers that the situation occurred at a moment in time. But the dispute that underlies the stand the people made at the Pines has gone on for hundreds of years. As I write today, I acknowledge that it is not yet resolved. This stands as testament again to the illusive nature of justice for Kanien'kehaka peoples in their relationship with Canada.

During the summer of 1990, I did not actively participate in the standoff. Pregnant with my second son, my teachers and Elders told me I had to stay away. My relations instructed me to not even watch the standoff on TV. But, I could not help myself, as I feared for the safety of the citizens of my nation (some of them friends). From time to time, I did make comments to the media when they contacted me at Dalhousie Law School where I was in my first year of university teaching. I was severely impacted by the struggle of my nation at Kanehsatà:ke and at the same time proud of their actions.

This is not to say that it was also not a terrifying time. There is also no doubt in my mind that my two oldest sons were also profoundly impacted by the events in the summer of 1990. My eldest son was forced to learn from a young age—just six years old that summer—that justice was illusive for our people. He wanted to play "Oka" with the neighbourhood kids. He would be the Mohawk warrior complete with kerchief over his face. As a mother, recognizing the impact on my oldest son raises both frustration and resentment that I don't imagine a non-racialized parent is forced to confront. And that acknowledgement is invisible for those who do not confront it. As Aboriginal parents, our quality of life is often diminished and few question this. However, as a result he is a strong and determined young man who would not hesitate to give his life up if meant others of his people would have the justice that has been denied to us. Again, this is another uncomfortable place for a parent to be.

Although not the topic of this paper, I want to acknowledge that the standoff at the Pines had a significant impact on an entire generation of our youth, more so for the youth growing up at Kanehsatà:ke, Kahnawà:ke and Akwesasne. Terror and fear of state violence is not a reality that many Canadian parents have needed to acknowledge as they raise their children, and for me it is another profound contour of the denial of our right to be safe. Briefly then, these are the personal impacts that my family experienced, although minimal compared to the impact on the youth and families of the communities. But it does demonstrate the far-reaching effect of the actions of one community. In our quest for change, we cannot forget that each of our actions has a ripple effect.

A long time ago I learned that there are significant differences in the way western cultures and Aboriginal cultures approach a concept like justice.[6] In fact, in some Aboriginal languages you cannot find a word that precisely means justice. Aboriginal Peoples are creative so we can come up with words to use but (and this is a big but) it is not the same concept that is being described. And I worry that it is only the Aboriginal people who participate in such a discussion in English or French that have access to the cultural nuances (some would call them differences) that becomes muted through speaking a colonial language.

In Kahnien'kehaka traditions our focus is not justice but living in the way of peace.[7] When talking from within our own justice frame of reference, we do *not* talk about offenders, criminals or crimes. Rather, we talk about balance and the multiple ways in which individuals and our communities have had their ability to live in the way of peace interfered with and imposed upon. If an individual is acting out, it means that the family, clan and nation are also impacted.[8] Transgression of the law (read peace), therefore, requires a multifaceted and multilayered response if it is going to be addressed. At home, misbehaviors or transgressions of our laws are often commented about with the phrase "he or she was not raised right." This situates all transgressions of the law in the community rather than on the backs of the individual involved (the one who would be labeled elsewhere as the "offender"). This, so far, has proved to be an insurmountable distance between the way Canada chooses to do criminal justice and the ways of my own people. The individualization of criminal responsibility is such an important divergence it requires further scrutiny.

The fact that Canadian criminal law is constructed on individualized responsibility is an important aspect required if developing an understanding of why a Kanien'kehaka person would be dissatisfied with this model of justice. It is reflected in my discomfort with words like "offender," "criminal" or "inmate." At a recent lecture at the University of Saskatchewan, Professor Khylee Quince (Maori) explained that western systems of criminal justice require at the outset a deficit model of thinking.[9] Deficit thinking requires one to classify people as having problems with alcohol and drugs, a lack of education, a lack of resources (financial and otherwise), possessing a propensity for violence, having problems with anger, and so the list goes on. Immediately, I recognized the thinking of Canada's supreme court in the *Gladue* decision in considering the list of "background factors" which should mitigate the sentencing process of an Aboriginal person.[10] Professor Quince then explained that this stood in stark contrast to Maori processes of justice because the Maori focus is to find the building blocks within both the individual and community, which provide the opportunity to help someone back, perhaps for the first time, to well-being. It is the western world's preoccupation with deficit thinking that stands oppositionally to Kanien'kehaka practices, traditions and wisdom. This in turn impacts on how the ideal of justice is realized.

One of the prisms, and there are many, through which we can reflect on the "Oka Crisis" is a consideration of what is just. The people at the Pines brought forward their grievance of some 270 years with the hope that it would be resolved. To date, there is no resolution or remedy to the underlying land issues. After the people at the Treatment Centre "surrendered," they were all taken into state custody by force. And for some, criminal charges were laid. This begs the question "what is a crime?" To assume that what we find codified in the criminal laws of Canada is the best list of serious harms that can be done to a person is an assertion that warrants serious scrutiny. From my position, actions such as racial hate (such as the stoning of Kanien'kehaka citizens in Chateauguay), the theft of Indigenous land and the continued stripping of her resources or the denial of colonial reality that shaped (and continues to shape) the foundation of this country by the representatives of the Canadian state[11] are far more serious transgressions of the peace (including what is just). To view criminal wrongdoing as a universally valid priorization of harm is misleading and denies to disenfranchised persons a voice and forum to bring forward their claims and understanding of what a serious harm is.[12] By allowing states to provide inadequate opportunities to resolve land disputes brought by Indigenous Peoples and nations in a timely fashion and then using the laws to criminalization the very people who have been denied access to any remedy (perhaps because their poverty forecloses the opportunity for legal action)[13] can only be seen as a transgression of the just relations an Indigenous person should be guaranteed. This form of behaviour should be seen as collateral genocide.[14]

The idea of individualized criminal responsibility is not an appropriate context in the knowledge systems of many Indigenous nations. Hence, we do not have the need for the idea of guilt, as our system of redress is not based on punishment but rather returning to the peace. Looking at the concept, justice, it is immediately clear that the idea of criminal justice is simply a small component of what is important to the Kanien'kehaka when we speak about justice. Justice, for me, is a broader concept intended to capture the idea that we can live at peace and live in balance with our relations. And relation is not a simple concept either. It refers not only to all our human relatives (of all races) but also to the animals, the birds, the water creatures, the thunders, the trees and plants, the earth. It includes all in our universe that has spirit. In the context of this discussion, justice includes the right to live by your own laws and traditions as well as having others respect the legitimacy of those systems. It is then, and only then, that the right to celebrate who you are exists.

A word on translation of concepts from Kanien'kehaka and other Indigenous languages is important here. It is important because it exposes the power that is embedded in the way knowledge is structured by so-called "civil societies." Indigenous knowledges are verb based.[15] Thus, everything is action. Justice, however, is a noun, and there are few if any nouns in Indigenous languages. In putting Kanien'kehaka ideas about justice into English, the doing that comes with being a verb is lost. Justice relationships are embedded throughout our languages. When I go home and people ask me "how are you" this is not what they are really saying although we allow that parallel to be created to the way things are done in "civil society. What I am really being asked is if the great peace is with me.[16] If, by chance, I have not been behaving well out here in Saskatchewan and my people back home have heard about it (and trust me they will) then people will only say one word to me: Sekon (hello). If they ask if the great peace is with me and I respond that it is not they are bound by their traditions to help me. This is a wonderful example of how complex (yet simple) "justice" things are for the Kanien'kehaka. Noticing that the people at home are only saying hello to me is my own responsibility. I must acknowledge that I need to get back to our ways before anyone is able to hold their hand out to help me. This is a fine example of the way in which the individual is embedded in the community and the community in the individual.

From the Canadian justice system's perspective many elements contained in understanding the term "justice" are also engaged when considering the events at Kanehsatà:ke in 1990. These include law and order, the rule of law, crime and punishment, the ability of the state to engage military force and protect what they perceive to be their territories. These concepts are believed to be essential to order in a "civil society." Yet they are engaged without any acknowledgement of the cultural assumptions on which they are based or the way they may reflect process of colonial relations, which were often delivered up to Aboriginal Peoples through law. This list includes the taking of land and resources, the denial of citizenship, the denial of the vote, residential schooling, the apprehension of children and the imprisoning of our youth, men and women. The assertion that the Canadian criminal justice system is based on neutrality appears nothing short of ridiculous to a traditional Aboriginal person.

Other basic tenets of the Canadian legal system or justice system are also engaged. Ideas like private property are assumed as superior and necessary for the construction of "modern" legal systems. For example, Vago and Nelson note that not every society has a formal legal system comprised of police, courts, judges, lawyers and jails (as though these western cultural things are the only things that can comprise formality). They continue uncritically purporting that

> ...for example, throughout the developing world, the formal systems of property rights taken for granted in advanced nations simply do not exist... traditional societies rely almost exclusively on custom as the source of legal rules and resolve disputes through conciliation or mediation by village Elders, or by some other moral or divine authority. As for law, such societies need little of it. Traditional societies are more homogeneous than modern industrial ones. Social relations are more direct and intimate, *interests are shared by virtually everyone, and there are fewer things to quarrel about.* Since relations are more direct and intimate, nonlegal and often informal mechanisms of social control are generally more effective.[17]

This vision of "civil society's" view of law is built on several assumptions about the structure of what they would have us believe are "primitive" societies. Vago and Nelson suggest that Aboriginal communities comprise people who share interests and therefore, there is no need to quarrel. (Apparently, the authors have never visited an Aboriginal community or joined us at the supper table.) Such a sameness amongst all suggests a simpleness that is equivalent to inferiority. It suggests, additionally, that to be an authentic "traditional" person belonging to a "traditional society" is a thing of the past when life was simpler. This reinforces another stereotype and also denies us a modern identity. The idea that all "primitive" peoples are the same is not only wrong but, frankly, is ridiculous. There is not only great diversity across Indigenous nations; there is also great diversity within those nations. Perhaps this is based on a fundamental misunderstanding of "man in nature"[18] where nature is seen as something to conquer and therefore, the only goal of primitive society can be basic survival. Furthermore, this is precisely the attitude of the superiority of private property systems and unquestioned assumptions that lay at the heart of the dispute at the Pines.

This is not an old text that is being quoted and it is used in many introductory sociology of law classes at many Canadian universities. It is a reflection on what our education system has to offer. Sadly, it does not ensure that students have the opportunity to learn to be critical about legal relations in this country and denies to students the opportunity to learn to critique. It places false boundaries around what is knowledge (that is, we superior people have it, you others do not). Yet, it ignores the influence of Indigenous Peoples on the very theories, such as Marx or Engels, that these university-based scholars quote.[19] My frustration grows not as much within the pain of living a colonized life and all the loses that entails, without remedy or sincere apology, but in the denial, ultimately a racist one, to share Haudenosaunee views of achieving justice (more accurately peace), teachings I feel that Canada would deeply benefit from at this point in their history.

Kanien'kehaka understandings rest on a different construction on what justice is. Common cultural understandings include ideas such as having a "good mind" and living in the way of peace. Peace is more than living without violence. It is about how you live your life every day with a commitment to living with a good mind. It is based on the ability of humans to be rational. Equally important, it is based on an ability to be forgiving. These are the ideas, as I have come to understand them, that ground Haudenosaunee law. The Great Law, which we must never forget, is a law about peace and was the basis of the resolution between the Canadian army and their leopard tanks, the Government of Quebéc, the Government of Canada and the people of many nations who stood together to defend the graves of our Ancestors. As I reflect on the events of twenty years ago, the importance of the Great Law of Peace in bringing to a resolution the force brought against the people of the Pines and their supporters, presents another irony. Although I am grateful for the visibility of our traditions in the media coverage of the days and days of violent confrontation the state chose to impose on the people, the result of following our way to peace brought us only the imposition of criminal laws and military force. Returning to the teachings of my daughter, I am reminded that we were not safe and are not safe. But I can now visualize the possibility of celebrating who we are and perhaps one day have the human right to be who we are as Kanien'kehaka. She left me a great gift, a gift that I share with you.

---

1 Law Reform Commission of Canada (1991), *Aboriginal Peoples and Criminal Justice* (Report 34), Ottawa: Law Reform Commission of Canada, p. 23.

2 From the time I started writing this paper, and its completion, I was suddenly and unexpectedly dealing with the death of my daughter. And a government report seemed to be quite meaningless. My definition and experience of justice began to evolve. At times, I am over come by anger and irony at being daughterless, having given my life to fight racism and seeking justice for Aboriginal Peoples. Then, to be left finding myself without my girl because of corporate indifference and racism is a cruelty that was once unimaginable. As a result, my questions and thoughts about justice have radically been shifted.

3 Law Reform Commission of Canada (1991), *Aboriginal Peoples and Criminal Justice* (Report 34), Ottawa: Law Reform Commission of Canada, p. 22.

4 I am using this word to remind people that the underlying land issues remain unresolved at Kanehsatà:ke. It seems fair and reasonable to conclude that as soon as the "inconvenience" of our "demonstration" is out of the world's lens, little progress is made. This is not just a statement about power (and justice cannot be discussed without acknowledging who has power and who does not) but also a statement that should frame our understanding of the choices that were made.

5 The author is a member of the Mohawk nation and is known as Aye-wah-han-day. My name means "getting things going with words."

6 Please see Patricia Monture-Angus (1995), "The Roles and Responsibilities of Aboriginal Women: Rethinking Justice" in *Thunder in My Soul: A Mohawk Woman Speaks*, Halifax: Fernwood Publishing, pp. 216–248.

7 For example, please see Douglas George-Kanentiio (2000), *Iroquois Culture and Commentary*, Sante Fe, Clearlight Publishing; Steve Wall (2001), *To Become a Human Being: The Message of Tadodaho Chief Leon Shenandoah*, Charlottesville: Hampton Roads Publishing; and Paul Wallace (1994), *The Iroquois Book of Life: White Roots of Peace*, Sante Fe: Clear Light Publishing.

8 For an early work in this area please see William B. Newell (Ta-io-wah-ron-ha-gai), *Crime and Justice Among the Iroquois*, Montreal: Caughnawaga Historical Society, 1965.

9 Khylee Quince (2009), "The Elephant in the Room: Ethnicity in Criminal Offending," Public Lecture delivered at the University of Saskatchewan, October 8, 2009.

10 *R. v Gladue*, (1991) 1 S.C.R. 688 at paragraphs 66 and 67.

11 And for the Prime Minister to suggest that he was speaking of Canada's economic relations shows how limited his understanding and knowledge of Canada's deep history of colonial relations is. Alcohol was used to increase the value extracted from Indigenous Peoples by fur traders or the settlers who went west to farm received advantages from both banks (in the form of loans for farm equipment) and governments (land grants) that Aboriginal persons were statutorily denied because their lands could not be mortgaged. And over time the early access to those benefits by settlers and not "Indians" has resulted in the accumulation of wealth by settlers that Aboriginal farmers cannot yet imagine. Yet, the "Indian" is frequently asked to forget the historic injustices and just get on with it.

12 For the understanding required to properly contextualize this analysis, please see Jeffrey H. Reiman (2007), *The Rich Get Richer and the Poor Get Prison: Ideology, Class and Criminal Justice*, Boston: Pearson/Allyn and Bacon.

13 Not only am I turning the focus on social responsibilities that impair our access to justice, but for a Kanien'kehaka citizen there is an ultimate irony of proceeding to a court of foreign jurisdiction (that would be Canada) who's Ancestors wrongfully to took land, to have them admit that the taking was unlawful even under their own rules.

14 I am using this term in the same way collateral violence is used.

15 Please see the discussion in Rupert Ross (1996), *Returning to the Teachings: Exploring Aboriginal Justice*, Toronto: Penguin Books, pp. 101–130.

16 I acknowledge the late Jake Thomas for sharing his understanding of the language and our ways.

17 Steven Vago and Adie Nelson (2008), *Law and Society*, Toronto: Pearson. Emphasis added.

18 Gender specificity is intended here.

19 Patricia Monture (2007), "What is Sovereignty for Indigenous People" in George Pavlich and Myra Hird eds., *Questioning Sociology: Canadian Perspectives*, Don Mills: Oxford University Press, pp. 253–265.

From Little Things...

KIERA L. LADNER

On a recent trip to Australia, I had the great honour of hearing a phenomenal mix of Indigenous artists in concert in Melbourne marking the closing of the 2008 World Indigenous Peoples Conference in Education. It is here that I first heard Archie Roach sing Paul Kelly and Kev Carmody's song "From Little Things Big Things Grow."[1] It is a song that tells the story of the Gurindji stockmen in Australia's Northern Territory in 1966, and how their seemingly small act of resistance changed Australia and Indigenous Peoples there, forever. It is a story of how a small group of Gurindji stockmen led by Vincent Lingairi walked off the job at cattle station on leased "Crown lands" (where they had been so poorly paid) to resolve their claims and attain the land rights that had been denied them since colonialism/occupation began. The occupation of Wattie Creek and the accompanying eight-year-long strike became one of the first "modern" land battles in Australia where Indigenous Peoples had historically had no "legal" rights to their lands and no political rights as nations.

Though there had been other movements and other acts of resistance, it was the Gurindji strike that put land rights on the national stage in Australia and began the long and unfinished process of transforming Indigenous rights in Australia and mobilizing Indigenous Peoples seeking change. These heroic acts of few serve as testimony, just as the song suggests, to the fact that "from little things big things grow." This is not to suggest that the Gurindji that "sat down" on their lands changed the world or transformed Australian land policy singlehandedly, for they did not. But they had a part in it, and, more importantly, they inspired others to act, to think, to mobilize, to imagine transformative change, to acknowledge their role in that change and to realize that there were others ready to stand and be counted. Even more important is the fact that the impact of such acts of resistance are not time-bound, but that the echoes of such resistance continue to inspire future generations.[2]

There have been and will continue to be countless seemingly "little things from which big things grow" on Turtle Island. Little things like the message of peace, power and righteousness that Hiawatha and the Peacemaker promoted among the Onkwehonwe and which became the foundation of the Great Law of Peace and the creation of a confederacy of nations founded on this message (the Haudenosaunee). Little things like Mistahimaskwa refusing treaty, citing the need for meaningful and trustworthy consultation and negotiation and reminding the representatives of the Crown that the Nehiyaw are a sovereign people, who will not (and have not) ceded their right to self-determination nor their territories, which they agreed to share with the newcomers. Little things like the women (including Sandra Lovelace, Jeannette Corbière Lavell and Irene Bédard) who refused to leave and/or returned to their reserves after they had married non-status men, gotten divorced or been widowed and who brought this gendered inequality to the streets, the Canadian Courts, the constitutional talks, the United Nations and the International Court of Justice. Little things like all of those parents and grandparents who refused to allow the state/church to take their kids to residential school and fought tirelessly for day schools, access to high school, integration and band-controlled education. Little things like Frank Calder and the Nisga'a Nation taking the Canadian Government to court in the 1970s in defense of their land rights and Aboriginal Title. Little things like all those fishermen (and women) like Dorthy Van der Peet and Donald Marshall Jr. who struggled for years on their rivers, their lakes and their oceans to maintain their fisheries despite being told that they were "fishing illegally" and knowing that they would end up in Canadian jails and courts. Little things like the Dene Declaration of 1975 and the corresponding mobilization of the nation in defense of their homelands. Little things like . . .

The echoes of these past resistances continue to be heard. I am sure that the echoes of past were heard that March at Kanehsatà:ke when a group of people decided to quietly block a dirt road in their community to raise awareness of the local golf course's intention of developing their community commons (a piece of land that had been claimed as part the Kanien'kehaka community since the from the outset when the Kanien'kehaka established that community and started to bury their people in those now iconic pines on the commons). Given that this was not the first attempt to have settler governments deal with the very same land issue that defined the 1990 resistance and given that this was not the first flashpoint or episode of mobilization in Kanehsatà:ke, I am quite certain echoes of the past were heard that summer as the Ancestors stood shoulder to shoulder with the generations of today.

The echoes of this resistance continue to be heard across the country and quite likely they reverberate throughout the world. The resistance at Kanehsatà:ke was a flashpoint that captured the attention of the world, and the hearts of minds of many. Generations past had their own defining and/or unifying moments, such as the standoff at Wounded Knee, the American Indian Movement, the closure of a residential school, the near nuclear standoff in the Bay of Pigs, the constitution train and the talks that led to the patriation of the Canadian Constitution with its Charter and its recognition of Aboriginal and Treaty Rights or those televised moments of the Aboriginal Constitutional Conferences in the 1980s where Trudeau belted out the lord's prayer in his attempt to drown out an Elders' Prayer. For many of my generation, the Kanehsatà:ke resistance is that place from which big things grew. This is not to suggest that the impact of those Kanien'kehaka blockades was generational, but rather that that this resistance was a defining moment for many and that its echoes inspired transformative dreams, actions and change and will continue to influence and inspire generations yet to come.

As a flashpoint event,[3] the summer of 1990 was not the start nor was it the end of the resistance at Kanehsatà:ke. But, as the main event on the news month after month that year and as the primary topic of discussion in the Red Lodge at the University of Calgary's and over lunches, coffees, beers and pool across the University and at home, the

"Oka Crisis" became a defining moment in my life. For me, its significance became not only the marking of a historical event or a flashpoint in Canadian history that caused the masses to take note, but the manner in which it caused me to question my life and my life's journey. Alongside the echoes and teachings of other moments in history, it made me and so many of my generation take note of the potential cost of our struggles to bring life to the treaty relationship and renew Indigenous sovereignty.

But it was not just people of my generation who took note. The events at Kanehawake and Kanehsatà:ke and the people of Akwesasne, Kanehawake and Kanehsatà:ke affected us all—Indigenous and non-Indigenous alike. The reason, as Ovide Mercredi explains. is quite simple:

> During the summer of 1990 we in Canada saw events and scenes that, depending on one's personality or politics, either raised consciousness or triggered the most primary emotions. Whether or not you are for or against the Mohawk Nation, the warriors, the Sûreté du Québec, the Canadian army, the Quebéc government, the Department of Indian Affairs or its Minister, the federal government, Premier Bourassa or Brian Mulroney, one thing is certain: none of us can escape the impact, the implications or the consequences of the imbalance in the relationship between Canada and the First Nations. We must live with that show of force against Mohawk people.
>
> As a result of the conflict at Oka all of us have come to at least one realization—that ignoring the rights and aspirations of the First Nations in this country will imperil the unity and stability of Canada.[4]

Though I would argue that that for most Canadians and their governments that realization was short lived (thus explaining the lack of change and the continued necessity of flashpoint events), there is no denying that that show of force against Kanien'kehaka—against people most Canadians (wrongly) identified as fellow citizens—was troubling, to say the least. In short, it was Canada's wake up call. It was a "public announcement" of sorts, warning of the cost of action and inaction.

Regardless as to whether the message was ever really heard, at the time, it was impossible for Canadians and Indigenous people alike not to think about the cost of action and inaction. It was impossible no matter who you were, where you lived or on what side of the metaphorical blockade you would stand. There were blockades. There were rocks. There were tanks, guns, bayonets, helicopters, snipers and anything else that the Canadian army and the Quebéc paramilitary provincial police force could imagine. There were Elders and children who had their cars pelted with rocks or who were beaten (even bayoneted) as they attempted to leave their communities. And then, of course, there were the people who stood on their lands protesting the development of their lands (a commons which held the trees their Ancestors planted and the bones of their Ancestors) for yet another golf course and parking lot. They were the people—the women, children, Elders and men—behind the blockades and on our television sets every night talking about their Ancestors, the treaties that they signed with the newcomers, their lands/the Pines and the violence that besieged them on the blockades, in the neighboring towns, by Quèbècois, Canadians, their army and the Sûreté du Québec (the sq).

For many, the standoff came with at least one more realization—what was happening at Kanehsatà:ke and Kahnawà:ke could be happening in their community; it could be them. That time of crisis made those with commitments and responsibilities ask, what would I do? I asked myself that very questions many times that summer as I watched events unfold across the country at Kanehsatà:ke and Kahnawà:ke and closer to home as Milton Born With A Tooth and the Warrior Society of the Peigan Nation stood in vehement opposition to the destruction of their homelands with the building of the Old Man Damn. I have asked myself that very question so many times since. Thankfully, I never have had to make a decision as to whether or not I was willing to stand on a blockade nose to nose with the Canadian army. I have never had to decide what I was willing to sacrifice. I hope I will never be forced to make such a decision. But if that time should come calling, I know what the answer will be.

But while I have never been forced to decide whether I was willing to stare down the barrel of a gun or to stand before a tank, I nevertheless made a decision to stand up during that Indian summer. It is a decision that I live each and every day. It was a decision made as a university student experiencing the "Oka Crisis" through the media from half way across the country. It was a decision that was empowered by both experiences—university and the images of men, women and children facing an army as they held up their treaty and defended what was left of their land. It was a decision to stop thinking about what to do and to pick up the fight. But unlike the people standing on the blockades or the warriors of past, I would pick up neither arrowhead nor gun but learn to take up my responsibilities with pen and paper and write about the treaties, Indigenous sovereignty and in defense of those on the front lines. While I never imagined that such a decision would lead to the life I now live—making my living acting as a word warrior[5]—I am ever mindful of why I do this and I know that there are many others who, like me, took up this fight or who became warriors in different arenas because of what we saw that summer or our reflections thereof.[6]

Looking back, my memories of watching the reality of this long-standing land dispute at Kanehsatà:ke and the equally long standing struggles in Kanien'kehaka resistance and resiliency every night on television were both horrifying and a source of strength. The images of those women, children and men standing face to face with the army, the images of a young girl being bayoneted by an officer and the images of these amazing people standing up with such conviction and bravery on the lines, in negotiations and with reporters still have the ability to move people today thanks to filmmakers such as Alanis Obomsawin, artists such as Joanne Cardinal Shubert and authors such as Richard Wagamese.[7] It was, and continues to be (in classrooms and communities) a transformative moment for all of us as members of nations (settler, Indigenous and possibly both) as we watched a standoff consume Canada in a dialogue over basic human rights, capitalism and the pretenses of colonialism.

It is likely that the "Oka Crisis" will become one of those canadian historical events that once "whitewashed" gets recounted by television commercials and text book writers alike—one that will result in Indigenous Peoples (beyond the likes of Riel and Mistahimaskwa) finally making an appearance in canadian history books, post-fur trade. And so it should. It was a defining moment for both Indigenous Peoples and settler society separately, and collectively. We as peoples (Indigenous nations and settler societies) can never go back. Shortly after the crisis had ended (or what some called the end of Indian summer), Richard Wagamese wrote in his weekly column in the *Calgary Herald* of several lessons learned; lessons which if they were actually learned and understood, explain why we can never go back. Among the lessons leaned Wagamese includes:

> LESSON THREE: The situation is not over. Although the Oka stalemate has ended, native groups across Canada have become enlightened and encouraged by the Mohawks. There is a deep-rooted sense of Aboriginal solidarity that has never existed in Canada before.
>
> Oka has become a symbol, both to Indians and mainstream Canadians...
>
> LESSON FOUR: The standoff did not end peacefully. How peacefully can someone be thrown to the ground by six to 10 soldiers? How peacefully do platoons of soldiers fix bayonets and point them at unarmed civilians, including women and children.
>
> LESSON SIX: The Canada we felt we knew disappeared forever. The hardest lesson of all. The rumble of tanks through Oka spelled the end of the "true North strong and free." It meant that responsible government in Canada was willing to send its troops against its own [supposed] citizens in order that right, might and white could prevail.[8]

While Canada, its governments and many of its people may have never completely come to the type of realization that the likes of Wagamese forecasted, I do think that as a result of the resistance at Kanehsatà:ke and Kahnawà:ke, Canada's metaphorical blindfold was finally been removed and that faked sense of Canadian innocence trampled. This was our Wounded Knee. While we did not have agents of the state engaging a sustained gunfight, Marlon Brando taking up the cause in Hollywood or the likes of Neil Young and Buffy Saint Marie singing of it, it happened and we were all affected.[9] The false sense of innocence and admiration that Canadians had for themselves and their treatment of the "Indian problem" was crumbling (one could hypothesize that it would have been shattered had Kanehsatà:ke not been surrounded by Québec, for many Canadians simply blamed Québec). Its impact and influence was not limited to the actual events of the so-called "Oka Crisis," or to the dialogue that transpired in band offices, coffee shops, homes, boardrooms, offices, legislatures and classrooms across Canada (and the world). For many, the Indian summer of 1990 was a transformative moment marked by a standoff eerily similar to others around the world where students stood face to face with tanks and nations stood face to face with a military force and the corporate interests that they were to defend. It was a moment that defined. It was a moment that empowered. It was a moment that changed us. And for some, it was a moment that changed everything. All this despite the fact that, for the communities involved, many would say it changed nothing, as those issues that resulted in the resistance (issues such as the violation of treaties, disregard for Onkwehonwe land rights, non-consultation, non-negotiation, and poor relations with the federal government) have not only ensued, they have worsened.

Looking across the country "post-Oka," one will note that there appears to have been a dramatic uptake in mobilizing resistance within the public space. This apparent increase should not be confused with a actual increase in protest and resistance, for quantifying resistance is all but impossible and Indigenous Peoples have been engaging in politics of contestation since the invasion and occupation of the Americas began.[10] The difference is that both efforts to mobilize and the episodes of mobilization in and of themselves intensified. Combined with the media, Canadians and their governments started to pay more attention to such flashpoint events or episodes of resistance (or at least governments claim to do so in the media, legislatures and international arenas). Paying attention or any such claims thereof, however, should not be confused with intentions—or for that matter even efforts—to effectively deal with the issues that underline such acts of resistance.

Indigenous Peoples have been engaging in politics of contestation and resisting colonization since the arrival of the first settlers (this may even date back to the first explorers). Indigenous Peoples continue to engage in such politics every day. In fact, as so many have said, to be born Indian is to be born political. As Taiaiake Alfred suggests, this may even be more exaggerated for Mohawks.[11] Aside from the major organizations (band, tribal, provincial and federal) it is only when opportunities arise (or are created) that the masses mobilize, "kitchen table" networks are engaged, wider networks are rekindled and the movement becomes organized.[12] Episodes of mobilization have varied and will continue to vary in orientation, issue, the level of mobilization (elite or popular), the ability (and desire) to organize and create organizational capacity, as well as the domains of mobilization. Though using different methods, it is almost always the same issues that are being contested and questioned in every flashpoint event and this has been constant through history, as Indigenous Peoples have taken up matters of citizenship, territoriality, development and Canadian sovereignty.

The issues at hand have not changed. Indigenous struggles have been and will continue to be defined by or predicated on considerations of nationhood and decolonization.[13] Though overwhelmed with frustration and while they know that they are fighting a battle representative of a modern-day matching of David and Goliath, people have not given up. Even after the "Oka Crisis" and the constant bombardment of images in the media of the settler governments sending in the army with its tanks, foot soldiers, snipers and helicopters to deal with people whom they claim as their citizens—imagine what would happen if they actually saw Kanien'kehaka as enemy aliens or terrorists (though they have attempted to use this label since). Rather than devastating efforts to mobilize or stalling their momentum, the people that stood up at Kanehsatà:ke and Kahnawà:ke and those communities as a whole empowered and strengthened the dedication, perseverance and commitment of others. It is as if the voices of the people involved joined the voices of other flashpoints and the voices of the Ancestors in song—honouring, empowering and encouraging others in their struggles. It is as is said in Cree, Kwayask ê-kî-pê-kiskinowâpahtihicik, which means that "their example will show me the way." I can absolutely say that in that Indian summer (the summer of 1990, which for activists at Kanehsatà:ke seems to have started in March when the snow was still on the ground), their example did indeed show us the way.

Indeed, I have heard such comments expressed from sea to sea, in a variety of forums including "kitchen tables." Throughout Indian Country people continue to be empowered by these memories. Like the authors and artists in this book and beyond, people are empowered by the courage and dedication of those women, those children, those Elders and those men who stood up for what they believed to be their right and thus, their responsibility. By the courage and compassion of supporters from all nations. By the nations (however divided) that reminded us who we are as Indigenous Peoples and/or Canadians and who provided each of us with timely lessons in strength, responsibility, shame and humility. While the echoes of these lessons wane from time to time, they are constantly picked up by others and given new life on a new "kitchen table," on a blockade, in another community or through a new initiative in classrooms, in research, in Canada and even internationally.

There are many conflicts between Indigenous Peoples and the settler state. While most elected Indigenous leaders have been engaged in bringing their issues to the forefront of Canadian politics. Many Indigenous people have been engaged in bringing issues of concern to the "tables" of their nations and have engaged in the rebuilding of their nations—politically, economically and socially. Indeed, in my travels across Indian Country I have come across many "kitchen tables" in private homes, coffee shops and offices as well as in gathering places, ceremonies and longhouses where unelected leaders (many will cringe by my mere suggestion that they constitute leaders) and traditional leaders (traditional governments and otherwise) of the community gather to address issues of concern to their nation. In many cases, there is no table—kitchen or otherwise—but simply a discussion within traditional venues and/or a directive from such structures. Such was the case in the Kanehsatà:ke resistance. There was no kitchen table. Instead, there were discussions in the Longhouse and (many) people who acted headed the call of their Longhouse to assert sovereignty and protect Kanien'kehaka territory.

Still, the idea of the metaphorical "kitchen table" is utilized to emphasize the fact that these are not state officials (*Indian Act* governments or bureaucrats) but individuals who—often because of circumstance—take on leadership roles and who, as a result, are often found meeting formally or informally among themselves and/or with community members at kitchen tables in the community (not in the usual boardrooms, band council offices or community halls). In many ways, the metaphorical kitchen table and the kitchen table resistance that results is an expression of traditional governmental processes and Indigenous political philosophies. For instance, the Anishinaabe, Niitsitapi (Blackfoot) and Nehiyaw created incredibly complex systems of governance while at the same time embracing situational leadership thereby allowing for flux and enabling people to take up their responsibilities as leaders situationally. But while kitchen tables represent the new webs or the contemporary iterations of traditional practices whereby individuals take up their responsibilities to act and/or to lead and do so in a manner that upholds their sovereignty, this is not always the case. Kitchen table resistance is not always grounded in tradition (strategically, philosophically or structurally). It is, however, always a mobilization at the grassroots which may or may not include traditional governments.

Today, these kitchen table resistances are what they are, as there is no discernable absolute—only people who, as individuals or collectives, take on leadership roles outside of band governance or who decide to mobilize. They are the fishers who decided collectively to continue fishing under the darkness of night when Canadian governments disregarded the treaties and their sovereignty by banning Indigenous fisheries, who regulated themselves and who mobilized to create their own fisheries officers to ensure their safety. They are the Clan Mothers who made the decision after hours of discussions at various tables (in kitchens and a local restaurant) to go fishing. They are the numerous people who have dreamed and organized the re-occupation of provincial parks, ceremonial space and construction sites. They are the traditional leaders and governments who dreamed, mobilized their people and organized blockades and occupations to stop development or resource exportation. They are the academics who from time to time have opportunities to gather around metaphorical kitchen tables (metaphorical since such gatherings often involve multiple venues and phones) to dream, strategize and mobilize as "word warriors." Such metaphorical kitchen tables and the action they provoke arise out of frustration. They represent an acknowledgement of responsibility. They speak to the issues and problems that underline Indigenous politics and thus, are predicated on considerations of nationhood and (de)colonization. They arise out of defense of tradition, territory and a right to live as a nation. They speak to the economic realities of communities but also of the realities of development and the pending destruction of territory. The represent a reckoning of those involved.

In my travels, I have heard tell of conversations had and decisions made—decisions that were empowered and influenced by the echoes of the resistance at Kanehsatà:ke and Kahnawà:ke. Decisions made at the peak of their own frustration or at the height of their own crisis that others had done it, survived and brought the nation to its couches where it sat and watched the crisis play out on their television sets. For instance, I remember a conversation at Esgenoôpetitj or Burnt Church about how the women involved in resistance at Kanehsatà:ke were a great source of strength and their echoes were there in the decision to go fishing (the events that started the so-called "Lobster Wars"), in their decision to create a blockade, and then again during the crisis as they dealt with a home-grown warrior movement, federal officers, police brutality, public insurgencies against them in the surrounding communities and a federal government that was unwilling to negotiate (but at least it was at the table, unlike in 1990 where the federal government refused to involve itself in the crisis or its dissolution). For the women that started the Lobster Wars or the Burnt Church resistance, for the communities involved and for the women, Elders, men, and children (warriors included), the "Oka Crisis" was a source of strength, inspiration and guidance.

This has been the case in other communities as people sitting around the kitchen tables of that nation made the decision to stand up, to quit talking and to do something. It must be noted, however, that it is not as if those people who made the initial decision to stand up from their metaphorical "kitchen table" at Kanesatà:ke (which was never a table, but rather a discussion within the Longhouse) or those who made a similar decision that summer at Kahnawà:ke were the first to be inspired to do as that Nike ad suggests—just do it. Here too, the discussion in the communities that resulted in the "Oka Crisis" also drew on the echoes of the past and on an example of another community's efforts in its decision to mobilize. But it also has to be noted that while the echoes of the past and the examples of other are ever-present at those metaphorical kitchen tables, the echoes of the resistance at Kanesatà:ke and Kahnawà:ke (and as supported by and involving Akwesasne) are noticeably different. The "Oka Crisis" was different—it was televised. We were all there, watching, emotionally wrought as it happened from the comfort of our living rooms. But like many Americans say of the

Vietnam War, for the first time, it was if it were happening in our living rooms. Thus, from coast to coast to coast and to the coasts beyond that, for many the "Oka Crisis" was a personal experience.

As I have said, for me, this was a personal experience. Watching what was going on brought me to one of the most important decisions of my life—to choose a pencil rather than an arrowhead, or pen and paper instead of facing a bullet. It empowered the kitchen tables (desks and pub tables) that I sat at in 1990 as a student, asking what I could do and dreaming of a Canada that respected Indigenous Peoples and upheld its responsibilities under the treaties. It empowers the kitchen tables that I sit at now as a scholar where we sit and discuss these same issues and engage in battles time and time again as we to find or create a way forward that does not necessitate new flashpoint events. In this way, that Indian summer continues to be more than a memory—it became a way of life, a personal experience that defined us.

Though the "Oka Crisis" was a different, semi-personal experience for outsiders, for those inside the struggle, after the crisis came more of the same—only worse. Not only did the very issue which sparked this flashpoint event never get resolved, as the "ownership" of the commons in Kanehsatà:ke is still questioned, the Quebéc government established a provincial park on other lands claimed by the community and housing projects continue to eat up disputed lands (lands once treated as reserve lands) at an alarming rate. Add to this the continued maltreatment of community members by police and of the communities involved by both federal and provincial governments, and it becomes very clear why many think the resistance and/or their sacrifice achieved nothing.

True, the "Oka Crisis" was by and large a wake up call that was never heard. The Canadian government has yet to effectively respond to or even begin to resolve the land question at Kanehsatà:ke, not to mention the lingering question of Kanien'kehaka sovereignty (as recognized by treaty and thus, the Canadian constitution) or the difficult relationship that exists between the two nations. Similarly, the Canadian government has yet to effectively deal with such issues beyond Oka. As a result, communities from coast to coast to coast continue to assert their rights and responsibilities and will continue to seek resolution of their claims using a variety of mechanisms, including the resurrection of blockades across roads, train tracks and at the entrance to those lands rich in natural resources that corporate interests seek to exploit. Perhaps more importantly, beyond the communities themselves there are individuals—a growing population of young warriors—whose frustration nears the boiling point. Something must be done before this occurs.

But while this wake up call has not been heeded, and the key issues of sovereignty and land rights and the underlying considerations of nationhood and (de)colonization have not been fully addressed, we must not forget that the resistance at Kanehsatà:ke was a little thing from which big things grow. Beyond energizing and empowering others and beyond the tangible impact that the "Oka Crisis" had on Indian Country in terms of both individuals and their communities, the Kanien'kehaka blockades forced Canada to look at itself and to start thinking of the changes necessary for decolonization and to build a new relationship with the Indigenous nations whose territories it claims as its own. In doing so, the resistance created opportunities or windows of opportunity within which people could mobilize, challenge the status quo and advance their agenda (specific or general, most often defined by the ever-present considerations of nationhood and (de)colonization)—opportunities created by the resistance at Kanehsatà:ke and Kahnawà:ke and then used to create the Royal Commission on Aboriginal Peoples (RCAP) and the Charlottetown Accord. It is a ripple affect where such opportunities, when combined, continue to create other opportunities that are, in turn, used to create opportunities such as the residential school inquiry. To this end, we can see the ripple effect of the "Oka Crisis" in RCAP and through RCAP to the Truth and Reconciliation Commission.

Thanks to those individuals and those communities who showed such courage in 1990, and all those who joined in offering their support by setting up blockades and pickets across the country, the Canadian government had to act—it simply had to do something. But what? The federal government (and for that matter provincial) had no clue what the underlying issues that had been festering since colonization really were or what to do to respond; people were able to use this as an opportunity to lobby for the creation of a commission which would be charged with explaining the situation to Canadians and their governments and to begin the process of dreaming a new future. The

Royal Commission on Aboriginal Peoples succeeded in doing this— now if only Canadians and their governments would take heed and begin to at least grapple with understanding the bigger issues, engaging in decolonization, respecting Indigenous rights and responsibilities and transforming the relationship.

Similarly, with the image of the "Oka Crisis" and Elijah Harper fresh in their minds, leaders from across the country found it impossible to engage in constitutional dialogue without Aboriginal issues on the table. Indigenous leaders used the window of opportunity which was created by the Kanehsatà:ke resistance to push for Indigenous leadership at the table and, once there, to raise every issue possible and to make sure that an Aboriginal agenda with its underlying considerations of nationhood and (de)colonization was heard. And it was— loud and clear! Aboriginal leaders used whatever opportunities they had to become key players in the process and to make issues such as self-government and land rights a primary part of the agreement. Though the Charlottetown Accord failed and RCAP failed to be implemented, they nevertheless have had quite a substantial impact on Aboriginal and Treaty rights, the legacy of residential schools, and the relationship between Indigenous nations and the settler state. Still, while Canadians and their governments started down this path with some gusto, they have failed to stay the course.

As a result, as we reflect on this the twentieth anniversary of the Kanehsatà:ke resistance, we sing our Honour Songs to remember our collective responsibilities to imagine once again a new future and to chart a new course. We must come to a new understanding of the role of non-state actors (be they unofficial leaders or activists at a kitchen table or traditional leaders/governments) in sustaining our agenda, in protecting the people and their lands, in educating others, in inspiring hope and in creating change. We must refresh our support for those unofficial and non-state political spaces and political actors—for they are the little thing from which big things grow (in the case of the Kanien'kehaka resistance at Kanesatà:ke and Kahnawà:ke, big things like Charlottetown Accord, justice reform, the Royal Commission on Aboriginal Peoples— and now the Truth and Reconciliation Commission—and the inspiration and transformation that all of the authors wrote about in this book). They are the ones that we sing about. They are the ones that are, and have always been, the source of political mobilization and change in communities and they are the source of strength and inspiration for the wider (the local and the global) Indigenous rights movement. They are the Clan Mothers, the activists, the traditionalists, the word warriors, the speakers/revitalizers of the language, the dancers, the militants, the fishers, the grandmothers that write, sleep, eat and build their vision of hope and change. They are the ones that are uniting to make that circle stronger. So, it is to those people who stood up during that summer, to the communities involved and to all those who have heeded the call and who have shown that courage, that I sing my Honour Song.

1 Paul Kelly and Kev Carmody (1991), "From Little Things Big Things Grow" on *Comedy* (Kelly, and Carmody composers), Darlinghurst Australia: One Louder Entertainment; Archie Roach & Sara Storer (2007), "From Little things Big Things Grow" on *Rockwiz Vol 2*, Kelly and Carmody composers, Sydney, Australia: Liberation Music.

2 Neal McLeod (2007), *Cree Narrative Memory*, Saskatoon: Purich Publishing Ltd.

3 John Borrows (2007), "Crown and Aboriginal Occupations of Land: A History & Comparison," Research Paper prepared for the Ipperwash Inquiry, <www.ipperwahinquiry.ca>.

4 Ovide Mecredi and Mary Ellen Turpel (1993), *In the Rapids: Navigating the Future of First Nations*, Toronto: Viking, p 49.

5 Dale Turner (2006), *This Is Not A Peace Pipe: Towards a Critical Indigenous Philosophy*, Toronto: University of Toronto Press.

6 Thanks, Leanne, for reminding me of this fact.

7 For instace see Alanis Obomsawin (1993), *Kanehsatake: 270 Years of Resistance*, Montreal: National Film Board; Richard Wagamese (1996), *The Terrible Summer*, Toronto, Warrick Publishing; Propagandhi (1998), "Oka Everywhere" on *Where Quantity is Job #1*; Winnipeg G7 Welcoming Committee; Douglas R. Nepinak (2001), "The Crisis in Oka, Manitoba," performed at the Winnipeg Fringe Festival.

8 Wagamese (1996), pp. 75–76.

9 Neil Young (1979), "Pocahontas" on On *Rust Never Sleeps*; Buffy Saint Marie (1992), "Bury My Heart at Wounded Knee" on *On Coincidence and Likely Stories*.

10 Kiera L. Ladner (2008), "Aysaka'paykinit: Contesting the Rope Around the Nations' Neck" in Miriam Smith ed., *Group Politics and Social Movements in Canada*, Peterborough: Broadview Press.

11 Taiaiake Alfred (1995), *Heeding the Voices of Our Ancestors: Mohawk Politics and the Rise of Native Nationalism*, Toronto: Oxford University Press.

12 Ladner (2008).

13 Ibid.

Wísakedják and the Colonizer

PAULA SHERMAN

What follows is a contemporary story written in the Omamíwínini tradition, exploring the themes of colonialism, decolonization, dissent and mobilization. It was written 16 years after the "Oka Crisis" and it is included here as a broad, creative reflection on the nature of colonialism and resistance.

WÍSAKEDJÁK WAS WALKING ALONG A WELL-WORN PATH through the forest that lay adjacent to the banks of Kiji Síbí in the territory of the Omamíwínini (Algonquin) people. He paused for a moment, breathing in deeply. It is mid autumn and many of the trees were bold and colourful. The smell of cedar was all around him. Birds were chirping in the distance, but there were no animals or people there to greet him. He called out to his relatives in the Natural World.

"Aandi nda-nwendaagnog?" Nothing but silence greeted him.

Wísakedják walked a little further on the path and paused in a clearing next to a large flat rock. He looked around him and through the forest for signs of life. Nothing stirred.

"Anishinaabeg! Anishinaabeg! Aandi Anishinaabeg?" Where are the Anishinaabeg? Where are my relatives, he wondered. He looked around the clearing, hesitating to go further.

"I guess I'll just wait here for them."

Wísakedják flopped down on the flat rock. He stretched out with his legs hanging over. He began to hum softly as he watched the clouds float by. A turtle shaped cloud drifted across the sky so slowly that he was able to follow it with his right hand. Before he knew what was happening, his body followed and he fell off the rock and hit his head.

"Ouch! That hurt." He rose up from the ground like a snake with his head peeping over the top of the rock. It was at this point that he heard the swish, swish, swish of flapping wings echoing through the treetops above his head. Wísakedják grew excited as he turned his head upward in anticipation. A flock of geese were coming his way. Glancing up from his hiding position, Wísakedják watched a goose swoop downward and land in the clearing. Two others followed. They circled him and then stopped a few feet away.

"Kwey Nika! Aandi nda-nwendaagnog?" Wísakedják said. The geese were so beautiful; their feathers were so clean and glistened in the sun. "Where is everyone?"

"Some of your relatives still live here," one of the geese replied, "but many of us have been knocked off over the years…"

One of the other geese chimed in just as the first one trailed off. "The land and water no longer sustains as much life as before. The humans have caused a lot of damage, you know, in many places."

"It is hard for us now to find a clean resting place. We are even prohibited from some areas because of their flying machines," the third geese exclaimed, lifting his left wing to indicate the spot where some feathers were missing.

"How could such a thing happen? Where are the Omamíwínini?" Wísakedják asked. Perhaps they were mistaken; it was possible, he thought.

The first goose moved a little closer as he replied, "They are scattered about the land but they no longer protect this place like they used to."

"What do you mean?" he said. "I gave the teachings to the original people, why aren't they using them to protect their homeland?" How could this be? He had visited them so many times in the past. He was sure they knew and understood their responsibilities.

"We don't know, Wísakedják," the second goose replied, "but I gotta warn ya, they're not the same people as the last time you saw them."

"What has happened to them?" he asked.

The third goose shook his head sadly. "They've been changed by the newcomers."

"I want to see them, but I can't seem to find them."

The first goose gestured in the direction of the cliff. "We saw a family when we were flying over; they are camping over by the cliff."

"I'll go then as soon as I have a bit of lunch. Say, you wanna stay and have some lunch with me?" Wísakedják said as he moved a little closer. "I've been on a great journey since you last saw me. I have some stories of your relatives in the north." He moved very slowly toward the first goose and then suddenly lunged for him.

Wísakedják missed him, though, and the geese scattered. As they flew away they sang a two-step song:

"Beware of Elder Brother,
when your invited to lunch,
his stories are fantastic,
caressing to your heart,
lots of excitement,
and laughter to behold,
but by the end, hey yah,
you could be his lunch,
hey ya hey ya hey yah,
hey ya hey ya hey yah,
hey ya hey ya hey yah,
we won't be his lunch!"

Wísakedják watched them fly away and then sat down on the flat rock again. He drew his knees up to his chin as he sat contemplating his empty stomach. "All those geese did was remind me that I'm starving!" he said. "Lunch would have been nice. What I wouldn't give though to have a nice plump duck...mmmm."

Wísakedják rubbed his belly and began to fantasize. He made a fire and constructed a spit. He placed a plump duck on the spit and sat watching the duck roast to perfection. He began to hum as he turned the spit. There was nothing like a plump juicy duck for lunch. When the duck was roasted to perfection he took it off the spit and laid it down on the rock. He cut off a piece with his knife, but just as he lifted a piece to his mouth for a bite, the duck disappeared and he was alone again with nothing but his empty stomach.

The sounds of splashing water and children's laughter in the distance shook him from his fantasy. "That must be the humans the geese told me about," Wísakedják said as he got up. He moved along quickly in that direction. When he arrived at a clearing he hung back, not wanting to reveal himself until he had a chance to figure out the best way to approach the humans. Pausing behind a tree, he peered around its expanse and discovered a campsite that seemed to be empty. The aroma of roasting meat greeted his senses and told Wísakedják all he needed to know about the location of the people. Slowly he left the safety of the tree for a closer look.

Walking out into the clearing, Wísakedják paused next to a tent that was erected at the edge of the camp. Not seeing anyone, he moved around the tent and stopped short. His eyes took in the sight before him. There were several people in the camp, including a young girl who was roasting a hot dog over a fire pit. A grandmother was shucking corn at a picnic table while a man sat in a lawn chair reading the *Globe and Mail*. A teen boy was slouched in a chair listening to an iPod. There was a sense of separation between the campers that was obvious to Wísakedják but he was not quite sure what to make of it. No one seemed to notice him as he inched closer. It was no great surprise to him that no one saw him as he approached; he was really good at sneak up.

As he moved nearer, Wísakedják began to sing and he moved in sync, dancing a sneak-up geese dance around the people in the camp. He was so fixated on them, though, that he tripped over a pile of firewood and fell forward on all fours, landing with a resounding thump. Wísakedják lifted himself from the dirt and continued the dance. The humans, however, were not staring at him with amazement or awe. Had they not heard that commotion? Boy he was really good at this sneak-up.

He focused his dancing on the people. "Hey you'se! This can be a round dance. Anyone wanna join?"

No one answered. He was startled by that fact and it made him loose his concentration and he missed a step in the dance. It was strange that the people were acting this way. It was rude not to acknowledge him or to say hello. He stopped dancing and paused in the camp, looking around. He had made a lot of noise and had danced for them and sang for them. What was going on here? Then something occurred to him and Wísakedják smiled. Of course, that was it, they were playing a game. The humans were pretending not to see him or hear him so they could trick him. He laughed out loud. It was a good game he conceded. He loved games, there was no doubting that. This was especially true if the game ended with food and a full stomach for him. Wísakedják would just play along for a bit so they would think they had succeeded in fooling him. He would then draw them into his own game. After all, who was better at games than he? It would be a spectacular game.

Wísakedják walked around the circle humming and pretending that he did not know they could see him. The object of his game was to make them admit that they could see him. When they admitted that they were tricking him, then he knew he could convince them to feed him. It was a good plan. Wísakedják wondered how he could make them admit that they were tricking him though. Suddenly he remembered the laughter he had heard from the camp earlier. Humans could not help laughing when they thought something was funny. If ever there were someone capable of creating laughter in humans and animals, Wísakedják knew that it was he.

First Wísakedják tried standing on his head and walking around the fire inside of the circle. Surely they would find this stunt funny. After a while, Wísakedják grew dizzy from being on his head and fell over in the circle. Sitting up, Wísakedják noticed that no one was laughing or even looking his way. Disappointed, Wísakedják walked around the circle and peered closely at the people. This had never happened before. Usually when he wanted humans to see him they grew very excited and they usually always fed him. What was wrong with these people? Didn't they know that they were supposed to acknowledge him when he wanted them too? Wísakedják was still hungry, however, and was not prepared to give up on the game just yet. With renewed determination, Wísakedják walked up to the man reading the paper. He sat down in front of him facing away and laid his head on the man's lap. He swatted at the paper and stared upward into the man's eyes. He was certain that this would work. How could it not?

"Hey you!" Wísakedják yelled. "Is there anyone home in there?"

The man, however, said nothing as he continued to stare through Wísakedják as if he were not there. Wísakedják wondered how it was possible for the man to ignore him in this position. Why was this man not reacting to Wísakedják's invasion of his space? He must be really, really good at this game to be so skilled. Untangling himself from the twisted position, Wísakedják sat down on the ground in front of him and stared at the man through the newspaper. He got up from the ground and walked over to the grandmother who was picking silk from the corn she had just shucked.

"Surely you will acknowledge me. I am your relative," he said. Looking down at the corn, an idea occurred to him. "Say, can I help with the corn? I am an expert at roasting it."

She did not reply or look up at him. Wow, he thought, she was very very good at this game. He imagined that the man must have learned from her. He turned away and looked at the others. Children! Yes, this would work; children were more susceptible and not as capable of ignoring him. The smell of roasting meat settled over him and he turned to the young girl with excitement.

"Hey, what's that you're roasting? Can I have a taste? I've never tried that before."

When she didn't answer, he reached over and grabbed the stick she held in her hand and took the hotdog off the end. He hadn't anticipated the burning pain that shot through his fingers, though, which caused him to drop the meat in the fire. He jumped around shaking his hand in the air. He stopped suddenly and blew on it to try and stop the intense pain. When that didn't work he began to jump around again. None of the commotion he was making did anything to trigger the girl's attention. She left the fire and then returned a couple minutes later with another hotdog to roast.

Wísakedják stood in the same spot until the pain subsidised in his hand. Angrily he turned away from the girl. He spotted the teen boy who was still lounging in the chair. Wísakedják approached him slowly, watching how his head bobbed from side to side for no apparent reason. There were strange cords hanging from his ears and he held a white device in his hand. He seemed to be focused on the white device. Wísakedják wondered at the purpose of the device, and why it seemed to be causing him to move his head and shoulders. He paused next to him and leaned his head down, watching carefully. He began to bob his head in unison with the boy. Suddenly the boy sat up when the grandmother called to him and took the cords out of his ears. He sat the cords and the device in the chair and made his way over to his grandmother.

Wísakedják picked up the device and put the cords into his ears like he had seen the boy do and then looked down at it, nothing happened. He ran his fingers over the smooth surface of the device and must have hit something because suddenly the loudest sound he had ever heard filled his ears. Super loud drumming and singing pierced his eardrums and he yanked the cords from his ears. They dangled from his hands as he shook his head to clear the ringing in his ears. What in the world, he thought, was this device? He lifted the cords near his ears but did not put them back in. The sound was not as loud and was quite pleasant to his ears. He must have accidentally hit something else on the device because suddenly the song changed to strange music he had never heard before. It had a very interesting beat and he found himself swaying and dancing with the beat. Suddenly he heard a high voice, which at first he thought was a woman, but then realized was a man. He listened carefully to the language and the words and then began to sing them back as he danced around.

> "I'm Bringin Sexy Back . . . ya!
> Them other boys don't know how to act . . . ya!
> I think it's special what's behind your back!
> So turn around and I'll pick up the slack . . ."

Wísakedják swung around still dancing and noticed a toddler jumping up and down in a playpen. Where had he come from? Wísakedják had not noticed him before. Had he been sleeping and just awoke? Wherever he had come from, he was pointing at Wísakedják and yelling toward his grandmother. Wísakedják moved toward him, excited that someone had actually acknowledging him.

"Aaniin! At last! Someone sees me. Tell your family that I have come back?"

"Na . . . na . . . na . . . na . . . na!"

Wísakedják looked at the toddler and realized he could not tell his grandmother that he was there. The baby didn't have enough language yet. Suddenly Wísakedják knew he needed to take his place. He picked up the child and rolled him up in a protective covering and hung him from a tree. The toddler rocked back and forth in the breeze and quickly fell asleep. Wísakedják dropped down into the playpen and awaited the grandmother who was making her way over to the child.

"What's up with you my little chatterbox? Are you talking to your imaginary friend again?" The grandmother said as she leaned over the playpen and patted his head.

Wísakedják leaned forward in anticipation as he looked up at the grandmother.

"Na...na...na...na..."

The grandmother motioned to the table. "I'll be right back with your blanket."

"NA...NA...NA...NA!" Wísakedják yelled.

"Oh geez you, I'll be back in a minute." She placed a kiss on his forehead and then walked away.

Wísakedják jumped up from the playpen after she left and returned with the child who he placed back inside. It was no use keeping up the charade; she had not acknowledged him at all. "I guess I will have to look for others."

He made his way out of the camp. He had interacted with every human in that camp and none of them had let on that they could see or hear him except the toddler, and he was too young to do anything about it. This was indeed a really good game. One of the best he had ever seen. Surely there were other humans nearby who were not playing games. "That was a good game you!" he shouted back to them as he left the clearing and headed along the path. He continued walking for quite a while. He paused when he came upon another clearing where there was a large building with lots of cars parked. Wísakedják knew there had to be people and food here because there were more cars scattered along the road. He stepped on the cars and jumped from hood to hood, looking inside each vehicle for food. All the people must have been very hungry too, however, because he found nothing to fill his empty stomach.

Crossing to the building, Wísakedják peered inside the open door and saw lots of people, some standing, some in chairs, all focussed on a table at the front of the room where four people sat. A man stood and introduced himself as an official from the Ministry of Northern Development and Mines. The official turned then to the man on his right and introduced him as the president of a uranium exploration company. Next to him sat a man with really fancy clothes. He was introduced as the company's lawyer. No one at the table looked at the woman or made any move to introduce her. This bothered Wísakedják because she appeared to be the only Anishinaabe at the table. Wísakedják crossed the room and sat next to her in an empty chair.

Turning to her, he smiled and said hello. "Thanks for saving me a seat. Say, who are these strange people?" He looked around the table and was not impressed by their carefully guarded expressions. He turned back to the woman; she appeared to look through him, her gaze fixated on the three men at the table. Wísakedják could tell she was nervous and he placed his hand over hers, wanting to ease her fear. Suddenly, one of the men from Mining and Northern Development stood up and looked away from the table toward the crowd who had gathered in the room.

"Is the community representative here? We would like to get started."

The woman at the table rose from her chair, her voice steady as she spoke. "I am the community representative."

The man laughed nervously as he turned to her. "Where are the men?"

"Excuse me?" She glared at him. "I was designated by the community to be here."

"Fine then," said the company lawyer. "Let's get on with it."

The woman let her gaze wander over the people in the room before sitting down and settling her eyes back on the government officials and the company president. "I am here because our land has been staked for uranium exploration. This is unacceptable to us. We don't support this type of development."

The official from Mining and Northern Development leaned over the table toward her. "Calm down. I'm sure we can protect your sacred sites if you tell us where they are."

"That will never happen!" she snapped back, her eyes darkening. "All of our land is sacred. What happens in one part has an effect on the rest."

"You need to be sensible," he said. "The company has a right under the Ontario Mining Act to explore for minerals."

"Uranium exploration is banned under Algonquin law." She shook her head at him. "We can't allow it to happen on our land."

Wísakedják watched as the company lawyer jumped up and glared at her. "The only law here is Canadian law. You are violating that by prohibiting my client from carrying out his lawful activities.

You will vacate the site you are occupying or we will press charges and have you arrested."

"We will not leave the site until we are properly consulted and our land is protected."

"We said we would protect sacred sites," the official reminded her.

"That is not enough; all of our land must be protected." She was getting angrier and angrier Wísakedják noticed. Not that he could blame her. How could they propose such a thing? She was right to stand up to these newcomers.

"Be sensible," the official said again. "Staking has already occurred. We are willing to mediate the impacts but you must cooperate. Blocking access to the site is illegal." He shared a nervous glance with the president of the company and lawyer before turning back to her for a response.

"We will not leave until our conditions are met."

"You're a bunch of criminals!" the company president yelled as he shook his fist at her.

Any possible response by the woman was cut off by the official from Mining and Northern Development who suggested possible benefits. "What about your community's needs. Surely you understand that cooperation could result in economic opportunities."

"What we understand is that we were not consulted about this project at all," she began. "Our land was staked without a word from the province. There was no move to talk to us until we decided to go camping on our land."

"But the company is even willing to hire members from the community?" he added.

"We don't want their money! We want our homeland to be protected," she returned sharply.

"Fine then," the company lawyer shot back. "Get off the site or we will have you arrested."

"You do what you have to do and so will we!" she countered him.

The company president jumped up and shook his finger at her. "If you don't get off the site we will use paramilitary troops like we did in Africa. They kill people, you know!"

Wísakedják had to check his own anger at that remark. He stood up, watching as the company president and the woman glared at each other. He began to stomp his feet on the ground and then jumped between them. Turning to the man he let him have it. "You would kill her because she protects the land? I can't take this anymore!" He turned away from him and stared down into the woman's face. She appeared to be on the brink of tears because she was so upset. "Why don't you let me help? I can help if you would just acknowledge me."

No answer was forthcoming. She continued to look through him at the men at the table. I've had enough, Wîsakedjâk thought. I can't deal with this. He fled the room and ran as fast as he could back down the path he had come. When he arrived back in the clearing he paused to get his bearings again. He spotted the family and moved toward them. They were all sitting at the picnic table eating supper. There was no seat left for him. "There is no place for me at your table. I don't understand why you protect the land but not me. Am I not a part of the land the same as you?"

No one responded or looked at him. The family cleaned up and then went into their tent for the night. As they laughed and chatted among themselves, Wîsakedjâk sank onto the cold hard ground. He bowed his head and began to weep. All I have is my own heartbeat, he thought. He shivered as the wind picked up and lightning flashed in the distance. What has happened here? Could they have really forgotten me? They used to tell stories about me. Have they forgotten the stories too? Lightning flashed closer, and suddenly the great cliff was illuminated in front of him. He saw the images that were left there as teachings by the Ancestors.

"That's me on that rock!" Lightning flashed again and thunder sounded off. He looked skyward. "I have come home!" he yelled. "But no one knows me anymore."

He took sema from a pouch around his neck and laid it on the earth. He looked upward into the Skyworld as he said a silent prayer. He dropped his head again looking at the earth around him. He heard great claps of thunder and then suddenly saw four large beings land and circle him. The Thunderbirds moved in around him. They circled closer as they danced, sending him their strength. He suddenly began to feel his body lighten. They moved in closer still. As they danced away from him again he felt himself being lifted from the ground. His movements were sluggish, but as the Thunderbirds lifted their wings in splendid movement, he was able to move about more freely. Their movements reenergized him and before he knew it he is was dancing. As he flew around the clearing a peaceful calmn overcame him and he got lost in the dance.

"I'm such a good dancer, my feet are so light and my movements are so smooth. I can't help but admire myself. Am I not great!?"

He stopped dancing when he noticed he was the only one still moving. The Thunderbirds were glaring at him. He looked back at them sheepishly.

"Don't play around, Wísakedják," the leader of the Thunderbirds admonished.

"You have important work to do," the second one said pointedly.

"Much is at stake!" said the third Thunderbird.

"The morning has come and the people are waiting," the forth Thunderbird remarked.

"What can I do? The only one who can see me is the baby and he can't talk." The seriousness of the issue reminded him that he was very frustrated.

"You must help the Omamíwínini, Wísakedják; you must help them find their way back to the teachings," the leader of the Thunderbirds replied.

"How can I do that?" he asked.

"You will go back and help them find their path," she said.

"How can I help them find their path when everything has been destroyed?" The frustration was clear in his voice.

"You must travel deep within their hearts. You will find the answer there," she offered.

"The answer...?" He didn't understand.

"The answer to why they don't see you anymore." The words were soft to lessen the blow.

Wísakedják felt that truth in his heart and very being. They did not see him or hear him anymore. They had not been pretending or playing a game. They simply didn't know he was there. The realization was much worse than any trick he had ever seen and the implications made his eyes fill with tears as he looked at the leader of the Thunderbirds. "How will I do this? How will I get to their hearts?"

"Take this medicine and make a tea," the leader of the Thunderbird replied. She stepped forward and placed it into his open hand. "You must drink it before you approach them," she said. "You may then enter their hearts."

One of the other Thunderbirds stepped forward and touched him on the shoulder as he spoke. "Take care Wísakedják! There is much pain there."

"Miigwech! I will be very careful!" Wísakedják said. He thanked them for their support and help as they flew away.

Although he was very hungry, Wísakedják put that aside and spent the night resting for what he knew would be a difficult journey in the morning. When he awoke, Wísakedják found that he had to wait until the Omamíwínini were again settled in their chairs before he could really proceed with his plan to find out what was in their hearts. Most of the morning was gone before they finally settled in the chairs again. Wísakedják approached them loudly in the hopes that things would be different. Sadness overwhelmed him as he realized that they had no papers or music to distract them and he still remained invisible to them.

He drank the tea he had made the night before and divided himself into two smaller beings as he drew closer to their chairs. The two smaller Wísakedjáks looked right through the outer flesh of the Omamíwínini people seated there. The two Wísakedjáks stepped forward into the bodies of the man and the grandmother. They travelled for a while through the veins of the people which eventually brought them into the hearts of the Omamíwínini. As they went deeper and deeper into the hearts, the two Wísakedjáks looked for any sign that the Omamíwínini people still believed.

They travelled so deep within the recesses of their hearts that they could no longer discern where they were. Suddenly, each Wísakedják encountered repressed memories in the hearts of the man and the grandmother. They found that the memories stored there were hard to circumvent, but eventually they pushed their way past the memories of violence, alcohol and substance abuse in the Omamíwínini people. They made their way past the images of residential schools, the *Indian Act* and the *Royal Proclamation*. Further and further back they travelled into the depths of the hearts of the people until they saw a light in the distance. They followed the light until they realized that they were following the path of the rising sun. Astonished, they noticed that they were standing on the banks of a great river.

The smaller Wísakedjáks combined themselves again and he scanned the forest and river around him for signs of why he had been brought to this place. Wísakedják caught a glimpse of a silhouette in the distance, against the backdrop of the great river. He could not make out the man's identity, but the man and the ship looked familiar. Wísakedják stared at the ship but did not move any closer.

"Why am I here with this strange man? Where am I?"

Just then, Wísakedják heard noises in the forest, and then saw a woodpecker approaching. The woodpecker landed on a log, and Wísakedják turned to her excitedly. "Kwey, I'm so happy to see you! No one other than the birds and baby has acknowledged me in a long time."

"Heelllooo, I saw you from that ship over there. Why have you come here, Wísakedják?" she said.

He took in the unfamiliar surroundings. "I'm not sure where I am, but I have travelled a long way. I am here to find out what happened to my people. They can't see me anymore in the future," he said.

"That must make you very angry. Did you turn them into birds too?" she admonished.

"Oh . . . it is you?" he said sheepishly.

"Yes, it's me, the woman you turned into a woodpecker," she said sternly.

He looked at her calmly. "I did that because you would not share with others. I came to you several times as various beings and still you denied me."

"Yeah, yeah . . . I don't have time to talk right now, Wísakedják," she mumbled, turning away.

"Wait!" he exclaimed. "What is going on with that ship and who is that man on the deck?"

"He could be anyone. How should I know?" she shrugged.

"You must know, Woodpecker, you were just there," he pointed out.

"Well why should I help you? You've made it very hard for me to gather food," she said contritely.

"Yes, you are right. You don't have to help. . ." he trailed off. "But if you don't help me, there won't be any trees left in the future from which to gather food to feed your children and grandchildren," he offered in his most serious tone.

"No trees! How can that be?" she asked.

"Many things change in the future. Perhaps you will not exist if you don't help me," Wísakedják said.

"What! Oh my. Very well, I will help you," she said grudgingly.

"Miigwech! Miigwech!"

"Don't get so excited! I'm not doing it for you," she shot back.

"Oh, ok."

"I will help, what do you need?" she asked.

Wísakedják thought for a moment before replying. "Well, the Thunderbirds told me to come here. When I arrived I found this ship. Do you know why the ship is here?"

"I was listening to their conversations on the ship before I flew over. The man on the ship says this land is his," she offered.

"What?" he stammered. "This land belongs to the Omamíwínini."

"He doesn't like them. He calls them savages."

"Who is this man and why does he talk so about my people?" he asked angrily.

"His name is Samuel de Champlain."

"He's an explorer?" Wísakedják asked.

The woodpecker flapped her wings around anxiously before replying. "Yes, and let me tell you, explorers are nothing but trouble. I heard this one say that he wants lots of furs from the people here."

He looked at her intently. "Are they giving them to him?"

She nodded. "Some are."

"Oh no, this is not good. There is only one ship here now, but in the future . . . this land is covered with his people. Everything is different and my people are like ghosts on the land," he informed her. How could this have happened? He wondered.

"How could that be?" she asked. "Do you think he is responsible?"

"I don't know, but I am here to find out." He paused momentarily and then moved closer to her. "Do you think he would speak with me?"

"I don't think so, Wísakedják," she said. "He favours his own people. He is rude and arrogant."

"How will I find out what has happened then?" he asked.

The woodpecker thought for a moment, then turned to Wísakedják. "You could disguise yourself like you did with me; he would not know it is you," she said. "You could then speak to him."

Wísakedják nodded. It was a good plan. "I have a great many disguises. What shall I become?"

"You must become a Frenchman; he will be compelled to talk to you then," she insisted.

"Oh, yes, that could work," he said. "But which Frenchman would be best?"

"A priest could work," she said. "It would have to be a special priest though, because he talks badly about them too."

"Perhaps a priest is not the best option if he does not believe in them," he countered.

"Oh, he is a Christian and prays all the time," she reassured him. "He just dislikes the Jesuits because they interfere with trade."

"Which priest do you suggest?"

"My choice would be Saint Francis of Assisi, he is the saint who watches over animals." She suggested, offering words of encouragement. "You can do it, Wísakedják, you just need a robe and a hairy face."

"Ok, but do I have to have a hairy face. It sounds itchy!"

"All of the men on the ship have hairy faces," she said, motioning in that direction with her left wing.

"Oh, ok. I guess if I have too." He sighed. "I will also need a dwelling for a confessional and a way to draw Champlain there." This part was important and would need to be just right to draw him in.

"See that dwelling there?" she asked. When he nodded, she continued. "The men on the ship use it. Champlain comes to it every afternoon. He sits inside and talks to himself. If you go there and wait, he will be along shortly."

"Miigwech, Woodpecker!"

After Woodpecker waved goodbye and flew away, Wísakedják wasted no time in closing the distance between him and the dwelling. Upon his arrival he noticed a particular odour coming from inside that was unmistakable. The dwelling was a duel outhouse. What a perfect confessional, he thought. It just needs a bit of work to make it complete. The first thing he needed was a covering so Champlain would not see him. Looking around, he spotted Bulrushes by the water and quickly moved in their direction.

"Kwey, my brothers," he said as he approached them. "May I use a few of your stems to weave a covering for my dwelling?"

The Bulrushes who had been swaying back and forth in the breeze, calmed their stems as they greeted him. "Yes, we will share with you, Wísakedják," they said in unison. "Be careful to weave it tightly or you may be seen."

Wísakedják took sema from his pouch and laid it down on the earth before he took a few stems and began to weave them together. When he was finished he attached it to the outhouse, admiring his work. "That should do nicely."

Wísakedják turned then and walked to a basswood tree where he also laid down sema. "Kwey! May I have a bit of your inner bark to make a robe?

"I guess I can spare a bit," the tree remarked, "as long as you only take a small amount."

"Of course!" Wísakedják said and proceeded to take what he needed to make his robe. When the robe was complete and he had covered his body with it, he walked around for a bit. As he paused to tie a belt around his waist, he saw his reflection in a pool of water on the ground. Touching his face, he remembered that he needed to have a hairy face. Hmmm, how would he manage that? He heard a high-pitched sound as he looked around the clearing but couldn't locate the source. He turned and began back in the other direction when he tripped over a rock and fell flat on his stomach. Looking around he saw green moss all over the ground and rocks.

"Sorry we had to trip you, Wísakedják, we thought you might like some of our lushness for your beard. It will certainly disguise your face," Moss said.

"Well, you didn't have to trip me," he said, sitting up. "That hurt!"

"We called to you and you didn't hear us Wísakedják," Moss said.

"Oh, I wondered what that high pitched sound was, he acknowledged. "I'm sorry."

"It's ok," they said. "We are used to being ignored."

Wísakedják offered them sema and then took the moss they put aside for him. He applied it to his face with a bit of a sticky substance they offered and stood up fully ordained with a green beard. He limped over to the outhouse using a stick that he had fashioned into a cane. He sat down on one side and pulled the covering in place to hide his presence. Before long, he heard a commotion in the forest nearby and footsteps. Wísakedják quickly took up the violin he had carved and began to play. Holy music began to fill the outhouse and the surrounding area.

Champlain approached the outhouse and paused outside an incredulous expression on his face. "What is this great pleasure!" he voiced. "It is like the music of the great cathedral in Paris."

"It is the sound of the angels," Wísakedják offered. "We have been waiting for you Monsieur."

Champlain was perplexed and looked around the clearing. "But ... but ..."

"No worries, my son," he said. "Come inside and sit and I will hear your confession."

Champlain stood firmly, his nose in the air. "What game do you play? This is an outhouse, not a confessional."

"There is great urgency Monsieur," he urged. "You must begin the confession right away."

"You insult me!" Champlain stated. "I will not confess in an outhouse!"

Wísakedják sat back for a second to consider his options. Champlain would not come inside unless he was forced to do so. Wísakedják sent his voice outside in such a way that it seemed to come back into the clearing from far away. Champlain, on his part, heard loud piercing war woops in the distance and jumped out of his skin. He shrieked and began to shake with fear as he banged on the outside wall of the outhouse.

"There are savages about, Mon Pere!" He yelled. "We must run for our lives!"

As he moved to run away, Wísakedják reached outside the covering and grabbed his arm. "No wait!" he urged. "You are safe, Monsieur, as long as you remain here with me."

Champlain quickly moved into the other side of the outhouse and sat down. He pulled the covering closed and sat shaking inside. "We are never safe with the savages about. Who are you?"

Wísakedják paused for effect and then replied, "I am Saint Francis Asissi."

"Assissi?" Champlain questioned. "That is not possible; he is dead!"

"Death is relative. I was somewhere else and now I am here," Wísakedják said.

"That is not possible. Who are you reeaallly?" Champlain insisted.

"I am Asissi! I was sent here to take your confession."

"Sent by whom? His Majesty?" Champlain questioned.

"No," Wísakedják said. "I answer to a much higher power."

"Why have you come here, Mon Pere? You believe I have committed some offense?

Wísakedják hesitated and then replied, "Yes, I believe that you may have committed sins here."

"Sins!" Champlain exclaimed, "I have no sins!"

"If you are sin free, why have you come to this place?" he asked.

Champlain was indignant. "I have come to pursue the fur trade with the savages."

Wísakedják nodded. "They invited you to trade in their homelands?

"Absolutment!" Champlain confirmed. "We have been here since the days of Monsieur Cartier when France claimed this land by right of discovery."

"There were people here already. You can't discover someone else's homeland."

Champlain leaned forward. "There was nothing here but vast wilderness when we arrived."

Wísakedják also leaned forward, almost making out Champlain's features in the small holes in the woven cover that separated the stalls on the outhouse. "What about the people you trade with? Is this not their home?"

"Indeed! The savages wander the forest," he admitted.

"This is their land then?" Wísakedják asked.

"No, this land belongs to his Majesty the King of France! The savages have no permanent settlements. They move with the animals," Champlain answered.

"You are really fond of these lands, are you not?"

"Absolutment!" Champlain exclaimed. "The forests are full of fur bearing animals. We are very interested in expanding trade."

Wísakedják paused for effect before answering. "The original people of this land have concerns about your presence. They say you only care about furs."

"Our presence here is a good thing for the savages. They live in sin and barbarism. Just the other day, I caught them frolicking in the waterfalls. Naked," Champlain condemned.

"You watched them bathing?" Wísakedják accused.

Champlain laughed at the accusation. "Of course I watched...it is against God to run around in such a state. I had to record my observations for His Majesty."

"His Majesty must know about their nakedness?" What leader would request such a thing? Wísakedják wondered.

"Of course!" Champlain insisted. "The savages expose themselves this way because they are in league with the Devil, he rules their hearts," he said, explaining further.

"The French are not?"

"How dare you insult me so! I am Catholic," Champlain swore.

"If you wish to be absolved of your sins you must confess," Wísakedják insisted.

"I have nothing to confess. I am a good Christian," he said.

"If that is so, tell me what happened with the Omamíwínini," Wísakedják shot back.

"O...ma...ma...wi...who?" Confusion filled Champlain's voice.

"You call them Algonkin."

Champlain was disgusted. "I do not see the need to talk about the savages. Really, Mon Pere, they are not like us!"

Wísakedják wondered how he could say that. "What makes the French think they're superior to my people...I mean God's people? Are they not his creation?"

Champlain began to laugh. "You jest? They are children. They do not possess reasoning or logic."

"Yes they do."

"No they don't," Champlain answered. "They need our help, Mon Pere, that is why God sent us here."

Wísakedják shot him a questioning glance. "I thought you were here for furs?"

"Absolutment!" Champlain exclaimed. "Converting the savages is a good way to expand the fur trade."

Wísakedják took the violin propped against the wall and began to play. Holy music flooded the outhouse. The sound startled Champlain and he cowered back against the wall. Wísakedják continued to play as he moved forward with the questions. "Do tell, Monsieur, how is this beneficial?"

"It is quite simple," Champlain offered. "The Jesuit Fathers wanted to conduct their missionary activities with the savages. I sent them into the interior with instructions to map out all the territories they visited."

"What is the purpose of these maps?" Wísakedják asked.

"I will send them on to His Majesty and he will add these territories to his claims," Champlain admitted, pleased with himself.

"Isn't that underhanded?"

"Yes. The English are no wiser. Before they know it New France will expand across the whole country." Champlain laughed.

Wísakedják looked at him crossly. "My concern was not for the English. What of the original people? Did you purchase this land from them?"

Laughter erupted from Champlain again at the question. "Ha! One cannot purchase the land from the savages. They do not own it."

"Who owns it then?" Wísakedják asked.

"The French own it," Champlain informed him.

"Who did the French purchase it from?" Wísakedják asked more pointedly.

"The French claimed this land by right of discovery," Champlain reminded him.

"Who owned it before it was 'discovered'?" Wísakedják asked stubbornly.

"No one owned it," Champlain insisted.

"Someone owned it," Wísakedják countered.

"Yes...the French," Champlain shot back.

"Before that..." He would get him with this.

"We discovered it," Champlain insisted again.

"Who owned it before you discovered it?" Wísakedják said restating his question.

"No one!" Champlain shouted.

"Someone did," Wísakedják maintained.

"No they didn't," Champlain argued.

"Yes they did," Wísakedják sang.

"Really, Mon Pere!" Champlain grunted.

"Really, Monseiur! What sins you committed here?"

"Sins! I said I have committed no sins," Champlain retorted. "I created a settlement here and allowed the Jesuit fathers to come and bring the word of God to this country. "

"Yet, the original people dislike you," Wísakedják said, challenging his assessment of the situation.

"The sheep do not have to like the Shepherd, Father," Champlain argued. "God commands that we bring these people under his faith."

Wísakedják stopped playing the violin and set it aside as he leaned in and peered through the woven cover. "Let me ask you then . . . if the people here were Christian would they be human?"

"Absolutment!" Champlain stated. "Converting the savages to the word of God is our Christian duty."

"So then, if you convert them, they become human?" These French seemed less human than the Omamíwínini. Why did these people love themselves so, he wondered. Why did they condemn everyone else who was not like them? He was brought out of his musings by Champlain's answer.

"Yes, and their souls will be saved."

"So, conversion allows them to be human and to become French?" Wísakedják offered.

"No! No! No! Mon Pere. It does not mean that at all," Champlain countered.

Wísakedják was confused. "What does it mean then?"

"It means their souls will not go to the Devil," Champlain explained with great enthusiasm.

Wísakedják interjected, wanting to dig at his reasoning a bit more. "Their souls can go to heaven and be with God, but they can't own land?"

"Exactly, Mon Pere," Champlain said, happy that Wísakedják seemed to finally understand.

What kind of society had rules like that? Wísakedják shook his head. Regardless, it did not apply here. "You have committed a great sin, Monsieur."

"No. I haven't!"

"Yes you have! Ten Hail Mary's for you and ten lashings on my back!" Wísakedják took out a whip and began to beat himself on the back at the same time that Champlain fell to his knees in the confessional and began to pray. Wísakedják cried out loudly with each lash.

"Hail Mary, full of grace.

The Lord is with thee.

Blessed art thou amongst women.

And blessed in the fruit of thy womb, Jesus.

Holy Mary, Mother of God,

Pray for us sinners,

Now and at the hour of our death,

Amen."

"Your soul will be saved, Father!" Champlain exclaimed. "You won't die in this heathen place. The savages will come to know and appreciate the great suffering we have endured as a result of our duty to them. Ah, the great suffering..." he left off.

Flies began to buzz around the outhouse. Champlain swatted at them. His wig was visible through the woven cover and Wísakedják saw bugs crawling in and out of the wig. He touched his own hair, grateful that it was not in that condition. Champlain's clothing was also ripe with smell and he had not bathed in weeks. The outhouse smelled of stench and the powder perfume that Champlain wore.

"What is that smell?" Wísakedják asked, plugging his nose.

"I don't smell anything," Champlain said.

"It's hard to concentrate with that smell." Wísakedják was sure he didn't smell anything. How could he next to that perfume? "Say, I need some answers for the big guy."

"Get to it then!"

"What good have you done here besides what you have already stated?" Wísakedják asked, reminding him of the purpose for his visit.

"I helped the Algonkin! I was here but a short while when they begged me to help them with their enemies, the Iroquois," Champlain offered.

"How did you help?"

"I went all the way down the river of the Iroquois to help them fight," Champlain insisted.

"Did you help them fight there?" Wísakedják asked.

"I tried. Superstitious cowards!" he spat. "They don't have the courage necessary to fight. I risked myself to kill some of the Iroquois devils."

"You killed them!" How could he have done such a thing?

"I had to because the Algonkin would not fight and defeat their enemies." Champlain defended his actions.

"They're not enemies," Wísakedják corrected him. "They have lived in their homelands a long time and have exchanged wampum and agreements."

"They are all enemies," Champlain complained. "The do nothing but fight and kill each other."

"I thought you said a bit ago that they wouldn't fight. Which is it?" Wísakedják challenged him.

"You say things to confuse me, Mon Pere," Champlain accused. "I said they would not fight. The whole night I was there with them was wasted with vulgar dancing and singing. They could have destroyed their enemies."

"Vulgar?" Wísakedják asked.

"Yes, you know." Champlain moved around in the confessional with his hand over his mouth, making strange sounds that Wísakedják did not understand.

"They are in league with the Devil in their dancing and singing," Champlain insisted.

"I'd like to kick his ass!" Wísakedják whispered, but considered a different option. "Hey Porcupine! Hey Skunk! My friend here would like to meet you."

"Porcupine? Skunk?" Champlain exclaimed. "Really, Mon Pere, I do not share your admiration of the animals."

Wísakedják pounded on the wall of the confessional. "Pay attention then!" He advised. "Violence isn't a good way to settle conflicts. These animals would agree."

"We are men, Mon Pere! Men fight as they have always done," Champlain stated.

"So violence is the answer?"

"Absolutment!" Champlain offered. "I told them to attack their enemies at the first sight of their camp, they refused. They preferred to sleep."

"They chose to rest?" Wísakedják countered.

"They chose to cower like women," Champlain stormed. "In the morning these fools were still standing, yelling at each other. I had to move things along myself."

"Oh, right, when you shot them?" Wísakedják could not believe he had done that. What kind of man does that kind of thing in other peoples homelands?

"I had to," Champlain reminded him. "I told you this already."

"Your actions had consequences for the Omamíwínini, Monsieur." Wísakedják wondered why he couldn't see that he was in the wrong.

"What consequences? Their enemies disappeared for a whole year," Champlain informed him.

"When they came back, they had guns. More people died." Wísakedják was getting very agitated.

"War is unpleasant." Champlain shrugged.

"Another sin! You started a war," Wísakedják declared.

"No I didn't," Champlain denied.

"Yes! You did," Wísakedják said, sure the accusation was sound.

"No I didn't!" Champlain yelled.

"Yes you did," Wísakedják sang.

"I don't believe you!" Champlain said, unwilling to accept it.

"You should," Wísakedják encouraged.

"Why should I?" Champlain resisted.

"Because I am Assisi!" he said sternly.

Champlain did not respond again immediately. He leaned forward and peered through the woven cover. His eyes grew large at the sight of what looked like green whiskers. Shaking his head in denial, he sat back against the wall. "All this talk of the savages, Mon Pere, do you protect the savages too?"

"Indeed, I do," Wísakedják acknowledged.

"Why do you fret so then? The savages have improved since our arrival."

"Many people have died!" Wísakedják interjected, denying his claim.

"You speak of the sickness." He nodded. "Large numbers have perished, disrupting trade."

"All of these lives lost... they are not important?" He couldn't say such a thing could he?

"The sickness is punishment from God," Champlain informed him.

"The sickness was brought by the Blackrobes," Wísakedják countered.

"The savages say that but it is not true," Champlain denied.

"The Omamìwìnini say they lost many people to the Blackrobes."

"The Algonkin?"

"The Omamíwínini." Wísakedják knew that their name and identity was important to them.

"Yes, it is unfortunate that trade with them has been affected." He sighed. "These Algonkin, why do you focus on them so?"

"I focus on them because they have been impacted by your presence in their lands." Why wasn't he getting this point, Wísakedják wondered.

"That is not so. I have helped the Algonkin," Champlain insisted. "They are much improved by our presence, Mon Pere!"

Wísakedják jumped up, not able to take it any longer. "They are not improved Monsieur. Something has happened to them!"

"What do you mean?" Champlain asked. "What has happened to them?"

"I don't know, but it's very bad." He shook his head. "They used to care about me, love me, and respect me. Now they don't even acknowledge that I exist." Tears flooded his eyes at the memory of his encounter with the family.

"Yes, this is the fate of all who die, Father," Champlain acknowledged.

"I have not left this place!" He yelled. "I am still here and will always be here."

"What? I don't understand," Champlain complained, "Riddles! It is always riddles with you."

"These past actions must be undone," Wísakedják insisted.

"Que Sera Sera." Champlain shrugged. "What has been done cannot be undone."

"But the past can inform the future," Wísakedják said.

"In what way?"

"The past provides knowledge to live in the future." Wísakedják offered.

"You are wasting you time then, Mon Pere." He laughed. "They have no knowledge, they live in darkness."

For the first time Wísakedják felt compassion for Champlain. "You're wrong." It was Champlain who lived in darkness and who did not understand.

"I'm not wrong," Champlain insisted.

"Yes you are. The darkness arrived with you." There he had said it. There was no taking it back now. Before Champlain could respond he was caught off guard by a large sphere of light that enveloped the clearing in front of the confessional.

"What magic is this?" Champlain asked fearfully as he shrank back against the wall. His eyes were drawn to the great sphere in spite of his efforts to avoid it.

"No magic!" Wísakedják said as he stepped out of the confessional. He held out his hand to Champlain. "This will show you what has been and what will be."

No, I will not go out there." He cowered inside against the wall of the confessional.

"You must do this my son," Wísakedják coaxed him gently.

Champlain reluctantly stepped from the confessional and looked at the light. Wísakedják took his hand again and they walked into the light together. Images and sounds flashed before their eyes. The sounds and images of creation filled the light and were then replaced with the practicing of ceremonies by the people. Champlain and Wísakedják saw the transmission of knowledge to new generations and the development of relationships within the land. They watched the arrival of Europeans and the divergent paths this created because of the violence, epidemics, genocide, slavery, and ecological destruction. It seemed like forever that the light continued to surround them and overwhelming them with images and sounds of colonization. Here and there they also saw images and sounds associated with various levels of resistance by the people and even allies. When the pool of light went dark they were aware that much had been lost along the way, but much had also survived. Champlain was so overwhelmed by what he had seen that he fell to his knees.

"Shocking isn't it?" he asked Champlain.

"Yes." The answer was simple and to the point.

"When the original people allowed you to come and stay in their homeland they expected that you would live in peace and friendship," Wísakedják noted.

"But . . . the French must live as French," Champlain said.

"The French can remain French and still respect the knowledge and wisdom of others," Wísakedják insisted.

"There is nothing here to show for such knowledge or wisdom," Champlain argued. "Where is your proof?"

Wísakedják looked at him sternly. "The proof is in the way they relate to the world around them. They see all as their relative."

"What do you mean, Mon Pere?" he asked.

"The original people were the last human beings to leave the Creator's side," Wísakedják said, offering an explanation he hoped Champlain would take to heart. "Their knowledge had guided them to live in their homeland without exploiting it."

"And the French do not have this knowledge?" Champlain questioned.

Wísakedják shook his head. "The French could have this knowledge, but they choose to believe they are superior to all life."

"Ah..." he nodded. "And your role here is to make me see this?"

"Yes, because the people have forgotten the knowledge and the teachings." Wísakedják went on, "They suffer in the future as a result."

"So you would like for this knowledge to be brought back to the people?"

Nodding, Wísakedják motioned to Champlain. "Yes, that is why you are here."

Champlain stood there looking at Wísakedják but not able to say a word in response. He had an epiphany. Finally, he found his voice. "Wait! I ... I feel something ... oh my God ... it feels so good! It has been here all along."

"What do you feel?" Wísakedják asked.

"I feel that ... that..." he was confused but trying to put it all together. "I mean ... I know ... that I'm here because the people no longer know you."

Wísakedják acknowledged his insight. "That is why we are both here!"

"I see it now," he said his voice beginning to loose the accent he had before. "You're not really Assisi. You're Wísakedják."

"Yes, that is true," he offered. "And you?"

"I'm not Champlain either." He stammered before his voice gained strength. "I'm really the spirit that dwells in the hearts of the people. I am ... part of you."

"What! You are?" Wísakedják took a step back. Wow, he hadn't expected that.

"Yes, I have been trapped and buried under all the pain," he said. "You have freed me Wísakedják. Miigwech!"

"Ah...yes. Their hearts do need us, you know." Wísakedják nodded. "That's why I had to come back and get you." He knew that now. Finally he understood what had happened to the people. They had lost their spiritual connection to the land and to him.

"We'd better get back to them."

Wísakedják and the spirit disrobed and tossed their clothing inside the outhouse. They laid down sema and then burned the confessional to the ground. They begin the long journey back to the present. There was something new there, it was small but it was hopeful. They followed it through the twists and turns that the people took to the present. When they reached the end they were on one path. They paused there to offer sema then exited the bodies of the man and woman. They two beings combined themselves again to become one. Wísakedják looked around realizing that he was once again in the camp of the family. He took note of the people wondering about the camp. Four chairs were arranged in a straight line.

Wísakedják embraced the camp. He danced around, his arms wide open. It was definitely different. He heard a startled exclamation and turned toward it. He saw the grandmother he had seen earlier, approaching him. She was wearing a shawl with the colours of a woodpecker. Wísakedják smiled.

"Waynaboozhoo," the grandmother said.

"Ah, you are talking to me...finally!" Wísakedják was so excited that he jumped up and down.

"You have travelled far for us Wísakedják," she said, holding out her hand to him. "I have been saving this for you."

She offered him a plate of food, which smelled and looked delicious. Wísakedják smiled and took the plate. He danced around with it holding up his gift for the world to see. Finally he stopped in front of the grandmother. "You know me! I can't believe it."

"Yes," she said. "There are a few of us who survive to carry forward the teachings that you left for us so long ago."

Wísakedják looked around the site at the others who were now gathered there. They watched the grandmother talking, but it was obvious that they still did not see him. They thought she was talking to the Ancestors. "What of the others, why do they not see me?"

"They are not ready yet," she said simply. "It's hard to get the young ones to understand the importance of the stories and teachings but we are trying."

The grandmother nodded in the direction of a boy who approached. He carried a bowl of strawberries and offered them to his grandmother. She turned and offered them to Wísakedják. He smiled brightly as took a bite. Wísakedják chatted with the grandmother for quite a while before taking his leave of the camp. He was just about to depart but paused to ask one last question.

"If you had one wish for the people what would it be?" he asked her.

"My wish would be that the young would begin to understand how important they are for the future; that they would feel the importance of learning their language and maintaining their traditions," she said with great compassion.

Wísakedják nodded. He understood the importance of the wish. "A strong wish," he said. "Keep up the good work and it will come to pass."

She nodded as he said goodbye. "Baamaapii."

"Baamaapii. Oh, one more thing Elder Brother," she said before he could leave the camp site. When he nodded she continued. "Please refrain from turning anyone else into a woodpecker! There are plenty of them now."

Wísakedják laughed as he walked away. The grandmother danced back to the picnic table, her colourful shawl spread out on her back. She sang a travelling song to wish him a safe journey. Wísakedják continued along the path, taking in the sights and sounds around him. He smiled. His belly was full and there was life all around him. He came upon a turtle and a frog who were sunning themselves on a rock next to the river.

"Say, what a beautiful shell you have, Turtle," he began. "And what fantastic legs you have, Frog."

"Not today, Wísakedják," the Turtle and Frog said in unison. "We know that your games mean we could be your lunch!" The Frog and the Turtle looked at each other and then jumped in the water and swam away. Wísakedják smiled and rubbed his belly as he skipped away.

"No worries," Wísakedják said. "There's always tomorrow."

Epilogue

Fraudulent theft of Mohawk Land by the Municipality of Oka

Kanehsatà:ke Mohawk Territory
July 11, 2009

It has now been 19 years since the "Oka Crisis" when the Municipality of Oka and developers, in collusion with the Federal and provincial governments, attempted to defraud the Mohawk peoples of Kanehsatà:ke of our ancestral Pines to make way for the expansion of a nine-hole golf course and a condominium development.

Nineteen years later, nothing has changed as the Municipality of Oka, with the approval of federal government, continues to defraud Mohawk peoples of our land and its resources through housing developments, the nationalizing of Oka Park and through the Kanesatake Interim Land Base Governance Act (KILBGA).

Since June 6, 2008, I have written three letters to the Municipality of Oka, with the inclusion of both the federal and provincial governments as well as the Governor General of Canada, Michaëlle Jean, regarding my concerns of the fraud being committed by the Municipality of Oka and developers. To date I have not received any response from any level of government or individual.

The issue that sparked the Crisis of 1990 was the blatant theft of our homelands, the Mohawk peoples' sovereignty over those lands and the continued efforts by governments to undermine and defraud us of our international human rights to our homelands.

The acceleration of development since 1990 is astounding and has exploited the hardship and violations of human rights that the Mohawk peoples and their allies suffered during the Crisis of 1990. In fact, no level of government, in particular the Municipality of Oka, has apologized for the blatant human rights violations, which included the denial of food, medicine and safety of the Mohawk peoples. Mohawk men were beaten and tortured by the Sûreté du Québec and members of the Canadian Army. Mid August 1990, Kahnawà:ke community members were assaulted with stones when they tried to leave their community via the Mercier Bridge while the SQ stood idly by. Mohawk effigies were burned nightly by racist citizens in Chateauguay who refused to understand that the blocking of the Mercier Bridge protected the community of Kanehsatà:ke from a police and army attack. To date, the Governments of Canada and Quebéc, the Sureté du Québec and the Municipality of Oka have yet to apologize for their casual disregard of human rights violations during the 1990 "Oka Crisis."

The Mohawk peoples have been waiting for over 300 years for a peace that never seems to come. A peace blocked by arrogant, racist governments and their forced assimilation policies concealing their coveting of our lands and resources through their legislation.

And so in the past 19 years, what has changed? It is evident that very little has changed and that there is a continuation to defraud not just the Mohawk peoples of Kanehsatà:ke of our lands and access to those resources, but all Indigenous Peoples living in Canada. Therefore the following recommendations are being put forward to the Government of Canada and those levels of government that fall under its jurisdiction:

1. That a legal caution be placed on all current and future development plans on Mohawk Territory, particularly those taking place within the Municipality of Oka, especially "Oka Park," Pointe Calumet, Ste. Marthe, St. Joseph, St. Eustache et. al.

2. That the Kanesatake Interim Land Base Governance Act (KILBGA) be rescinded as the validity of the process is questionable and adversely affects the rights of the Kanienkehá:ka peoples

3. Furthermore, that a legal review be conducted by an international human rights tribunal on the process used by Canada to pass S-24 and that Canada pay for the cost of the tribunal.

4. That the Kanienkehá:ka (Mohawk) nation, and in particular the community of Kanehstatà:ke, be accorded the time to begin the process of a strategic plan that will protect our lands and its resources for future generations.

5. That a process begins to create a policy for the approval of development by the traditional government of the Iroquois confederacy on our territories.

6. That an apology for the human rights abuses and all propaganda criminalizing the Mohawk people be given by the Canadian Government, the Government of Quebéc and the Municipality of Oka as quickly as possible in order to begin the process of reconciliation.

7. That an environmentally friendly sustainable development program be implemented throughout Kanienkehá:ka (Mohawk) Territory.

8. That Government of Canada implement the norm of free, prior and informed consent for any policy, legislation or development that has the potential to adversely affect the rights of all Indigenous Peoples in Canada.

9. That the Government of Canada be accountable for the money it holds in trust for Indigenous Peoples, including the Six Nations Trust Fund, and that this accountability be made public in an honest and transparent manner.

These are only a few of the necessary recommendations required for the process of reconciliation and for the rule of law to be respected by the Government of Canada. Nothing short of this disavows the honour of the Crown.

In Peace,

Ellen Gabriel
Turtle Clan Kanienkehá:ka of Kanehsatà:ke

Contributors

DAINA AUGAITIS has been Chief Curator/Associate Director since 1996 at the Vancouver Art Gallery, where she plays a leadership role in developing the exhibition and collection programs.

REBECCA BELMORE was born in Ontario (Anishinabe) and works in a variety of media, including sculpture, installation, video, and performance. Currently living and working in Vancouver, Belmore has long been creating work about the plight of the disenfranchised and marginalized in society. In her poignant and dramatic performances, the artist's own body becomes the site of historical, cultural, and political investigations as she explores self and community, boundaries between public and private, chaos, and linear narrative. The official representative for Canada at the 2005 Venice Biennale, Belmore's work has been exhibited internationally since 1987 and can be found in the collections of the National Gallery of Canada, Art Gallery of Ontario, and the Canada Council Art Bank. In 2004, Belmore received the prestigious VIVA award from the Jack and Doris Shadbolt foundation.

JUDY DA SILVA is Anishinabe from Asubpeeschoseewagong Anishinabe Territory (Grassy Narrows). She is a mother of five children and is one of the protectors of the land in her area. She works on many issues related to Mother Earth including environmental contamination studies, anti-mining workshops, water protection initiatives, and Anishinaabe cultural teachings/learning. Judy has been an active participant in the ongoing blockades in her territory to stop clear-cut logging.

RICHARD J.F. DAY is an anarchist activist and scholar based in Kingston, Ontario. He is Associate Professor of Sociology at Queen's University, and is the author of two books: *Multiculturalism and the History of Canadian Diversity* (University of Toronto Press, 2000); and *Gramsci Is Dead: Anarchist Currents in the Newest Social Movements* (Pluto Press, Between The Lines, University of Michigan Press, 2005. Also in Italian, Greek, and Turkish translations). His current work focuses on relations between settlers and autonomy-seeking Indigenous Peoples in the Americas, with a particular interest in resonances between anarchism, indigenism, and feminism.

GKISEDTANAMOOGK is Wampanoag and lives at Punawabsket-Wabanakik. He is married to Miigam'agan and has three children. As a practioner in ceremonial and experiential knowledge, he is also an Adjunct at the University of Maine, having degrees in both political science and law. In 2000, he witnessed the Department of Fisheries and Oceans' siege of Burnt Church, and was alongside his Esgenoôpetitj family as they stood up in defense of their responsibilities as Mi'kmaq.

SHEILA GRUNER is an activist-educator who lives and works in Northern Ontario. She can be found teaching at Algoma University, working toward her PhD at OISE/UT or spending time in the Far North.

GREG A. HILL is a multidisciplinary artist primarily working in installation, performance and digital imaging. His work explores his Kanyen'kehaka (Mohawk) and French-Canadian identity through the prism of colonialism, nationalism and concepts of place and community. Born and raised in Fort Erie, Ontario, Hill is a member of the Six Nations of the Grand River First Nation.

AL HUNTER is a spoken word performer and the author of two books of poetry, *Spirit Horses* and the *Recklessness of Love*, both published by Kegedonce Press.

ROBERT HOULE holds a BA degree in Art History from the University of Manitoba and a BEd in Art Education from McGill University. He is currently an instructor at the Ontario College of Art and Design.

An exhibitor in group and solo shows internationally since the 1970s, Houle has shows at the Museum of Contemporary Art, Australia; the Canadian Cultural Centre, Paris; and the Stedelijk Museum in Amsterdam, amongst others. In Canada, he has shown work at the Mendel Art Gallery, Saskatoon; the Museum of Contemporary Canadian Art, Toronto; the Carleton University Art Gallery, Ottawa; the Agnes Etherington Art Centre, Kingston; the Winnipeg Art Gallery and many more. Robert Houle was Curator of Indian Art at the National Museum of Man in Ottawa from 1977 to 1980. He was a visiting artist at Hood College, Maryland; Gettysburg College, Pennsylvania; the Heard Museum, Phoenix; the McMichael Canadian Collection, Kleinberg; the Winnipeg Art Gallery; and the International Canada Council studio in Paris in 2009. His work is included in most major Canadian museums and galleries, including the National Gallery and the Art Gallery of Ontario. He won the Visual Arts Prize during the 2001 Toronto Arts Awards.

WAB KINEW is a one-of-a-kind musical talent, becoming one of the artists "to watch for" from the western Provinces. He is a hip-hop artist and CBC radio producer/host based in Winnipeg, Manitoba. Wab exemplifies what it means to be multicultural in Canada today, holding both a Bachelor of Arts degree in economics and training in the traditional Medicine ways of his Anishinaabe people.

ARTHUR KROKER is Canada Research Chair in Technology, Culture and Theory, Professor of Political Science, and the Director of the Pacific Centre for Technology and Culture at the University of Victoria. One of his most recent projects is the monograph *Born Again Ideology: Religion, Technology and Terrorism*. His books include *The Will to Technology and the Culture of Nihilism*, *The Possessed Individual*, and *Technology and the Canadian Mind*. With Marilouise Kroker he is the editor of *Critical Digital Studies: A Reader* as well as the international, scholarly review, *CTheory* (www.ctheory.net).

KIERA L. LADNER is an Associate Professor and Canada Research Chair in Indigenous Politics and Governance in the Department of Political Studies at the University of Manitoba. Alongside Leanne Simpson, she held a position at Trent from 2000–2002. She is a scholar in the field of Indigenous politics and is widely published in Canada, Australia, the United States and Mexico. She is currently writing a book on

Indigenous constitutions and constitutional politics and is working on projects on political decolonization in Cananda and in Hawai'i.

MELINA LABOUCAN-MASSIMO is Lubicon Cree from Northern Alberta. She has been working as an advocate for Indigenous rights for the past nine years. She has worked with organizations like Redwire Media Society, Indigenous Media Arts Society and has also produced short documentaries, researched, and worked on topics ranging from the tar sands, inherent treaty rights, water issues to cultural appropriation. She has studied and worked in Australia, Brasil, Mexico, and Turtle Island focusing on Indigenous rights and culture, resource extraction and international diplomacy. Before joining Greenpeace as a tar sands climate and energy campaigner in Alberta, Melina was pursuing her Masters in Environmental Studies at York University.

DAMIEN LEE is a citizen of the Anishinabek Nation and grew up in Fort William First Nation. For the past ten years he has worked on environmental issues with Indigenous communities, locally, nationally and internationally. He is the founder of the Anishinabek Gitchi Gami Environmental Programs, the first citizen-led, community-focused environmental not-for-profit organization on a First Nation reserve in Canada. Damien is currently a student in Indigenous Studies at Trent University, where he is studying inherent Anishinabek forms of contention.

NEAL MCLEOD's first book of poetry, *Songs to Kill a Wîhtikow*, was nominated for several Saskatchewan book award including book of the year in 2005. In 2007 it was nominated for book of year at the Anskohk McNally Aboriginal Literature Awards, and won the poetry book of the year by unanimous decision of the jurors. He has published *Cree Narrative Memory: From Treaties to Contemporary Times* (Purich Press, 2007). His most recent book of poetry, *Gabriel's Beach*, was published by Hagios Press in 2008. His current research is exploring Indigenous conceptions of land and space. Neal is also a visual artist and has exhibited across Canada and Europe.

JUNE MCCUE is a member of the Ned'u'ten People located along Lake Babine in northern British Columbia. Professor McCue graduated from the UBC Graduate Law Program in 1998. Professor McCue has been the Acting Director of First Nations Legal Studies since 1998 and joins the Faculty as an Assistant Professor and Director of First Nations Legal Studies on July 1, 2000. Professor McCue has directed the development of a First Nations Legal Studies Academic Plan and supervised the process to create the conceptual development for the Centre for International Indigenous Legal Studies. From 1999–2005, Professor McCue was the founding Chair of Environmental-Aboriginal Guardianship Through Law and Education (EAGLE). Professor McCue's current efforts are focused on research, writing and teaching in the Indigenous law field.

GERALD MCMASTER has been the Curator of Canadian Art at the Art Gallery of Ontario (Toronto), since the fall of 2005. Before arriving in Toronto, Dr. McMaster worked at the Smithsonian's National Museum of the American Indian as Deputy Assistant Director for Cultural Resources from 2000–02, and from 2002–04, he was the Director's Special Assistant for Mall Exhibitions responsible for all the Museum's permanent exhibitions. He co-edited *The Native Universe: Voices of Indian America.* In 2004, Dr. McMaster co-edited and co-curated *First American Art: The Collection of Charles and Valerie Diker* at the NMAI's George Gustav Heye Center, in New York City; in 2005–06 he edited and curated *New Tribe: New York*; and in 2007 he co-curated *Remix: Multiple Modernities in a Post-Indian World.* From 1981–2000, Dr. McMaster was Curator at the Canadian Museum of Civilization, in charge of exhibitions, acquisitions, and publications of contemporary Indian art. From 1995–2000 he was made Curator-in-Charge of the First Peoples Hall. While with the CMC he curated many leading-edge exhibitions, including *In the Shadow of the Sun, Indigena, Edward Poitras Canada XLVI Biennale di Venezia,* and *Reservation X.* His awards and recognitions include the 2005 National Aboriginal Achievement Award; the 2001 ICOM-Canada Prize for contributions to national and international museology; Canadian Commissioner to the world's most prestigious exhibitions, the XLVI 1995 Venice Biennale; and recently he was given our country's highest honour, Officer of the Order of Canada. Dr. McMaster is originally from Saskatchewan and holds a PhD from the University of Amsterdam and degrees from the Minneapolis College of Art and Design and Carleton University.

KATE MONTURE was 16 years old at the time of her passing in August 2009. She is Mohawk from Grand River Territory and also has ties through her father to the Thunderchild First Nation (Cree) in Saskatchewan. Her passions were writing, dance and soccer.

PATRICIA A. MONTURE is a citizen of the Mohawk Nation, Grand River Territory. She was educated as a lawyer in Ontario and now teaches sociology at the University of Saskatchewan where she is academic coordinator of the Aboriginal Justice and Criminology program. Her activism focuses on securing justice for Aboriginal Peoples. She is mother to Justin, Michael Blake, Kate and Jack. She has just co-edited her third book published by Inanna and titled *First Voices: An Aboriginal Women's Reader*.

WANDA NANIBUSH is an Anishinabe-kwe curator, writer and media artist from Beausoliel First Nation. She has curated exhibitions such as *Chronotopic Village at Modern Fuel* in Kingston, *Rez-Erection* at Artspace in Peterborough, *post-Colonial Stress Disorder* at WARC in Toronto. Her work examines relationships between western and Indigenous philosophies/ theories around time, space, subjectivity, gender, humour, and trauma.

DOUGLAS RAYMOND NEPINAK was Saulteaux Indian from the Pine Creek First Nation. He was a second-generation residential school survivor. Doug spent six years in the Navy travelling the world (he was stationed in Germany for three years) before coming back to Winnipeg to get his BA Honours English from the University of Winnipeg. The summer of 1990, Doug was reporting for *Weetamah*, a small Aboriginal newspaper in Winnipeg, and spent almost every day at Peace Village. Profoundly affected and seeking understanding for the degree of violence and racial hatred that exploded so quickly over "just a golf course" Doug wrote *Crisis in Oka, Manitoba*. A self-proclaimed poet, playwright propagandist for the cause (inspired by the warriors, and Ellen Gabriel specifically) he continued writing until his death August 13, 2005. He was a loving husband, and father to three beautiful children.

SHELLEY NIRO is a member of the Six Nations Reserve, Mohawk, Turtle Clan. Niro was born in Niagara Falls, NY, 1954. She currently lives in Brantford, Ontario. She graduated from the Ontario College of Art with honours in visual arts. She received her MFA from the University of Western Ontario. In 2001, she became an Eiteljorg recipient at the Museum of Western and Indian Arts, Indiana, Indianapolis. She has participated in the Women in The Director's Chair Program at the Banff Centre for the Arts, 2003. In the fall of 2006, Shelley was se-lected to be a fellow with Women in Film and GM Accelerator Grants. Niro has finished her feature film *Kissed By Lightning*. You can find works of art in the Museuem of Civilization; the National Gallery and the Indian Art Centre; Contemporary Photography Museum of Canada; the Portrait Gallery, Ottawa, Ontario; The Rockwell Museum, Corning New York; and the University of Seattle, Library.

MICHAEL ORSINI is Associate Professor in the School of Political Studies at the University of Ottawa where he specializes mainly in health policy and politics and the role of the civil society in policy processes, including the role of Aboriginal Peoples. He is the co-editor (with Miriam Smith) of *Critical Policy Studies*, UBC Press, 2007. Following his undergraduate degree in Journalism from Concordia University in Montreal, he worked as a reporter for the *Montreal Gazette* in the early 1990s.

JACOB OSTAMAN is from Kitchenuhmaykoosib Inninuwug (KI), where he is the Director for Lands and Environment for the community. He is also an advisor to the KI Chief and Council with respect to lands and resources issues.

JANE ASH POITRAS, RCA is an internationally acclaimed visual artist whose work has been showcased in numerous solo and group exhibi-tions around the world and can be found in many prestigious public, private and commercial collections. She is a graduate of the University of Alberta with degrees in microbiology and printmaking and has a Master of Fine Arts in Painting and Sculpture from New York's Columbia University. She is a longtime lecturer at the University of Alberta and a much-in-demand guest lecturer across North America and overseas. Respected for her generous support of Aboriginal and community causes, her numerous honours include the Alberta Centennial Medal, the National Aboriginal Achievement Award for Arts and Culture, and the University of Alberta Alumni Award of Excellence.

THOMAS RYAN RED CORN, Wa.zha.zhe (Osage) holds a Bachelors of Fine Arts from the University of Kansas in Visual Communications with an emphasis in Graphic Design. During his time at KU he produced multiple short films, was a two-time First Nations Student Association co-president, and was awarded the Big XII Conference Native American Graduate Student of the Year Award for Leadership. Shortly after graduating, Ryan started freelancing his graphic design skills and making T-shirts, which quickly became Red Hand Media, Inc., and Demockratees.com—entities that catered to and outfitted the activist and non-profit communities, both in Native America and on a global level. In 2007, he co-founded Buffalo Nickel Press and Distro, which acts as a printing and distribution hub for all of his business ventures. Buffalo Nickel doubled sales in its first two years in business, and, in 2008, Red Hand Media received American Indian Chamber of Commerce Business of the Year honours for the Tulsa Chapter. His client list includes the Native American Rights Fund, National Museum of the American Indian, United States Dept. of Defense, Osage Nation, Standing Rock Nation, Sauk & Fox Nation, Chickasaw Nation, National Congress of the American Indian, Lucky Star Casino, and Sony. Ryan is member of the Osage Nation, Tsi-zho Wa.shta.ke Clan (Gentle Sky/Peacemaker). He currently sits on the presiding Wa.hxa. ko'lin districts drum keeper's In.lon.shka committee. Ryan lives and operates his business from Osage Nation Territory, Pawhuska, Oklahoma.

HARMONY RICE is a publisher, writer and multimedia artist who has been named to *Chatelaine's* Top 80 influential Canadian women to Watch. harmony, a Pottawatomi woman from Wasauksing First Nation, was the publisher of *SPIRIT Magazine*, an identity, arts and culture-based magazine that was distributed across Canada. Mother to a young daughter, harmony is an active cultural advocate and community builder and was raised as a jingle dress dancer, hand drum singer and ceremony girl in her community of Wasauksing. harmony was recently published in a motherhood anthology called *Between Interruptions* (Key Porter Books, 2007) and is the host of a television show called *When the Music Speaks* (APTN, SUN TV). She was named 2008 youth entrepreneur of the year by the Waubetek Business Development Corporation. Her most recent venture, Roots & Rights Media, focuses on communications, creative production and education of various land and culture related issues in Canada.

WAUBGESHIG RICE is a broadcast journalist and writer currently based in Winnipeg, Manitoba. He's originally from Wasauksing First Nation, a beautiful Ojibway community on Georgian Bay in Ontario. He developed a passion for storytelling at a very young age, learning about his culture and traditions through stories the Elders told. His journalism career began when he spent a year as an exchange student in Germany at 17. He sent stories about his experiences as an Ojibway kid in Europe to a local Ontario newspaper. He graduated from Ryerson University's Journalism program in 2002 and has since been published in national newspapers and magazines. He currently works as a television reporter for CBC News. He cites growing up on the rez as his greatest learning experience.

PETER H. RUSSELL is a Professor Emeritus of political science at the University of Toronto where he is now Principal of Senior College. He has served as President of the Canadian Political Science Association, the Canadian Law and Society Associations and the Churchill Society for the Advancement of Parliamentary Democracy. He chaired the Research Advisory Committee of the Royal Commission on Aboriginal Peoples and was a member of the Research Advisory Committee for the Ipperwash Inquiry. He has published widely in the fields of Aboriginal, constitutional and judicial politics. His book, *Recognizing Aboriginal Title: The Mabo Case and Indigenous Resistance to English Settler Colonialism* won the 2006 American Political Science Association's C. Herman Pritchett Award.

ROBINDER KAUR SEHDEV is an Assistant Professor in the Department of Gender Equality and Social Justice at Nipissing University. She holds a PhD in Communications and Culture from York University where she researched the involvement of popular cultural representational practices in the normalization of the myth of the innocent settler state. Her current work focuses on the politics of solidarity in decolonial action amongst Aboriginal and other racialized peoples.

CHARLIE GREG SARK is a cross-blood from the east coast of North America. His poetry is inspired by the persistence of colonial constructs in western society.

PAULA SHERMAN is Omàmìwinini (Algonquin) and Family Head on the Ka-Pishkawandemin, the traditional council for Ardoch Algonquin First Nation. She has been actively involved in the resistance against uranium exploration and mining and she is the author of *Dishonour of the Crown: The Ontario Resource Regime in the Valley of the Kiji Sìbì*, published by Arbeiter Ring Publishing. Paula holds a PhD in Indigenous Studies from Trent University where she is currently a tenured professor and director of the PhD program.

LEANNE BETASAMOSAKE SIMPSON is a writer, educator and activist. She is a citizen of the Nishnaabeg nation and holds a PhD from the University of Manitoba. Leanne is the editor of *Lighting the Eighth Fire: The Liberation, Resurgence and Protection of Indigenous Nations*, published by Arbeiter Ring Publishing. She currently teaches at Athabasca and Trent Universities, and she lives in Nogojiwanong (Peterborough, Ontario) with her partner and her two children, Nishna and Minowewebeneshiinh.

CLAYTON THOMAS-MULLER, of the Mathais Colomb Cree Nation also known as Pukatawagan in Northern Manitoba, is an activist for Indigenous rights and environmental justice. With his roots in the inner city of Winnipeg, Manitoba, Clayton began his work as a community organizer, working with Aboriginal youth. Currently based out of Ottawa, Clayton is involved in many initiatives to support the building of an inclusive movement for Energy and Climate Justice. He serves as board chair of the Collective Heritage Institute (CHI), which hosts the annual Bioneers Conference in Marin, California. Recognized by *Utne Magazine* as one of the top 30 under 30 activists in the United States, Clayton is the tar sands campaign organizer for the Indigenous Environmental Network. He is also a gifted poet and rap artist. Clayton is happily married and is a proud father of two sons.

Index

Bold numbers indicate illustrations